Getting Started With Microsoft Excel 5.0 For Windows

Getting Started With Microsoft Excel 5.0 For Windows

Babette Kronstadt
Pace Computer Learning Center
School of Computer Science and Information Systems
Pace University

Babette Kronstadt
David Sachs
Series Editors
Pace Computer Learning Center
School of Computer Science and Information Systems
Pace University

JOHN WILEY & SONS, INC.
New York / Chichester / Brisbane / Toronto / Singapore

Trademark Acknowledgments:

Microsoft is a registered trademark of Microsoft Corporation
Excel for Windows is a trademark of Microsoft Corporation
Windows is a trademark of Microsoft Corporation
Word for Windows is a trademark of Microsoft Corporation
Microsoft Access is a registered trademark of Microsoft Corporation
1-2-3 is a registered trademark of Lotus Development Corporation
WordPerfect is a registered trademark of WordPerfect Corporation
IBM is a registered trademark of International Business Machines Corporation
Paradox is a registered trademark of Borland International, Inc.

Portions of this text were adapted from other texts in this series and from Pace University Computer Learning Center manuals.

ISBN 0-471-12055-3

Printed in the United States of America

10 9 8 7 6 5 4

Preface

Getting Started with Microsoft Excel 5.0 for Windows provides a step-by-step, hands-on introduction to *Excel*. It is designed for students with basic PC and Windows skills who have little or no experience with *Microsoft Excel 5.0 for Windows*. Basic skills are taught in short, focused activities which build to create actual applications.

Key Elements

Each lesson in *Getting Started with Microsoft Excel 5.0 for Windows* uses eight key elements to help students master specific worksheet and *Excel* concepts and skills and develop the ability to apply them in the future.

- **Learning objectives**, located at the beginning of each lesson, focus students on the skills to be learned.
- **Project orientation** allows the students to meet the objectives while creating a real-world application. Skills are developed as they are needed to complete projects, not to follow menus or other artificial organization.
- **Motivation** for each activity is supplied so that students learn *why* and *when* to perform an activity, rather than how to follow a series of instructions by rote.
- **Bulleted lists of step-by-step general procedures** introduce the tasks and provide a handy, quick reference.
- **Activities with step-by-step instructions** guide students as they apply the general procedures to solve the problems presented by the projects.
- **Screen displays** provide visual aids for learning and illustrate major steps.
- **Independent projects** provide opportunities to practice newly acquired skills with decreasing level of support.
- **Feature reference** at the end of the book allows students to have a single place to look for commands to carry out the activities learned in the book.

Stop and Go

The steps for completing each *Excel* feature introduced in this book are covered in two ways. First they are described clearly in a bulleted list, which can also be used for reference. Then the steps are used in a hands-on Activity. Be sure to wait until the Activity to practice each feature on the computer.

Taking Advantage of Windows

Getting Started with Microsoft Excel 5.0 for Windows provides a balanced approach to using a Windows application. The use of the mouse, buttons, and icons for carrying out commands is emphasized. However, familiarity with the menus is developed so that students can take advantage of the greater options often available in menu commands.

Shortcut menus and shortcut keys are introduced when appropriate. The convenient **Feature Reference** at the end of the book summarizes menu commands and mouse and keyboard shortcuts for each of the features covered in the lessons. Students can use this both to review procedures or learn alternate ways of carrying out commands.

Flexible Use

Getting Started with Microsoft Excel 5.0 for Windows is designed for use in an introductory computer course. As a "getting started" book, it does not attempt to cover all of the features of the software. However, the topics included in later lessons allow instructors to provide opportunities for individualized or extra credit assignments or use the book in short courses focused specifically on *Excel.* While designed to be used in conjunction with lectures or other instructor supervision, basic concepts are explained so that students can use the book in independent learning settings. Students should be able to follow specific instructions with minimal instructor assistance.

Data Disk

Data disks are provided to the instructors for distribution to the students. Many of the projects use files from the data disk so that the focus of the lesson is on the new skills being learned in each project. Initial projects require that students develop applications from the beginning, while later projects mix developing new applications with editing existing applications. Enough explanation and data entry is always included so that students understand the full application that they are building.

Acknowledgments

Getting Started with Microsoft Excel 5.0 for Windows would not have been possible without the support and effort of many individuals and organizations. Nancy Treuer, and Matthew Poli worked miracles with the layout and text formatting and graciously endured many revisions to the materials. Sally Sobolewski patiently tested all of the activities and provided valuable editing comments. Barbara Farrell shared her expertise in developing specific projects.

In addition Nancy, Matthew, Sally, Joe Knowlton, and Lynn Bacon provided great ideas for the design of *Getting Started with Excel* and its companion books on the Windows versions of *Word, WordPerfect, Lotus, Access* and *Paradox.* Finally *Getting Started with Excel* benefited greatly from the teamwork and ideas of the authors of these books, Sylvia Russakoff, Nancy Hale, Kitty Daniels, Janet Smith, Barbara Farrell and Henry Gaylord.

We received enormous institutional support from Pace University and the School of Computer Science and Information Systems (CSIS). In particular, much personal support and personal leadership for our work has come from the Dean, Dr. Susan Merritt.

From another perspective, this book is also a product of the Pace Computer Learning Center which is a loose affiliation of approximately 15 faculty and staff who have provided more than 7,000 days of instruction to over 60,000 individuals in corporate settings throughout the United States and around the world during the past nine years. Our shared experiences in the development and teaching of these non-credit workshops, as well as credit bearing courses through the Pace University School of Computer Science and Information Systems, was an ideal preparation for writing this book. In addition none of our books for Wiley would have been possible without the generous and continuing support of David Sachs, the director of the Computer Learning Center.

We have received many invaluable comments and suggestions from instructors at other schools who were kind enough to review earlier books in the *Getting Started* series and offer their suggestions for the current books. Our thanks go to Jack D. Cundiff, Horry-Georgetown Technical College; Pat Fenton, West Valley College; Sharon Ann Hill, University of Maryland; E. Gladys Norman, Linn-Benton Community College; and Barbara Jean Silvia, University of Rhode Island.

My thanks also go to the many people at Wiley who provided us with the support and assistance we needed. Our editor, Beth Lang Golub, and editorial program assistant, David Kear, have been very responsive to our concerns, and supportive of all of the Pace Computer Learning Center's writing projects. Andrea Bryant was invaluable in her management of all aspects of the production of this book.

Last but not least, I would like to thank my husband Eric for his support throughout the long writing process and my children Jessica and Gabriel, whose support extended to using their word processing skills to assist in the production of the book.

Babette Kronstadt
December, 1994
White Plains, New York

Contents

Students and Instructors

Before Getting Started Please Note:

WINDOWS INTRODUCTION

Getting Started with Microsoft Excel 5.0 for Windows assumes that students are familiar with basic Windows concepts and can use a mouse. If not, instructors may consider using the companion book, *Getting Started with Windows 3.1*, also published by Wiley. Windows has a tutorial which can also help students learn or review basic mouse and Windows skills. To use the Windows Tutorial: 1) turn on the computer; 2) type: **win** or select Windows from the menu or ask your instructor how to start Windows on your system; 3) press the **ALT** key; 4) press the **H** key; 5) when the **Help** menu opens, type a **W**; and 6) follow the tutorial instructions, beginning with the mouse lesson if you do not already know how to use the mouse, or going directly to the Windows Basic lesson if you are a skilled mouse user.

STUDENT DATA DISKS

Most of the projects in this book require the use of a Data Disk. Instructors who have adopted this text are granted the right to distribute the files on the Data Disk to any student who has purchased a copy of the text. Instructors are free to post the files to standalone workstations or a network or provide individual copies of the disk to students. This book assumes that students who use their own disk know the name of the disk drive that they will be using it from. When using a network, students must know the name(s) of the drives and directories which will be used to open and save files.

SETUP OF WINDOWS AND EXCEL 5.0 FOR WINDOWS

One of the strengths of Windows and *Excel* is the ease with which the screens and even some of the program's responses to commands can be customized. This, however, can cause problems for students trying to learn how to use the programs. This book assumes that Windows and *Excel for Windows* have been installed using the default settings and that they have not been changed by those using the programs. Some hints are given about where to look if the computer responds differently from the way it would under standard settings. If your screen looks different from those in the book, ask your instructor or laboratory assistant to check that the defaults have not been changed.

VERSION OF THE SOFTWARE

All of the screenshots in this book have been taken using Version 5.0 of *Microsoft Excel for Windows*. If you are using a different 5.0 version, the appearance of your screen and the effect of some commands may vary slightly from those used in this book.

Introduction

Objectives

In this lesson you will learn:

- What a worksheet is used for
- How to start *Excel*
- The parts of the *Excel* screen that are common to Windows programs
- The parts of the *Excel* screen specific to *Excel*
- Terminology used in worksheets
- How to use the **View** menu to change the appearance of the screen
- How to use the toolbars
- How to select a cell
- How *Excel* follows Windows procedures for using menus and dialog boxes
- How to use Help
- How to exit from *Excel*
- The typographical conventions used in this book

PURPOSE OF THE INTRODUCTION

In all of the other lessons in this book you will develop a specific project. This introduction is designed to teach you the basic concepts, terminology, and techniques that you will need to use *Excel* successfully to complete the projects that follow. This introduction will quickly review basic Windows concepts and terminology, but it will also indicate areas in which *Excel*'s procedures may differ from those used in other Windows applications.

The last section in this chapter describes the typographical conventions used in this book. In this chapter, more explicit instructions will be given. Most commands that you are to follow are given using the mouse unless a keyboard combination is particularly easy. However, the task list in Appendix A includes shortcut keys for most tasks that you will do in this book.

WHAT IS MICROSOFT EXCEL 5.0 FOR WINDOWS?

Excel is an electronic spreadsheet or worksheet. Worksheets are essential tools used by all businesses and can be used in your life as a student as well. A worksheet is an organized way to keep track of numeric data. It is used when you need to perform calculations to analyze the data. Oftentimes the data in a worksheet change frequently. One of the strengths of a worksheet is that after you create formulas to perform the calculations, they are automatically updated, or recalculated, whenever you update the data.

More importantly, the worksheet can answer questions about the data. What was the company's profit in the last quarter? Did actual revenues and expenses meet budget expectations? What was the total payroll for the week? What is the effect of different interest rates on the amount of money that can be borrowed?

Because worksheets recalculate automatically, they can also be used to make projections into the future. These projections are often called *what-if* analyses. *What* will be the effect on profits *if* the company can hold expenses for materials to 15%? *What* will be the effect on my grade *if* I get a 95 on the next exam?

Excel also lets you easily create *charts* that graphically represent your data. These charts let you quickly see changes and trends in the data. In addition, they too update whenever the data they are based on change.

Finally, since data in worksheets are often organized in a *list* (labeled rows containing similar sets of data), *Excel* can also be used to perform typical *database* tasks such as sorting data or filtering data to display just those sets that meet certain criteria. These tasks will not be covered in the lessons in this book, but sorting is introduced in Independent Project 3.4.

GETTING STARTED

Since *Excel* runs under Windows the appearance of the *Excel* window, and the methods of starting *Excel*, selecting commands from menus, completing dialog boxes, and performing basic file commands like opening, closing, and saving files are the same as those used for any other Windows application package. This introductory lesson will review these procedures briefly, but it is assumed that you are familiar with Windows and that you know how to use the mouse.

STARTING EXCEL

Since *Excel* runs under Windows, it is started in the same way as any other Windows application.

The steps for completing each *Excel* feature introduced in this book are covered in two ways. First, they are described in a **bulleted** list, that can also be used for reference. The steps are used in a hands-on *Activity*. Be sure to wait until the **numbered** instructions in the *Activity* to practice each feature on the computer.

To start Excel:

- Turn on your computer and start Windows.
- Open the *Microsoft Office* program group if it is not already open.
- Double-click on the ***Excel*** icon.

Activity I.1: Starting Excel

1. Turn on your computer and start Windows.
2. If the Microsoft Office program group is open (Figure I - 2), go to step 4.

3. If the Microsoft Office program group appears as an icon (Figure I - 1), point to the program group icon and double-click the left mouse button.

   If the program group icon is not visible on the screen, click on the **Window** menu. Click on **Microsoft Office** in the drop-down menu. If **Microsoft Office** is not listed, but **More Windows** is, click on **More Windows** and then click on **Microsoft Office.**

PROBLEM SOLVER: *If you are having trouble double-clicking the mouse button, point to the application icon, click the mouse button once and press* ***ENTER***.

PROBLEM SOLVER: *If your computer does not have a program group called Microsoft Office, look for one called Microsoft Excel or Excel or ask your instructor or lab assistant for help.*

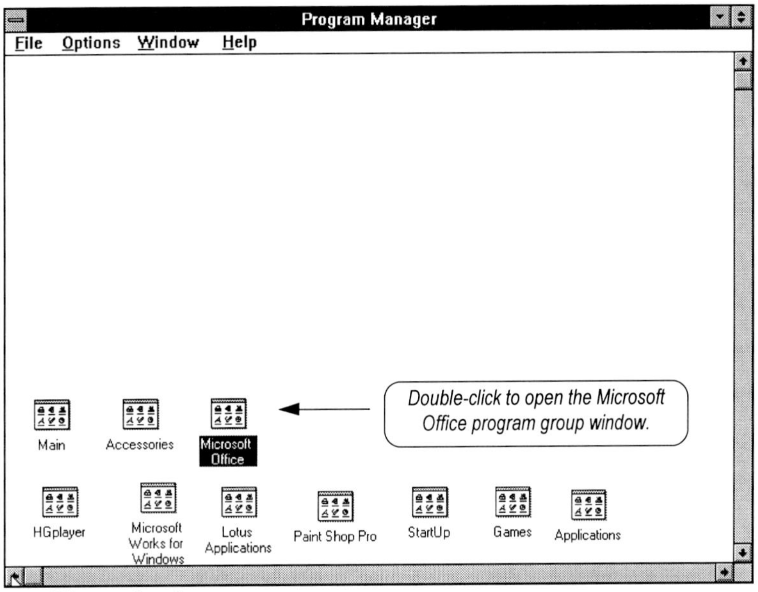

Figure I - 1

4. Point to the *Microsoft Excel* application icon (Figure I - 2) and double-click the left mouse button.

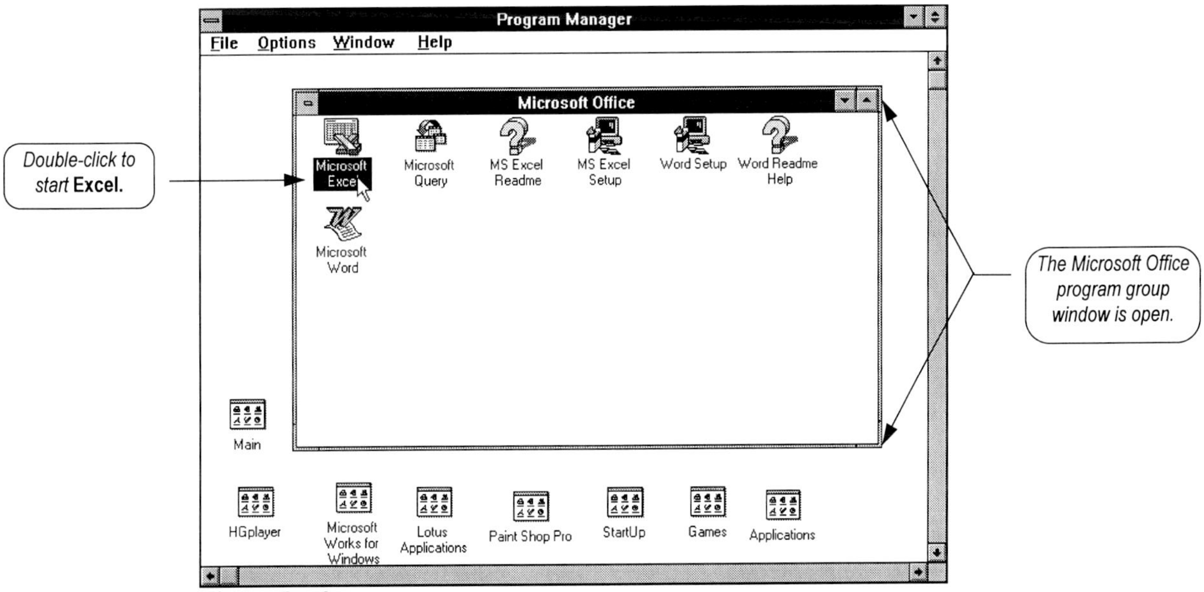

Figure I - 2

The Microsoft Excel window should be displayed (Figure I - 3).

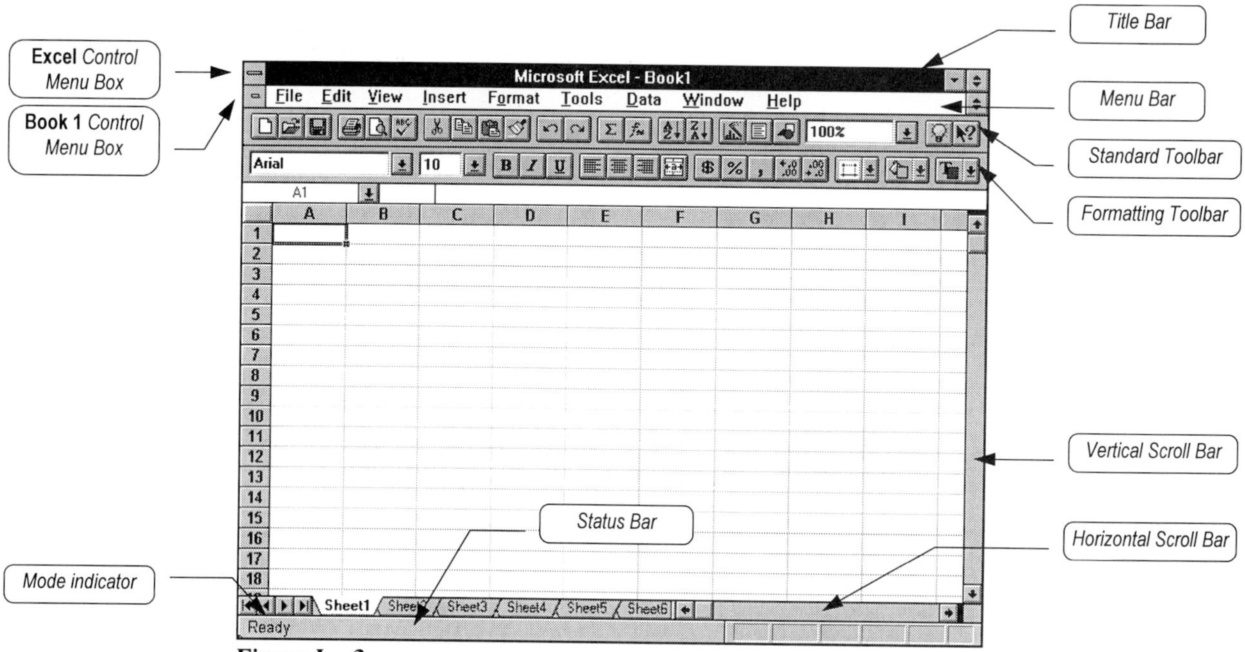

Figure I - 3

THE EXCEL SCREEN

Most of the *Excel* screen is made up of components that are familiar to you from other Windows applications. Other elements may be less familiar because they are specific to working with worksheets or with *Excel.*

Typical Windows Components

Figure I - 3 labels the parts of the *Excel* window that should be familiar to you from using Windows or from other Windows applications. Figure I - 3 shows the screen components that appear when *Excel* is first installed according to a standard setup. As is true with all Windows applications, your screen may look somewhat different than Figure I - 3 if someone has changed the default settings. Some of the more common changes, and ways of changing the appearance of your screen to match those used in this book, will be discussed in this lesson. As you work through this book if your screen differs from those in the book even after you have tried the techniques described in this chapter, check with your instructor or lab assistant.

The Title Bar

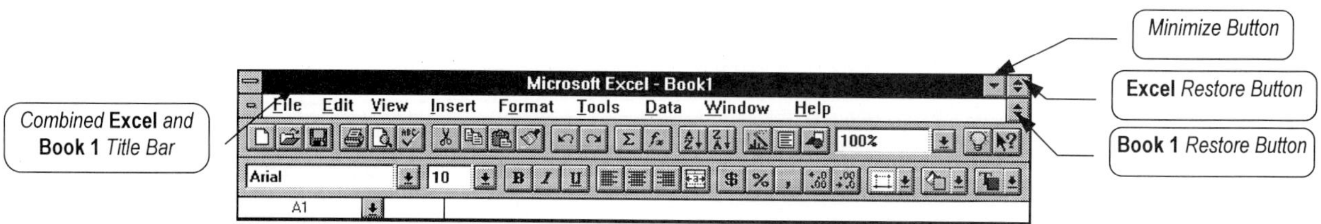

Figure I - 4

As in all Windows applications, *Excel* may have two title bars—one displaying the application name (*Microsoft Excel*), and one displaying the name of the document, or *workbook*, that you are working on. If your screen is using the *default* settings (the settings that are preset by *Excel*), the two title bars are combined into one (Figure I - 4) because the workbook has been maximized.

The right side of the title bar in Figure I - 4 contains the *minimize*  and the *restore*  buttons. The *minimize button* is used to shrink the *Excel* window to an icon. The presence of the *restore button* indicates that the window is already maximized. The *restore button* is used to return a maximized window to its previous size and location. Once a window is restored, the restore button is replaced by the *maximize button* . The *maximize button* is used to enlarge a window to its maximum size. If the Title Bar on your screen does not resemble Figure I - 4, complete Activity I.2. Otherwise skip to the next section on the Menu Bar.

Activity I.2: Maximizing the Excel and Workbook Windows

Do this activity if your title bar(s) resemble(s) Figure I - 5, Figure I - 6 or Figure I - 7.

1. If the **Maximize** button appears on the *Microsoft Excel* title bar, as in Figure I - 5 or Figure I - 6, then the application is **not** maximized. To maximize it, point to the **Maximize button** on the right side of the *Microsoft Excel* title bar and click once with the left mouse button.

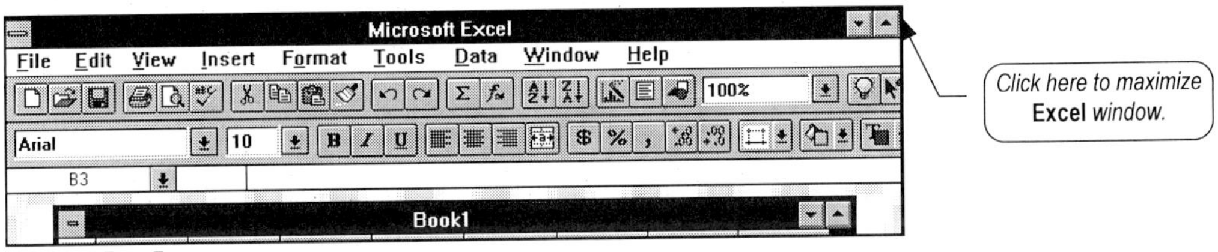

Figure I - 5

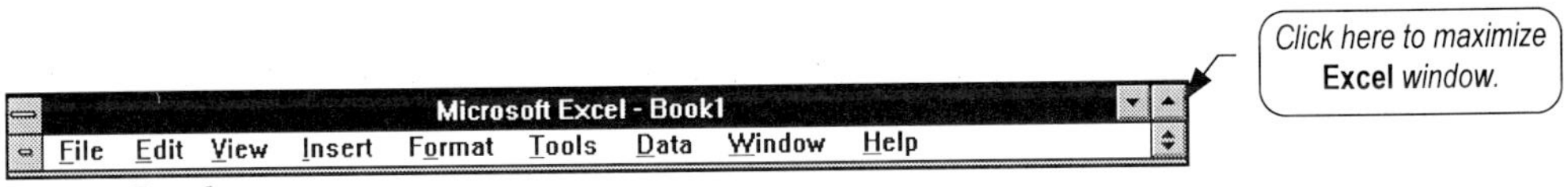

Figure I - 6

2. If **Book1** has its own title bar (Figure I - 7), point to the **Maximize** button on the right side of the **Book1** title bar and click once.

The workbook (Book1) and Excel title bars are now combined and the title bar should resemble Figure I - 4.

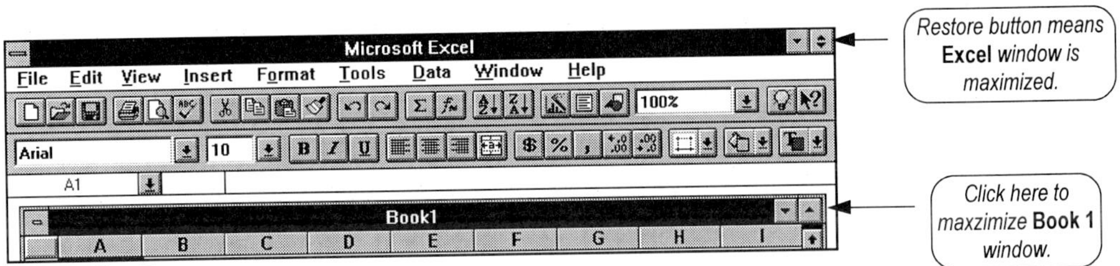

Figure I - 7

The Menu Bar

Immediately under the Title Bar is the Menu Bar (Figure I - 3). The Menu Bar contains the names of the menus from which you choose *Excel* commands. If you have used *Microsoft Word 6.0,* you may notice that all of the menu names except for **Tools** are the same as those in *Word.*

The Toolbar

Immediately under the Menu Bar are the Standard and Formatting Toolbars (Figure I - 3), unless the person who previously used *Excel* on your computer has chosen to hide one or both of them or to display additional toolbars. *Excel* comes with 13 toolbars, some of which are automatically displayed when you issue certain commands. Additional customized toolbars can be created. You will learn how to display the toolbars of your choice in a few pages. Each toolbar contains a set of buttons that perform related actions more quickly than if you used the **Menu** commands they replace. If you have used *Microsoft Word 6.0,* you will notice that more than half of the buttons on the Standard and Formatting Toolbars are identical to those used in *Word.*

Scroll Bars

Excel, like all Windows packages, includes *scroll bars (*Figure I - 3*)*, shaded bars along the right and bottom sides of a window, allowing you to move rapidly through a long worksheet.

Status Bar

The Status Bar (Figure I - 3) is the shaded bar along the very bottom of the screen that displays information about what you are currently doing. It is very important to get into the habit of looking at the Status Bar. When you are working with menus or toolbar buttons, the left side of the Status Bar gives you information on what actions the **menu** commands or toolbar buttons carry out. At other times the left side of the Status Bar gives a general description of the *mode* or type of task you are performing, or even instructions for completing a task. The right side of the Status Bar shows the status of important keys on your computer, such as **NUM LOCK, CAPS LOCK, SCROLL LOCK,** or **INSERT.**

Workbooks and Worksheets

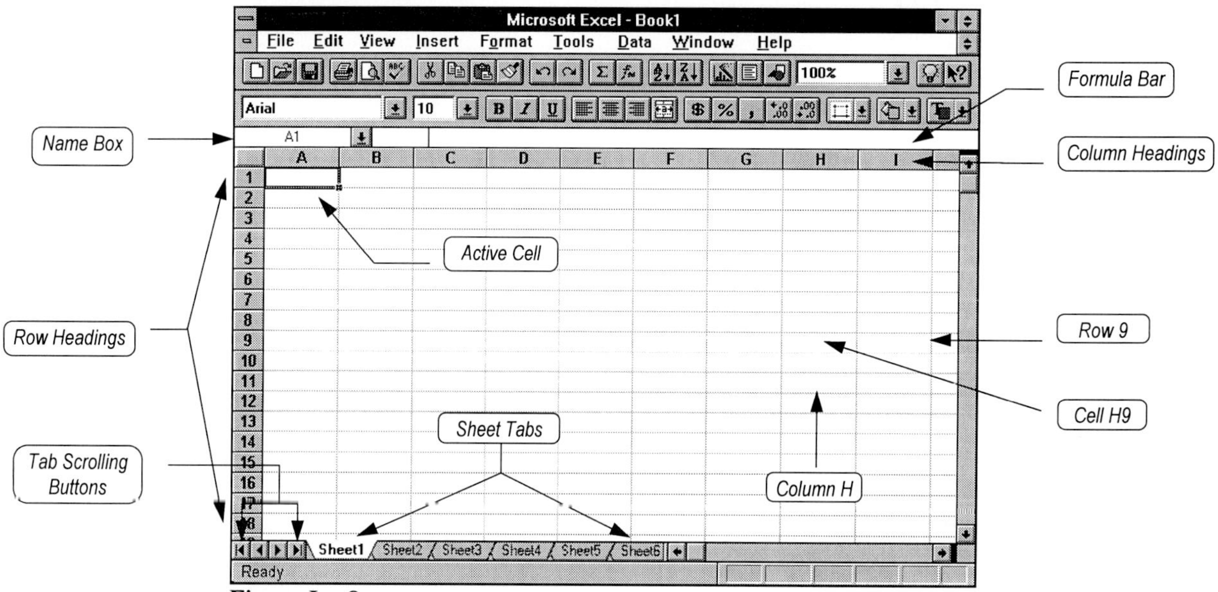

Figure I - 8

In *Excel 5.0* each new file is called a *Workbook.* When a new file is created, its default title is **Book1**, **Book2,** etc. A workbook is a container that holds one or more sheets. Each sheet can be a separate worksheet, a chart, or instructions used to automate working with *Excel.* Figure I - 8 shows a worksheet with its main components labeled. If some of the parts of the worksheet are not displayed on your screen, look at Figure I - 8 as you read the following descriptions. You will learn how to display missing parts of the worksheet in the section on using the **View** menu.

A *worksheet* is the main type of sheet used in *Excel* to store data, perform calculations on data, and otherwise manipulate the data. Most of the terms used to describe parts of the worksheet are described in this section. Unlike the parts of the window previously described, these terms will not be familiar to you unless you have used another worksheet package.

Important worksheet terms that will be used in this book are:

- **Columns** run vertically down the length of the worksheet; a single worksheet contains 256 columns.
- The **Column heading** is the shaded row at the top of the worksheet, which contains the names for each of the columns. Columns are named by letters (**A** through **Z**, followed by **AA** through **AZ**, **BA** through **BZ**, etc., ending with **IA** through **IV**.)
- **Rows** run horizontally across the width of the worksheet. A single worksheet contains 16,384 rows.
- The **Row heading** is the shaded column to the left of the worksheet, which contains the names of the rows. Rows are named by numbers, beginning with **1** and ending with **16, 384**.
- **Cells** are the individual locations on the worksheet. A cell is the intersection of a column and a row, so its name is the column name followed by the row name with **no** spaces (e.g. **A1**, **B62**, **BI203**). There are more than 4,000,000 cells on an each worksheet. The name of the cell may also be called the **cell address** or the **cell reference**.
- The part of the worksheet that contains the cells is sometimes called a **grid.** The **gridlines** are the horizontal and vertical lines that separate columns and rows. They may be removed from the worksheet, but their presence makes it easier to identify cells.
- The **active cell** is the cell in which you are working. It will receive any data you enter and will be acted upon by any commands you choose. It is surrounded by a dark border.
- The **Formula Bar** is a bar above the worksheet window that is used to enter or edit the contents of the worksheet. The **name box** on the left side of the Formula Bar usually tells you the location of the active cell. The rest of the Formula Bar shows you the cell contents.
- **Sheet Tabs** are used to switch between the different sheets in a workbook. A workbook may have as many as 256 sheets, but typically only 16 sheets are available when a new workbook is opened.
- The **Tab Scrolling Buttons** appear along the horizontal scroll bar. They are used to move the first, previous, next, and last sheet in the workbook.

THE MOUSE POINTER

As you move the mouse, a mouse pointer moves across the screen. The shape of the pointer changes depending on the part of the screen to which it is pointing. For example, the mouse pointer is an  when you are pointing to items on the Menu Bar, Toolbar or Status Bar, but changes to a  when it is pointing to cells on the worksheet grid so that you can select the cell(s).

More importantly, the shape of the mouse pointer may also change to indicate what activity will be performed if you press the mouse button. For example, if you point to certain parts of an already selected cell, the pointer will change from a to a or a + . When this happens clicking the mouse button will copy or move the cell contents rather than select the cell. As you follow the activity instructions in this book, look for descriptions of the shape of the mouse pointer and make sure the mouse pointer on your screen is the correct shape!

THE ACTIVE CELL—SELECTING A CELL

Before you can enter data into a cell or perform a command on the contents of the cell, you must select that cell (i.e. make it the *active cell*). The active cell is indicated by the heavy border surrounding it. The name of the active cell can also be seen in the **name box** on the left side of the Formula Bar.

To select a cell that is already visible on the worksheet:

- Move your mouse pointer to the cell and click with the left mouse button, *or*
- Press the **ARROW** keys (← ↑ → ↓) until the heavy border indicating the active cell surrounds the cell of your choice.

Activity I.3: Selecting a Single Cell

1. Point to the cell at the intersection of column **B** and row **3** (cell **B3)** and click with the left mouse button.

   *The dark highlight surrounds **B3** and **B3** appears in the **name box** on the Formula Bar (Figure I - 9).*

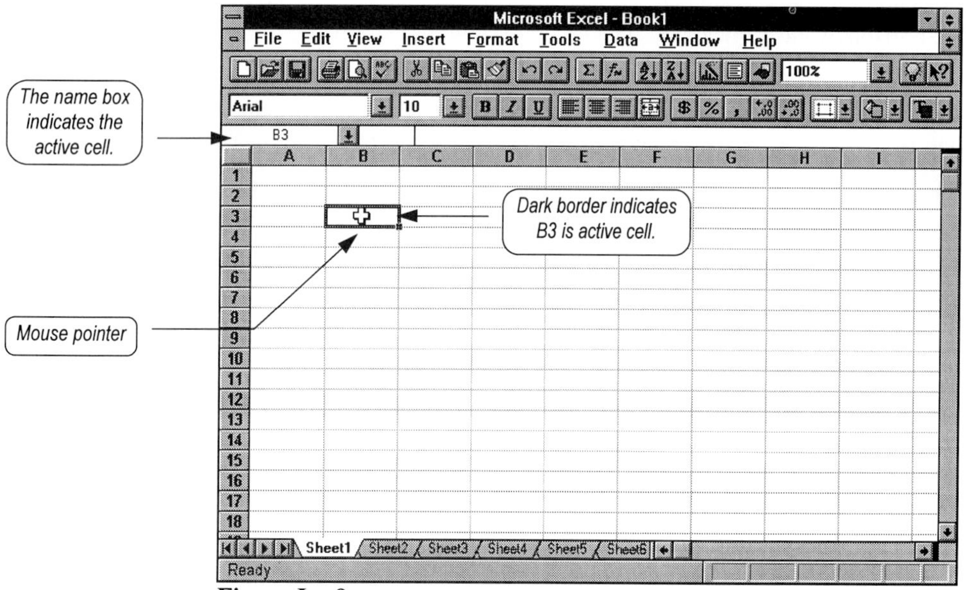

Figure I - 9

2. Press the **DOWN ARROW** key twice and the **RIGHT ARROW** key once.

   ***C5** should be selected as indicated by the dark border surrounding it, and **C5** is indicated in the **name box**.*

GIVING COMMANDS IN *EXCEL*

Commands in *Excel* can be given through the use of the main menus (and their related dialog boxes), toolbar buttons, shortcut keys, and shortcut menus. Instructions in this book will focus on the use of menus and toolbar buttons. Shortcut menus will be introduced in Lesson 2 and used in following lessons. Shortcut keys will be mentioned occasionally. Keyboard shortcuts for the main tasks covered in this book can be found in Appendix A. The menus and dialog boxes in *Excel* work the same way as in other Windows packages. Features that may not be common to all Windows packages will be introduced when first used.

To use the menus to give commands:

- Open the menu by pointing to the menu name and clicking the left mouse button.
- Choose a command by pointing to the command name and clicking the left mouse button.
  - If the command name is followed by an ellipsis (...), a dialog box will be displayed. Follow the instructions in Table I - 1 to complete the dialog box.
  - If the command name is preceded by a check mark, choosing the command will turn it off.
  - If the command name is followed by a triangle, choosing the command will display a submenu. Choose the submenu command the same way you choose the menu commands.
  - If the command name appears in light print, it cannot be used at that time. Choosing it will have no effect.

KEYBOARD ALTERNATIVES*:* To open a menu using the keyboard, press the **ALT** key and then type the underlined letter in the menu name. To choose a command from the menu, type the underlined letter in the command name.

KEYBOARD SHORTCUT: Key combinations that appear to the right of a menu command can be used as shortcuts for the command. They must be used, however, before the menu is opened.

To close a menu without choosing a command

- Point to the menu name or a blank part of the screen outside of the menu and then click the left mouse button.

KEYBOARD ALTERNATIVE*: Press the* ***ALT*** *key to close an open menu.*

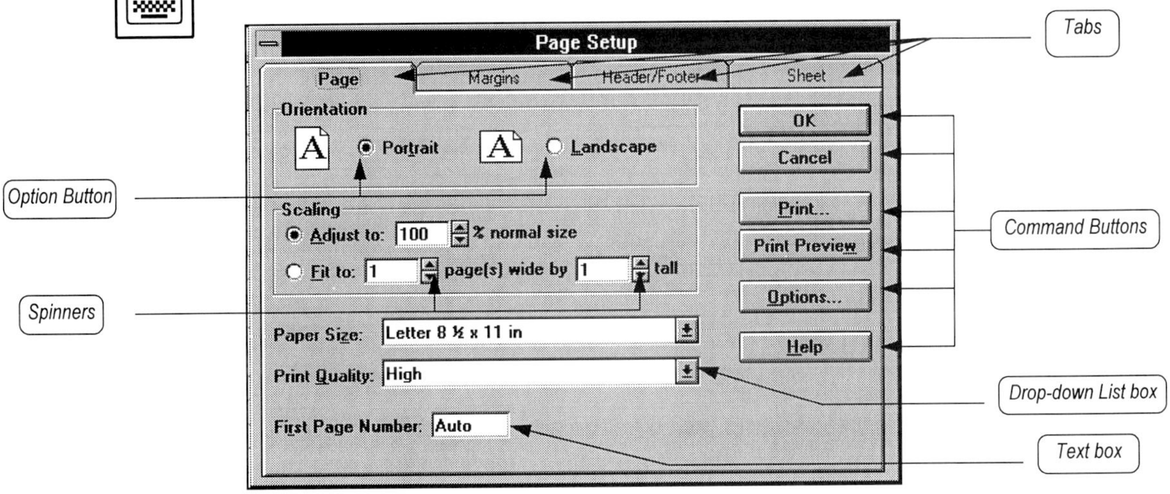

Figure I - 10

Task	Mouse	Keyboard
Tab (Figure I - 10)	Point to the tab and click the left mouse button.	Press **CTRL** and **TAB** until the tab is selected.
Text Box (Figure I - 10)	Double-click in the text box; then type the new information	Press **ALT** and the underlined letter in the text box name; type the new information.
Option (radio) Button (Figure I - 10)	Point to the option button and then click the left mouse button.	Press **ALT** and the underlined letter in the option button name.
Check Box (Figure I - 11)	Point to the square preceding the box name and then click the left mouse button to toggle the box on or off.	Press **ALT** and the highlighted letter in the check box name.
List Box (Figure I - 11)	Point to the list box item and click the left mouse button. If the item is not visible, click on the scroll arrows to move the list up/down one item at a time; click on the list item once it is displayed.	Press **ALT** and the underlined letter in the list box name; use the **UP** and **DOWN ARROW** keys to select the list item.
Drop-down List Box (Figure I - 10 and Figure I - 11)	Click the ↓ to the right of the list box and then follow directions for list boxes.	Press **ALT** and the underlined letter in the list box name to open the drop-down list.
Spinner (Figure I - 10)	Click the **UP** and **DOWN** arrows to the right of the box until the number you want appears in the box, or type the new number.	Press **ALT** and the underlined letter in the spinner name; press the **UP** or **DOWN ARROW** keys to change the numbers by the default amount or type the new number.
Command Button (Figure I - 10)	To execute or cancel the command, or display another dialog box, click on the appropriate command button.	Press **ESC** to cancel a command, **ENTER** to execute a command, or **ALT** and the underlined letter.

Table I - 1: Using Dialog Boxes

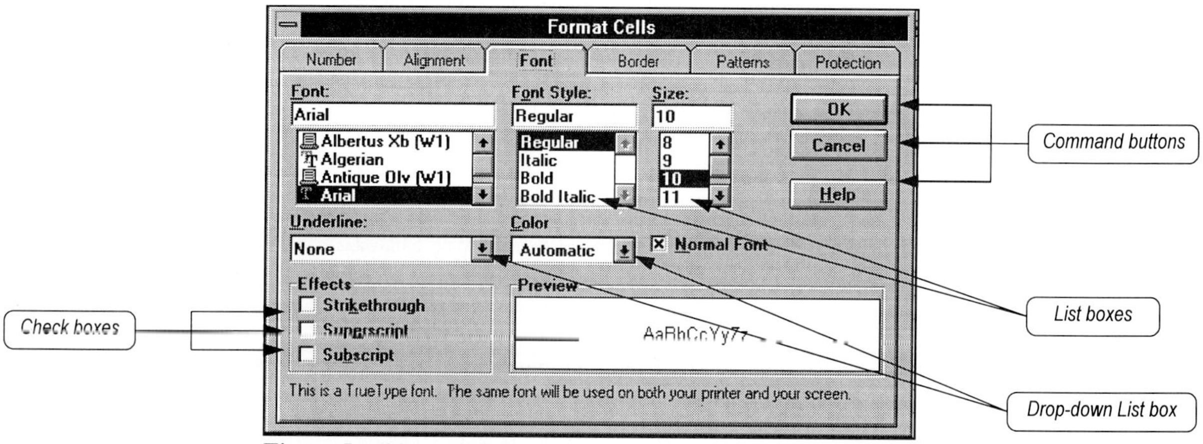

Figure I - 11

THE VIEW MENU

The **View** menu controls the appearance of the screen. If your screen has not contained all of the components described previously, the **View** menu is the first place to go to change the display.

To display the Status Bar and Formula Bar:

- Open the **View** menu by pointing to **View** with the mouse pointer and clicking on **View** with the left mouse button.
- If **Formula Bar** and **Status Bar** are preceded by check marks (√), they are already selected. If the one that you want displayed is not preceded by a check mark, click on it with the left mouse button.

To display/hide toolbars:

- Open the **View** menu.
- Point to **Toolbars** and click on it with the left mouse button.
- In the **Toolbars** dialog box, a toolbar preceded by a marked check box is displayed. Click on empty check boxes to display additional toolbars; click on marked check boxes to hide already displayed toolbars.

Activity I.4: Using the View Menu to Change the Appearance of the Screen

1. To open the **View** menu, point to **View** in the Menu Bar and click the left mouse button (Figure I - 12).

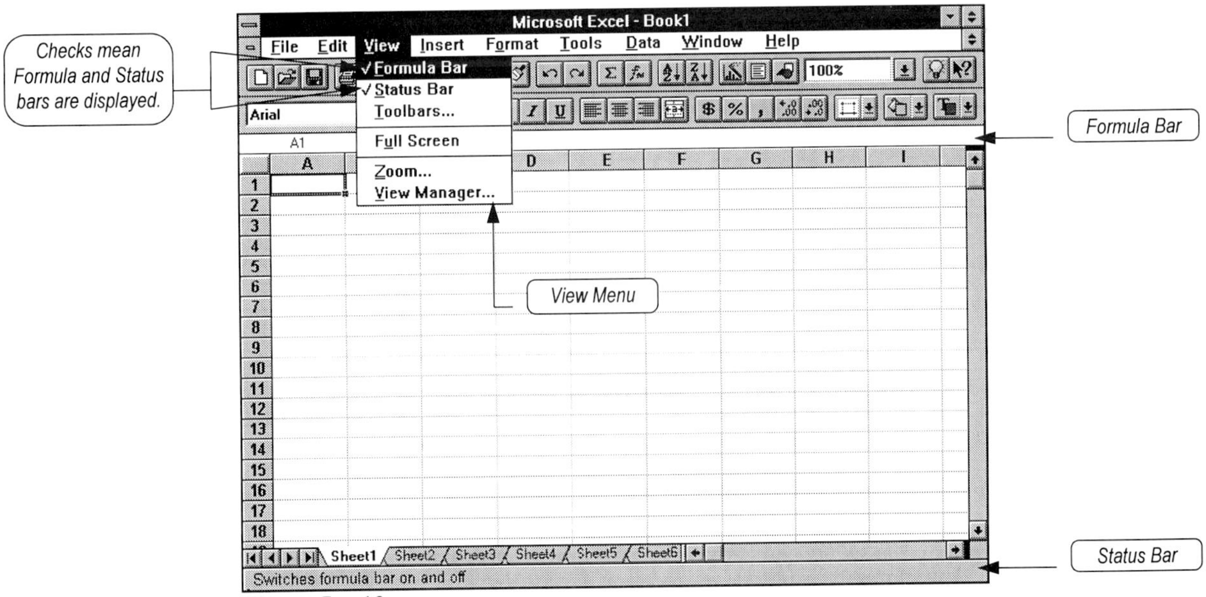

Figure I - 12

2. In Figure I - 12 **Formula Bar** and **Status Bar** are both preceded by check marks indicating that both are displayed. Point to **Status Bar** and click the left mouse button.

***Formula Bar** and **Status Bar** work like toggle keys — selecting them changes their state from on to off and vice versa. If the Status Bar was previously displayed, it will be removed as in Figure I - 13. If it was not previously displayed, it will now be displayed.*

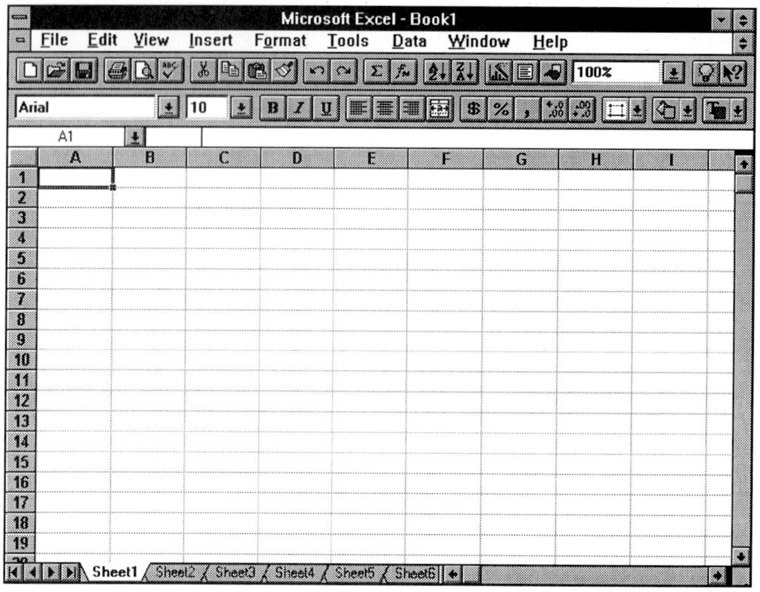

The Status Bar is no longer displayed.

Figure I - 13

3. Click on **View** again. If the **View** menu resembles Figure I - 14 and **Status Bar** is NOT checked, click on **Status Bar**. If **Status Bar** is already preceded by a check mark (as in Figure I - 12), click anywhere on the worksheet grid to close the menu.

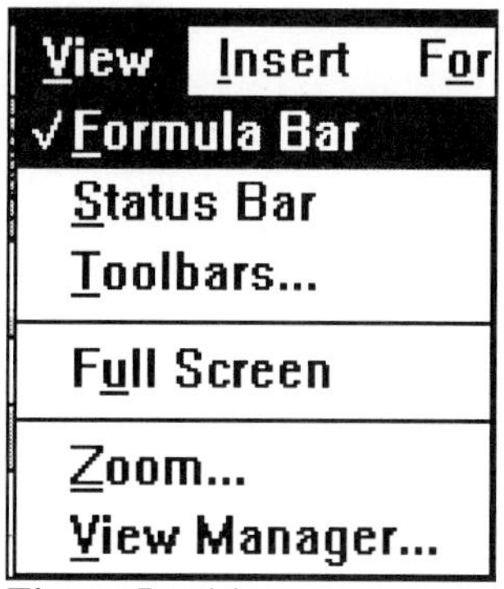

Figure I - 14

PROBLEM SOLVER: *If the Title Bar, Status Bar and other screen parts are not visible on the screen, and the **Full Screen** command on the **View** menu has been selected, click on it again to unselect it.*

4. Choose **View** again.
5. Choose **Toolbars** by pointing to it and clicking the left mouse button.

   *The **Toolbars** dialog box (Figure I - 15) is displayed.*

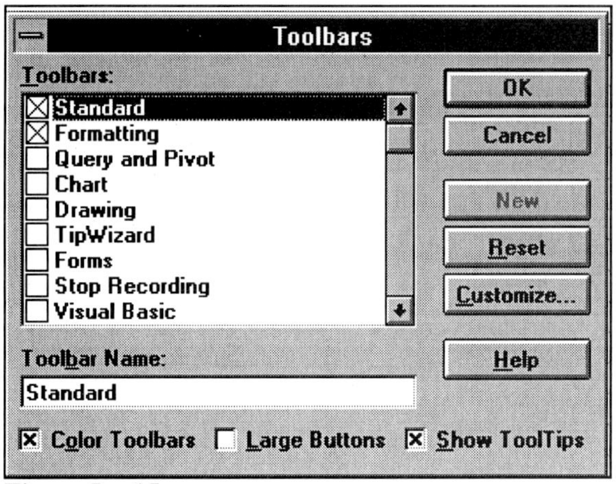

Figure I - 15

6. The **Standard** and **Formatting** check boxes should be marked as in Figure I - 15. If either or both are not checked, click on them to check them. If any other check boxes in the **Toolbars** section of the screen are checked, click on them to unmark them.
7. Compare the **Toolbars** dialog box on your screen with Figure I - 15. When it is identical (including the **X**s in the **Color Toolbars** and **Show ToolTips** check boxes) to Figure I - 15, click on **OK**.

   *Use the **View** menu through this book anytime the Status Bar, Formula Bar, or Toolbars are missing from your screen.*

USING TOOLBAR BUTTONS

Toolbar buttons can be used to perform many of the commands that the menus perform. While using the toolbars is quicker than using the menus, sometimes your choices are limited or you receive less information about the effects of your command.

One of the improvements *Excel* made in version 5.0 was the inclusion of **ToolTips**. When you point to a toolbar button, the name of the button appears in a colored box next to the button and a description of the button appears on the Status Bar. In Activity I.4 you used the **VIEW/Toolbars** command to make sure **Show ToolTips** would be displayed.

To use a toolbar button:

- Move the mouse pointer to the toolbar button and click the left mouse button.

To find out what a specific toolbar button does:

- Move the mouse pointer until it is on the toolbar button.
- Read the name of the button in the **ToolTips** box that appears next to the mouse pointer. Read a description of the button on the Status Bar.

GETTING ON-LINE HELP

ToolTips is one of many examples of the help *Excel* provides. Each of the dialog boxes also contains a **Help** button. Choosing that button displays help about the dialog box that you are currently using. The **Help** menu provides three ways of searching for help on a topic: **Table of**

Contents, **Search for Help on**, and an **Index**. In addition, **Quick Preview** and **Examples and Demos** provide tutorials on performing many tasks in *Excel*. The **TipWizard** button on the Standard toolbar displays the **TipWizard** toolbar, which contains tips on other ways to perform the tasks you have tried since opening *Excel*. Click on the **Help** button and then click on any part of the screen to get help on that part of the screen.

To get Help while working in a dialog box:

- Point to the **Help** command button in the dialog box and click the left mouse button.
- If the Help topic extends beyond the screen, click on the ↓ on the vertical scroll bar to see the rest of the topic.
- Any information on the screen that is green and underlined with a solid line is a *jump term*. If you move the mouse pointer to the jump term, the shape of the mouse changes to a hand. Click the left mouse button to display the Help topic.
- Any information on the screen that is green and underlined with dashes is a *term* for which *Excel* has a definition. Point to a term and click the left mouse button to display a definition of the term. When you have finished reading the definition, click the left mouse button again.

Activity I.5: Using Help

In this activity you will practice using **Help**.

1. Open the **Format** menu by pointing to **Format** on the Menu Bar and clicking the left mouse button.
2. Point to **Cells** and click the left mouse button.
3. If the **Font** tab is not on top, point to the **Font** tab and click (Figure I - 16).
4. Point to the **Help** command button (Figure I - 16) in the **Format Cells** dialog box and click the left mouse button.

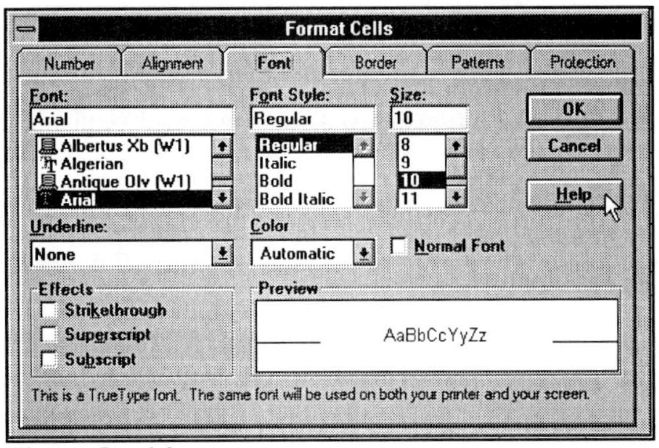

Figure I - 16

*The **Font Tab, Cells Command (Format Menu)** Help screen (Figure I - 17) is displayed.*

5. Click on the ↓ on the vertical scroll bar until **Normal Style** (in green print underlined) is displayed (Figure I - 18).

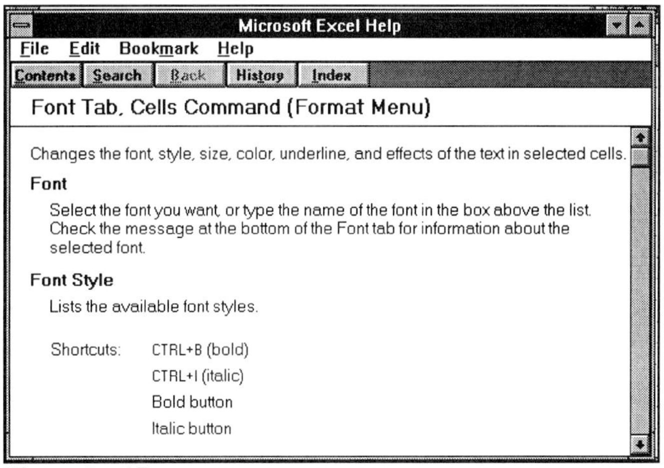

Figure I - 17

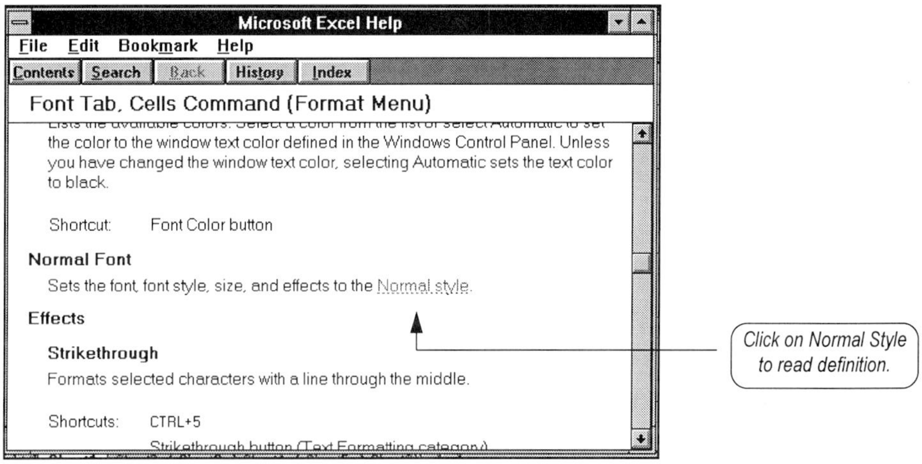

Figure I - 18

6. Since **Normal Style** is underlined in a green dashed line, it is a defined term. Move the mouse until it is pointing to **Normal Style** and has changed to a hand. Click the left mouse button.
7. Read the definition of **Normal Style** (Figure I - 19) and click the left mouse button again to close the definition box.

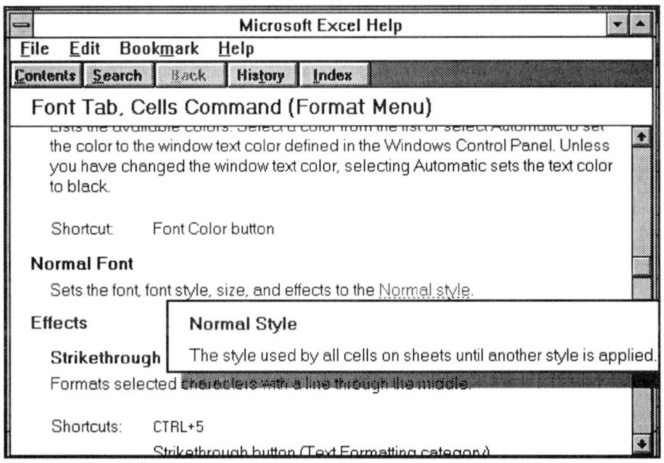

Figure I - 19

8. Scroll the screen until the **See Also** section of the dialog box appears. Click on the *jump term*, **Bold Button** (Figure I - 20).

   *The **Bold Button** Help screen is displayed.*

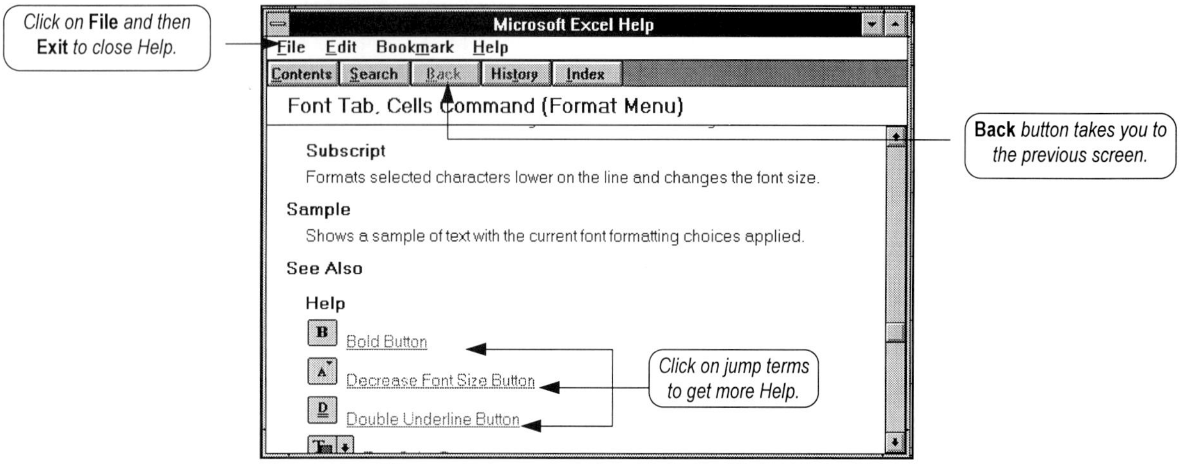

Figure I - 20

9. Read the **Bold Button** Help screen.
10. To exit from **Help**, click on **File** in the **Microsoft Excel Help** menu bar.
11. Click on **Exit** on the **File** menu.
12. Click on the **Cancel** button in the **Formal Cells** dialog box to close it.

EXITING FROM *EXCEL*

While you are working, *Excel* creates temporary files to help it with its work. Therefore, it is always important to exit correctly from a program, rather than to turn off the computer while in the middle of the program.

To exit from *Excel*:

- Point to **File** on the Menu Bar and click the left mouse button.
- Point to **Exit** on the **File** menu and click the left mouse button.
- If you have made any changes to the workbook and not saved your work, an *Alert box* containing four choices, **Yes, No**, **Cancel,** and **Help** will appear. To save changes to the file, click on **Yes.** To exit without saving changes to the file, click on **No**. To continue working in *Excel*, choose **Cancel**. To get help on how to use the alert box, click on **Help**.
- If you are finished using **Windows**, choose **FILE/Exit** from the Program Manager menu. When the prompt **This will end your Windows session** appears, click on **Yes**.

Activity I.6: Exiting from Excel

1. Point to **File** on the Menu Bar and click the left mouse button.
2. Point to **Exit** on the **File** menu and click the left mouse button.
3. If an Alert box asking **Save changes in 'Book1?'** appears, click on **No** to exit the program <u>without</u> saving the workbook.

SUMMARY

In this introduction you have seen the parts of the *Excel* screen that are common to all Windows applications and those that are specific to *Excel* or to worksheet software. You have seen how to use the **View** menu to change the appearance of the screen. You have also reviewed the use of menus and dialog boxes and of using **Help**. As you work through this book, if you have trouble with basic worksheet terminology or the use of menus and dialog boxes, refer back to this chapter.

The two Independent Projects at the end of this Introduction introduce two parts of Help — **Quick Preview** and **Contents**—which may be slightly different from **Help** options that you have used in other Windows applications.

CONVENTIONS FOLLOWED IN THIS BOOK

Table I - 2 shows the way instructions are abbreviated in this book.

Task	Words used in this book	Explanation
Using the mouse	"click on" or "click the mouse button"	Move the mouse pointer to the item to be selected (cell, toolbar button, menu name, command name, etc.) and click the **left** mouse button.
Using the **right** mouse button	"click the right mouse button"	Every time the **right** mouse button is to be used instead of the left mouse button, the instructions will specifically include the word **right**.
Selecting a cell	"select *cell name*" where *cell name* is the name of a cell (e.g. select **A21**)	Move the mouse pointer to the cell and click the left mouse button, or press the **ARROW** keys until the thick frame surrounds the desired cell
Choosing a command from the Menu Bar	"Choose **MENU NAME/Command, Name, SubMenu Command**, or **Dialog Box tab"** (For example, "Choose **FORMAT/Cells, Font**")	• Point to the **menu name** with the mouse and click the left mouse button. • In the menu that is displayed, point to the **Command Name** and click the left mouse button. • If a SubMenu is displayed, point to the **SubMenu Command** and click the left mouse button. • If a tabbed dialog box is displayed, point to the desired tab and click the left mouse button or press the **CTRL** key and keep it depressed while pressing the **TAB** key until the tab that you want is on top.
Using two keys together	Press **ALT+letter** (for example, press **ALT+I**)	• Press the **ALT** key (or the **CTRL, SHIFT,** etc. key) and while keeping it depressed, type the letter.

Table I - 2

KEY TERMS

Active cell
Cell
Cell address
Cell reference
Check box*
Column
Column heading**
Command button
Default
Dialog box*
Drop-down list box*
Formula Bar**
Grid
Gridlines
Insertion point
Jump term
List box*
Maximize button**
Menu Bar
Minimize button**
Name box**
Option button*
Row
Row heading**
Sheet tab**
Spinner*
Status Bar**
Tab dialog box*
Tab scrolling buttons**
Text box*
Title Bar
Toolbar
Toolbar button*
ToolTip
What-If analysis
Workbook
Worksheet*

* Defined in Microsoft Help Definitions (see Independent Project I.2)
**Described in Parts of Microsoft Excel Screen (see Independent Project I.2)

INDEPENDENT PROJECTS

Independent Project I.1: Learning More About Help

In this project, you will use the **Getting Information While You Work** section of the *Excel* **Quick Preview** to learn more about Help.

1. Open *Excel.*
2. Choose **HELP/Quick Preview**.

   *The **Quick Preview** screen will appear.*
3. Click on **Getting Information While You Work** or press **ALT+I**.

   This tutorial will describe how to use the TipWizard, and the Search and Index Help commands and the Help screens.
4. Read each screen. Click on the **Next** button at the bottom of the screen or press **ALT+N** to display the next screen.
5. When the last screen is displayed, click on the **Close** button or press **ALT+C**.

   *The **Quick Preview** screen will be displayed.*
6. Click on the **Return to Microsoft Excel** button or press **ALT+R** to return to *Excel.*

Independent Project I.2: Using Help Contents

In this project you will become familiar with the **Contents** section of the **Help** Menu. Then you will use the **Reference Information** section of the **Contents** help screen to help you review terms and parts of the *Excel* window introduced in the Introduction and listed in the Key Terms section of the lesson.

1. Open *Excel*, if it is not already open.
2. Choose **HELP/Contents.**

*The **Microsoft Excel Help Contents** screen will be displayed (Figure I - 21).*

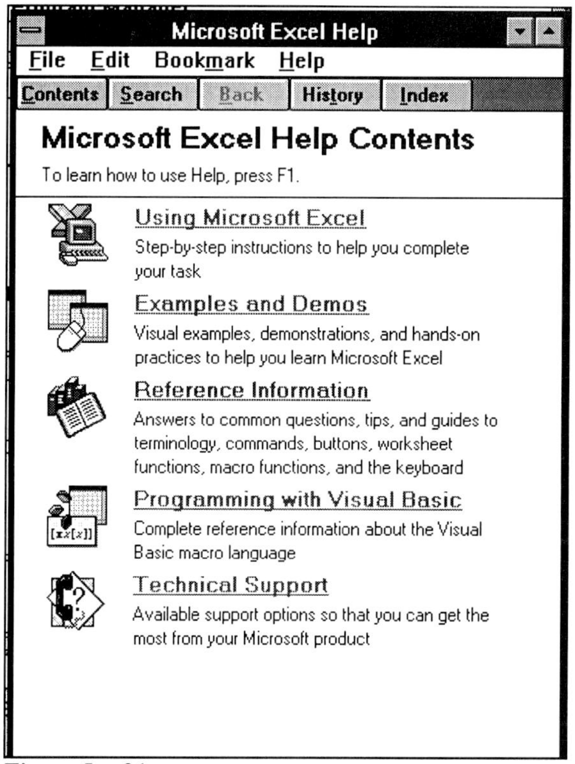

Figure I - 21

3. To choose **Using Microsoft Excel**, point to **Using Microsoft Excel**. When the mouse pointer changes to a hand, click the mouse button.
4. Read the **Using Microsoft Excel** topics. Keep these in mind if you need help later when working through this book.
5. Click on the **Back** button under the Menu Bar to return to the **Microsoft Excel Help Contents** screen.
6. Choose **Examples and Demos**.
7. Read the topics for which examples or demos are offered. Click on the **Close** button at the bottom of the screen when you are done.
8. Choose **Reference Information** from the **Microsoft Excel Help Contents** screen.
9. Choose **Definitions**. Click on each of the words from the Key Terms section of this chapter that is followed by a single asterisk (*). Read the definition and click again.
10. Click on the **Back** button at the top of the screen under the Menu Bar.
11. Choose **Parts of the Microsoft Excel Screen** from the **Reference Information** screen.
12. Choose each of the screen parts listed in Key Terms that is followed by a double asterisk (**). After reading about that part of the screen, click on the **Back** button to return to the **Parts of the Screen** window so that you can select another screen part.
13. Choose **FILE/Exit** to leave help.

Use **Reference Information** from **HELP/Contents** as you work through this book when you want to review definitions or basic procedures.

Lesson 1

Creating a Simple Worksheet

Objectives

In this lesson you will learn how to:

- Distinguish between text and value entries
- Enter text and values
- Correct errors
- Change column widths
- Enter formulas
- Edit a worksheet
- Undo commands
- Save, close, and open a workbook
- Print a worksheet
- Display formulas on the worksheet

PROJECT DESCRIPTION

In this lesson you will create your first project. ECAP Consulting, Inc. is a small consulting company that hires employees on an hourly basis and bills clients based on the number of hours worked by the employee. In this project you will create a worksheet to calculate the total salary and the total amount billed by each employee for one week, and to calculate the profit and % profit generated in the week.

In order to create this worksheet, you will perform most of the basic tasks involved in creating any worksheet — entering data, entering text that explain the data, performing calculations on the data, saving the worksheet, and printing it. By the end of this lesson, your worksheet will look like Figure 1 - 1. In Lesson 2, you will improve the appearance of the worksheet by changing the alignment of some of the data, formatting the numeric data with commas, dollars, and percent signs, and using lines and text enhancements to make different parts of the worksheet stand out.

Before you create this or any other worksheet in *Excel*, you must plan the worksheet.

PLANNING A WORKSHEET

Before you enter anything into the worksheet, you must first decide what the general objectives of the worksheet are and how you will design the worksheet to meet its objectives. The general steps in planning a worksheet, and how they are applied to our first project follow:

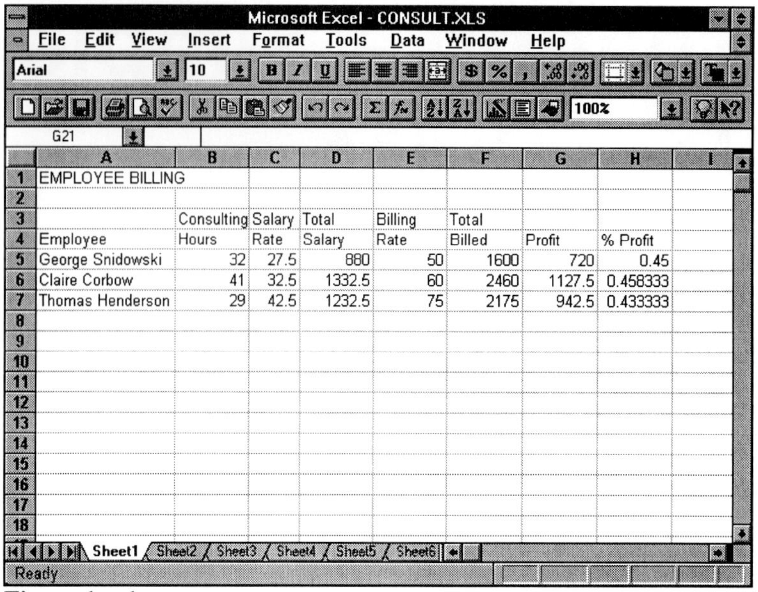

	A	B	C	D	E	F	G	H
1	EMPLOYEE BILLING							
2								
3		Consulting	Salary	Total	Billing	Total		
4	Employee	Hours	Rate	Salary	Rate	Billed	Profit	% Profit
5	George Snidowski	32	27.5	880	50	1600	720	0.45
6	Claire Corbow	41	32.5	1332.5	60	2460	1127.5	0.458333
7	Thomas Henderson	29	42.5	1232.5	75	2175	942.5	0.433333

Figure 1 - 1

To plan a worksheet:

- Define the general objectives of the worksheet.

  ECAP Consulting needs to determine the total salary and the total amount billed by each consultant, and the gross profits resulting from these billings.

- Define the specific results you want the worksheet to provide.

  The worksheet must provide: a) the salary due each consultant; b) the amount billed by each consultant; c) the gross profit generated by each consultant; and, d) the percent profit generated by each consultant.

- Specify and obtain the data needed to obtain the results.

  The required data are: a)names of each of the consultants, b)hours worked by each consultant, c)salary rate for each consultant, and d)billing rate for each consultant.

- Specify the calculations to be performed on the data:

RESULT	***CALCULATION***
Total Salary for each consultant	*Number of consulting hours times salary rate*
Total billed by each consultant	*Number of consulting hours times billing rate*
Profit generated by each consultant	*Total billed minus total salary*
Percent profit generated by each consultant	*Profit divided by total billed*

- Organize the worksheet on paper. Determine which data will go in each column and row. Choose a title for the worksheet and for each column and row. Indicate where the calculations will be entered.

Worksheet title							
Employee	Consulting Hours	Salary Rate	Total Salary	Billing Rate	Total Billed	Profit	% Profit
Data (Names)	Data (# hours)	Data (Salary)	Calculation	Data (Billing #)	Calculation	Calculation	Calculation
↓	↓	↓	↓	↓	↓	↓	↓
↓	↓	↓	↓	↓	↓	↓	↓

ENTERING TEXT AND VALUES

The first steps in creating a worksheet are to enter labels (or titles) that describe the contents of the worksheet, data (which may be either text or numbers), and formulas that perform calculations on the data. All of these cell entries can be classified as *text* or *values.*

Text

A text entry can generally be thought of as any entry made up of letters or letters and numbers. (*Excel* defines text as any entry that is not a number, formula, date, time, or logical or error value.) Text is used to identify the data that you will be putting into the worksheet. Text can appear anywhere on the worksheet, but is often used across the top of the worksheet as column labels or down the left side of the worksheet as row labels. You will use text in both ways in this lesson. If you accidentally include a text entry in a formula, it has the value of zero.

When you type text it is automatically *left aligned.* This means that the text starts at the left edge of the cell. You will learn how to change this alignment, should you choose to do so, in Lesson 2.

Values

A value is an entry that is a *number* or a *formula.* Values can be used in all mathematical calculations such as addition, subtraction, multiplication, and division. To enter a value, you typically type the value without any formatting symbols (dollar signs, percents, commas, etc.). Then you use one of *Excel's* formatting commands to enter these symbols automatically. When entered, values are automatically *right aligned* in the cell. An entry is considered to be a number if it contains only numeric digits and any of the following characters used as described below:

.	to indicate a decimal point
,	to separate the number into thousands; if you type a comma in the wrong place, it makes the entry a label
+	to indicate that a number is positive
-	to indicate that a number is negative
( )	to indicate that a number (not a calculation) is negative
/	to indicate a fraction
$	to display a number as currency
E e	to display a number in exponential format
%	to indicate that a number is a percent

Numbers (e.g. 54, -364) are sometimes also called *constants* because they cannot change unless they are edited or retyped.

Formulas are used to calculate. We will discuss them in a few pages when you are ready to use them.

Entering Text

Now you're ready to start creating your worksheet.

REMEMBER: Read the bulleted list that follows, but do not actually perform the steps until you reach Activity 1.1.

To enter text or values:

- Select the cell to contain the data by clicking in the cell or using the **ARROW** keys to move the highlight to the cell.
- Type the data. If you notice any errors while you are typing, press the **BACKSPACE** key until the error is removed and finish typing.
- Press the **ENTER** key or click on the **enter box** to enter the data. Alternatively, you may press an **ARROW** key or click on another cell to both enter the data and move the highlight.

Activity 1.1: Entering Text

First, you will enter text for the title of the worksheet, EMPLOYEE BILLING, and for the labels of each of the columns. Some of your column labels, such as Consulting Hours, are very long. To keep your columns as narrow as possible, when you have two-word column labels, you will type the first word in one cell and the second in the cell directly below it. See Figure 1 - 6 for an illustration of what you are about to do. After you enter the column labels, you will enter the row labels, which are the names of the employees.

1. Start *Excel*. Follow the instructions in the Introductory lesson, if necessary.

   *A blank worksheet will be displayed. Cell **A1** will be enclosed in a dark border. This border indicates that **A1** is the selected cell and that any data you type will be entered in that cell.*

2. If **Excel** or **Book1** is not maximized, maximize it. See Activity I.2 in the Introduction for instructions.

3. With the cursor still in **A1**, press the **CAPS LOCK** key and type: **EMPLOYEE BILLING**

   *As soon as you begin to type, three buttons – the **cancel box**, the **enter box** and the **Function Wizard** button appear on the screen. A blinking vertical line, called the **insertion point** appears in **A1** to show you where the next typed character will appear. As you type, the text is visible in **A1** and in the Formula Bar (Figure 1 - 2). The mode indicator on the Status Bar changes from **Ready** to **Enter**.*

4. Press **CAPS LOCK** again to turn off capitalization.

5. Press the **ENTER** key or click on the **enter box** in the Formula Bar.

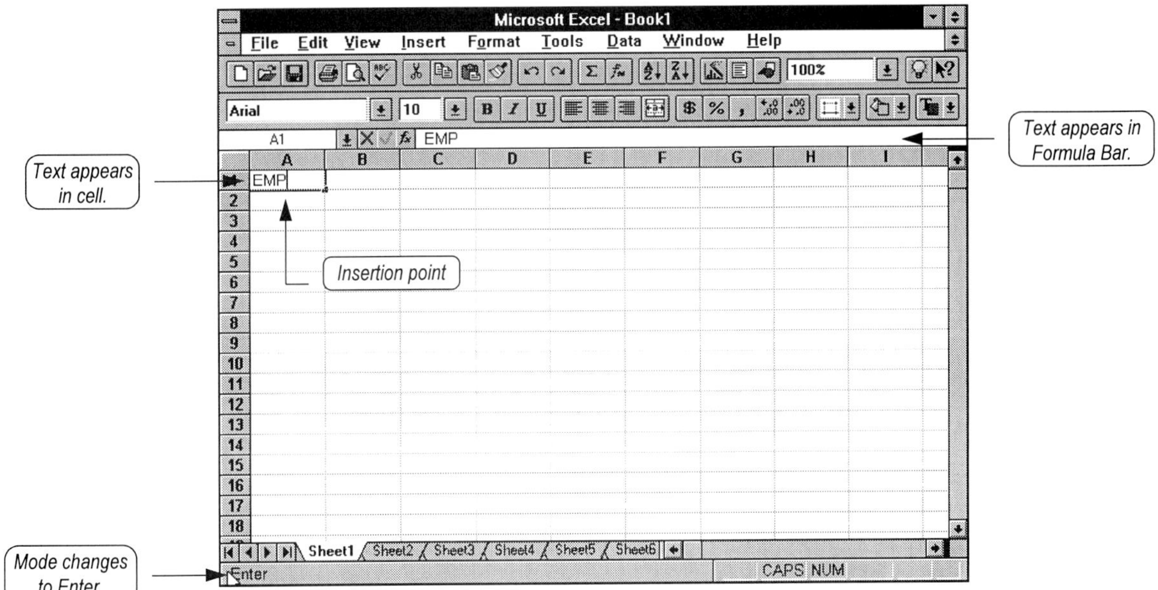

Figure 1 - 2

If the default settings have not been changed, clicking the ***enter box*** *will leave the highlight in cell* ***A1,*** *while pressing the* ***ENTER*** *key will move the highlight down one cell to* ***A2****. The movement of the highlight after pressing the* ***ENTER*** *key is controlled by the* ***TOOLS/Options,Edit*** *dialog box. If* ***Move Selection after Enter*** *is checked, the highlight moves; otherwise it remains in the cell.* ***Employee Billing*** *is too wide to fit in cell* ***A1****. Since its adjacent cell,* ***B1,*** *is empty, it overflows into that cell (Figure 1 - 3).*

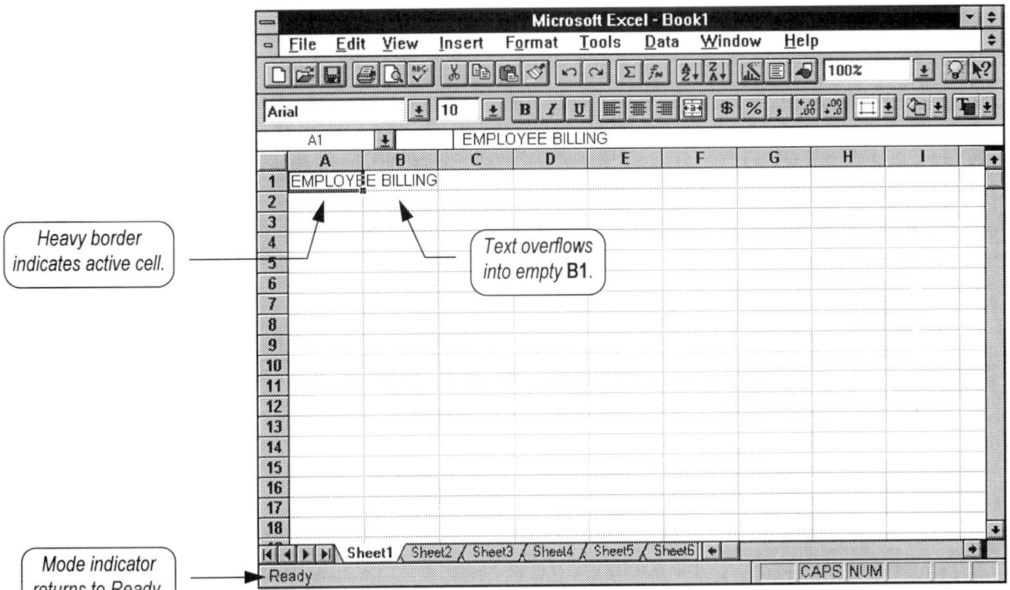

Figure 1 - 3

6. Click on cell **A4** to select it.

7. Type: **Employee** and click on the **enter box** or press the **ENTER** key.

   *Since Employee is text, it is left aligned in the cell. In Figure 1 - 4, the highlight remains in **A4**. The highlight on your screen will be in cell **A5**, if the **Move Selection after Enter** option is in effect and you pressed the **ENTER** key.*

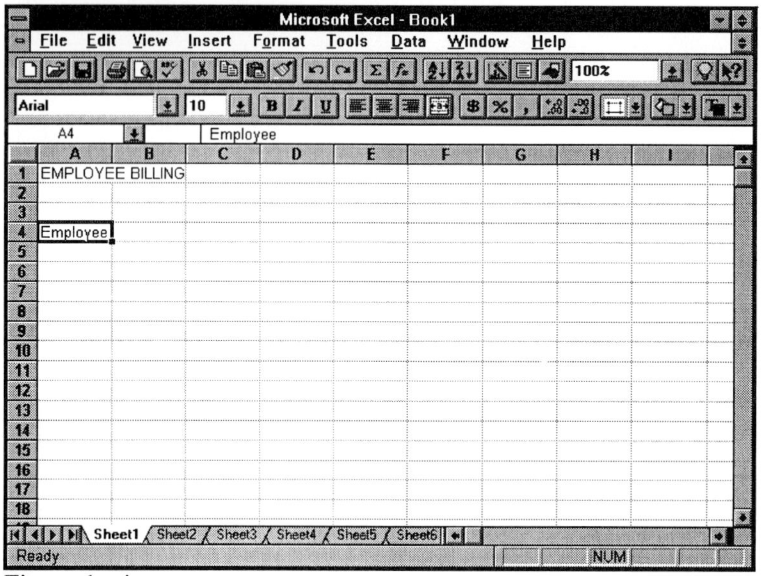

Figure 1 - 4

8. Click on **B3** to select it.
9. Type: **Consulting**
10. Press the **DOWN ARROW**.

    *The highlight will move to cell **B4**. Pressing any **ARROW** key enters the data and moves the highlight one cell in the direction of the arrow key.*

11. In **B4** type: **Hours**
12. Click on **C3**.

    ***Hours** is entered in **B4** and the highlight moves to **C3**. Clicking on a new cell enters the data in the original cell and selects the new cell.*

13. In cell **C3** type: **Salary** and in **C4** type **Rate** using the method of your choice to enter the data and move from cell to cell.
14. In cell **D3** enter: **Total** and in **D4** enter: **Salary**
15. In cell **E3** enter: **Billing** and in **E4** enter: **Rate**
16. In cell **F3** enter: **Total** and in **F4** enter: **Billed**
17. In **G4** enter: **Profit**
18. In **H4** enter: **% Profit**

    Your worksheet should resemble Figure 1 - 5. If you have made typing errors, don't worry; you'll learn how to correct them in the next section.

PROBLEM SOLVER: If you have entered data into a cell that should be blank, click on that cell and press the **DELETE** key to erase the data. If a cell contains the wrong information, click on the cell containing incorrect information, retype the entire cell contents and press the **ENTER** key or click on the **enter box.**

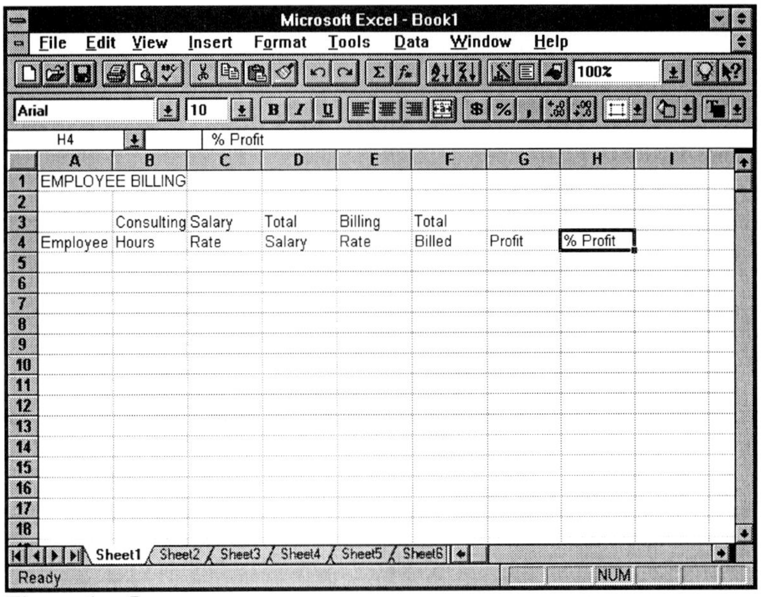

Figure 1 - 5

19. Move the highlight to cell **A5** and in cells **A5, A6, A7,** and **A8,** type the employee names listed below. After typing each one, press the **DOWN ARROW**.

    George Snidow

    Claire Carbow

    Thomas Hender

    Naomi Gold

*The employee names overflow into column **B**. You will correct this problem shortly. Your worksheet should resemble Figure 1 - 6.*

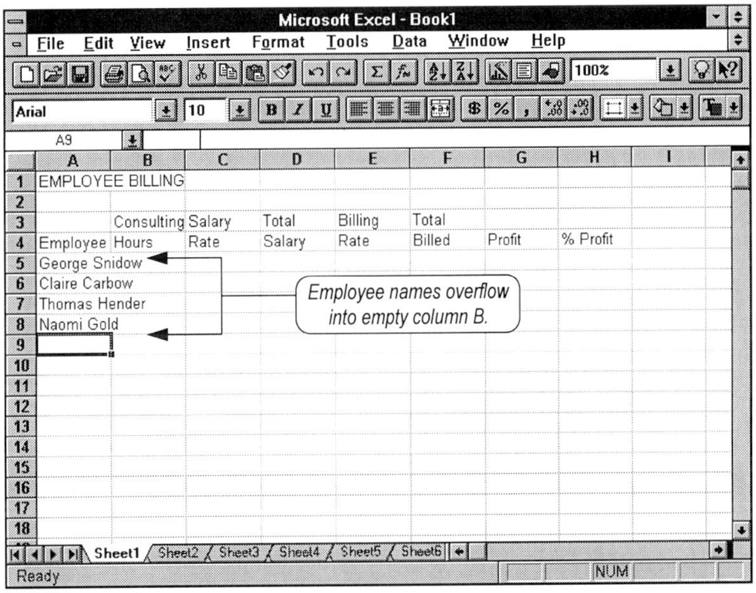

Figure 1 - 6

CORRECTING ERRORS

There are several different ways of correcting data entry errors. The best procedure to use depends on when you discover the error and how big the difference is between the data you typed and the correct data.

To correct errors:

- To correct an error that you discover *before* you have entered it into the cell (by pressing an **ARROW** key or the **ENTER** key or by clicking on the **enter box** or a new cell), press the **BACKSPACE** key until you erase the incorrect data. Type the rest of the cell contents and press the **ENTER** key or click on the **enter box**.

  *When you are entering data, you may not use the **ARROW** keys to move the cursor back to an incorrect character. When you press the **ARROW** keys, the data is entered into the current cell and the next cell on the worksheet in the direction of the arrow becomes the active cell.*

- To correct a major error that you notice *after* you have entered the data, select the cell in which you have made the typing mistake. Type the correct cell contents and then press the **ENTER** key or click on the **enter box**.
- To correct an error involving only a few characters, or to add to the cell contents, edit the cell contents using the directions for editing cells.

When only a small part of the cell contents is wrong, it is easier to *edit* the entry rather than erase or retype it. In Version 5 of *Excel*, you may edit directly in the cell. In earlier versions of *Excel* and in many other worksheets, you may edit only in the Formula Bar.

To edit cells:

- Double-click the cell containing the data you want to edit.

  *Excel will enter **Edit** mode. There are three changes to the screen: the word **Edit** replaces **Ready** in the far-left side of the Status Bar; the highlight around the cell changes from a double border to a single border; and the insertion point appears in the cell.*

- Click immediately to the left of the character to be changed or use the **RIGHT** or **LEFT ARROW** keys to move the cursor to the left of the character to be changed.
- To delete characters, press the **DELETE** key once for each character to be deleted. To insert characters, type them. To change characters, press the **INSERT** key. The letters **OVR** will appear on the Status Bar. Type the new characters.
- When editing is completed, press the **ENTER** key or click the **enter box.**

ALTERNATE METHOD: *To edit data in the Formula Bar, first click in the cell to be edited and then click in the Formula Bar immediately to the left of the characters to be changed, inserted, or deleted.*

KEYBOARD ALTERNATIVE: *Press **F2** to begin editing. The insertion point will appear in the cell at the end of the data. Move it to the character(s) to be changed and edit the data as described above.*

Activity 1.2: Correcting Errors

There are three errors in the data you entered. George's last name is Snidowski instead of Snidow, Claire's last name is Corbow, not Carbow and Thomas's last name is Henderson.

1. Double-click anywhere in cell **A5**.

*Your screen should resemble Figure 1 - 7, although the insertion point will appear in **A5** at the point you clicked rather than between the **G** and the **e** as shown in Figure 1 - 7.*

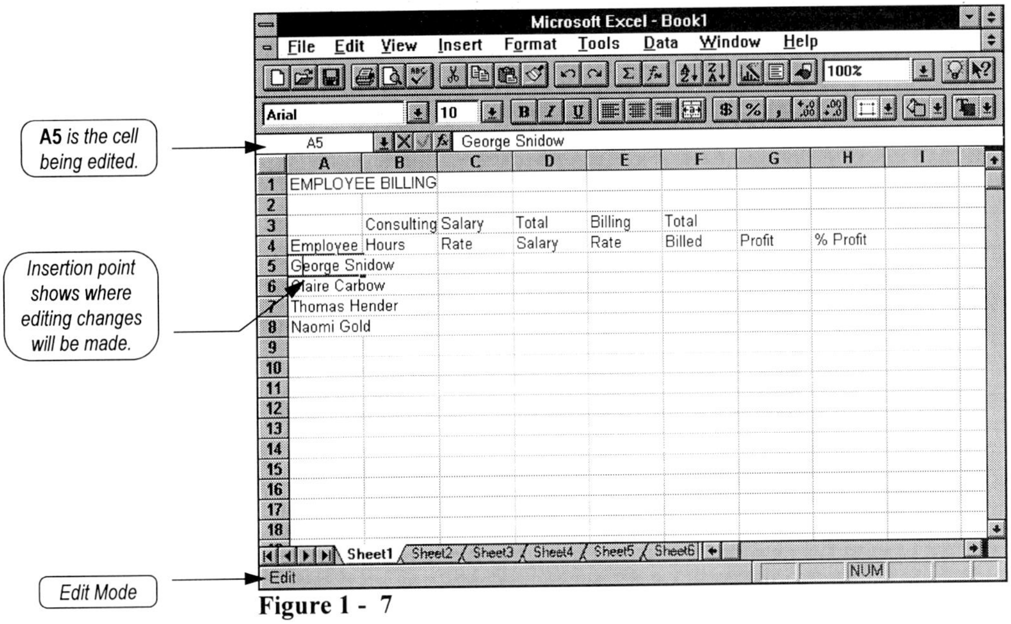

Figure 1 - 7

PROBLEM SOLVER: *Does the **name box** in the Formula Bar (left-side)indicate that the active cell is **A5?** Since George Snidow's name overflows into **B5,** if the mouse is pointing to the end of the name when you double-click, you will be editing cell **B5,** which is empty. To solve this problem, press the **ENTER** key, move the mouse so that it is pointing to cell **A5,** and double-click.*

2. Click to the right of the **w** in **Snidow**.

   The insertion point will be positioned to the right of Snidow as in Figure 1 - 8.

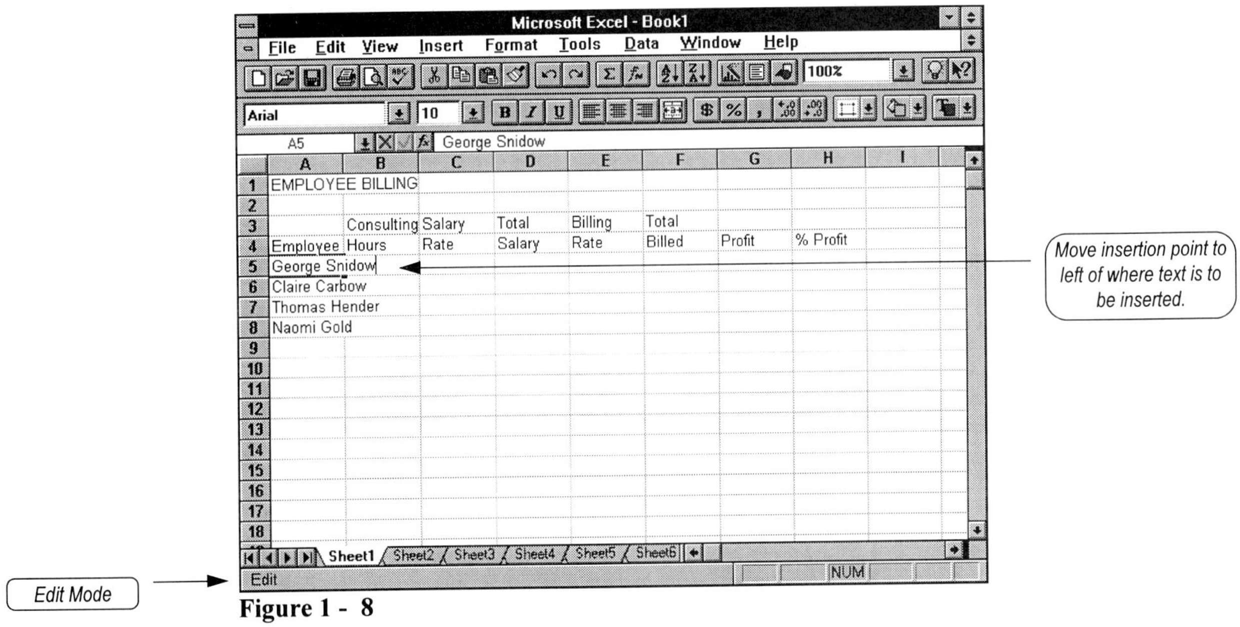

Figure 1 - 8

3. Type: **ski** and press the **ENTER** key or click on the **enter box**.
4. To change Carbow, double-click in cell **A6**.
5. Click immediately to the left of the **a** in **Carbow**.
6. Press the **INSERT** key.

   *The letters **OVR** should appear on the Status Bar and the letter **a** in Carbow in cell **A6** should be highlighted (Figure 1 - 9).*

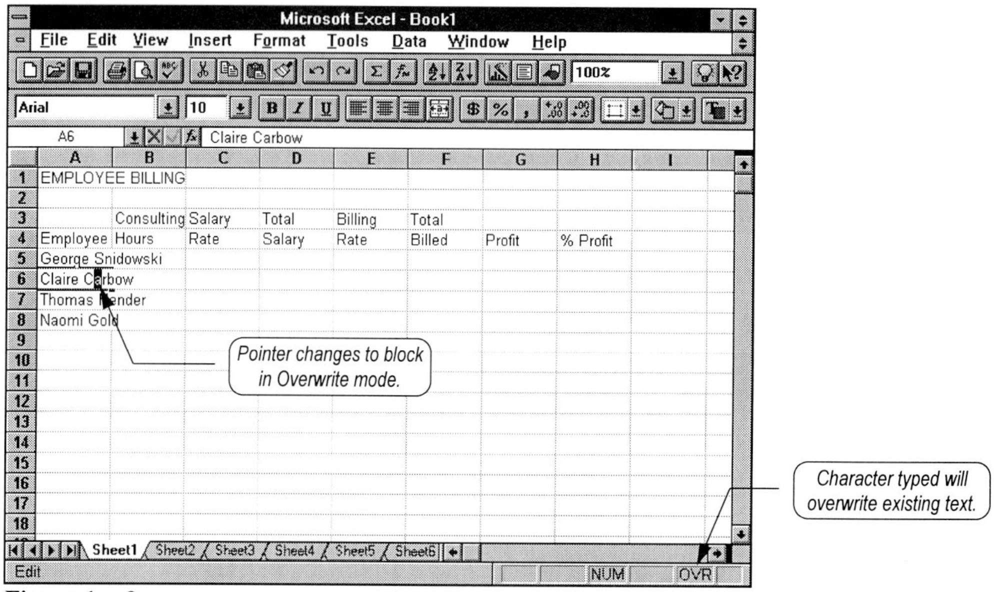

Figure 1 - 9

7. Type: **o** and press the **ENTER** key or click on the **enter box**.
8. Use the procedures in steps 1-3 to change Thomas Hender's name to **Thomas Henderson.**

   KEYBOARD SHORTCUT: *When you are in Edit Mode, pressing **END** moves the insertion point to the end of the cell and pressing **HOME** moves it to the beginning of the cell.*

Clearing Cell Contents

Sometimes you want to erase the entire contents of a cell. The easiest way to do this is to use the **DELETE** key.

To clear the contents of a cell:

- Click on the cell.
- Press the **DELETE** key.

Activity 1.3: Clearing the Contents of a Cell

After entering the employee names in the worksheet, you learn that Naomi Gold no longer works for the company.

1. Click on cell **A8**.

2. Press the **DELETE** key.

   *Cell **A8** should be empty.*

Undoing Actions

Excel lets you undo many commands if you realize your mistake immediately after making it.

To undo an action:

- Open the **EDIT** menu.

  *The top command on the **Edit** menu will either indicate the action that you can do (i.e., **Undo Clear**) or will indicate that you **Can't Undo**.*

- Choose **UNDO (action)**.

Immediately after **EDIT/Undo** or the **Undo** button  has been selected, *Excel* changes the **Undo** menu item to **Redo.** That way, if **EDIT/Undo** did not correct your problem, you may "undo" the undo!

To reverse EDIT/Undo:

- Open the **EDIT** menu.

  *If you have used **EDIT/Undo** and that action can still be reversed, the top menu choice will be **REDO (action)***

- Choose **REDO (action)**.

Activity 1.4: Undoing the Last Command

You decide that you don't want to delete Naomi Gold's name after all.

1. Click **EDIT** on the Menu Bar to open the **EDIT** Menu.

   *The first menu choice is **Undo Clear**.*

2. Click **Undo Clear**.

   ***Naomi Gold** should reappear in cell **A8**.*

3. To clear Naomi Gold's name again, choose **EDIT/Redo [U] Clear**.

ENTERING VALUES

You enter values in the same way that you enter text. However, *Excel* aligns values on the right side of the cell instead of the left side. In addition, when you type values, you have some additional choices in how you enter them. For example, should you type dollar signs or the commas that separate thousands? *Excel* gives you the option to type *formatting characters* such as dollar signs and commas when you enter the data, or to wait and add all of these characters at once. When you enter data in this lesson, only type the numeric digits and the decimal point. In Lesson 2 you will learn how to add the formatting characters.

Activity 1.5: Entering Values

You will enter the values for the Consulting Hours, Salary Rate, and Billing Rate columns.

1. Select cell **B5** and type: **32**

*As soon as you start typing, the part of George Snidowski's name that had overflowed into that cell disappears. Don't worry, it is still in Excel's memory. After you finish entering values, you will increase the width of column **A** so that all of the data is visible.*

2. Press the **DOWN ARROW**.
3. In cell **B6,** type: **41** and press the **DOWN ARROW**.
4. In cell **B7**, type: **129** and press the **ENTER** key.

   Your screen should resemble Figure 1 - 10.

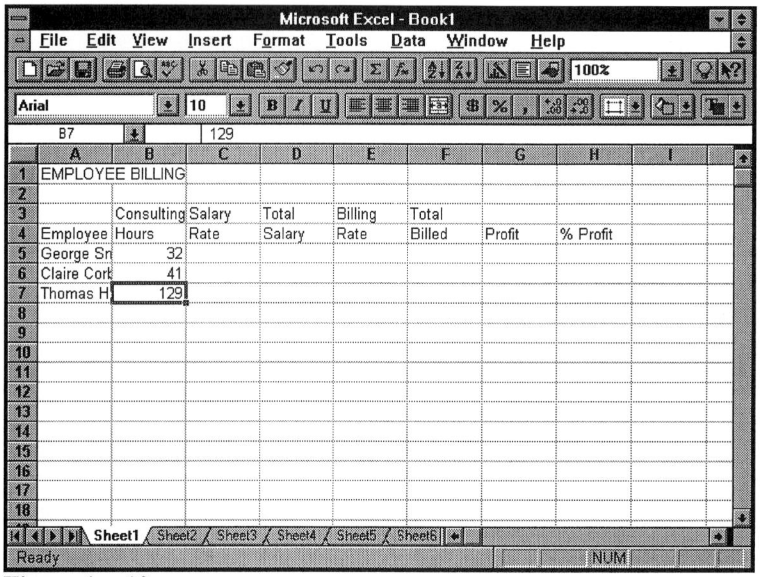

Figure 1 - 10

5. Select cell **C5**, and enter: **27.50**

   *As Figure 1 - 11 indicates, Excel enters 27.50 as **27.5**. In Excel's default format, digits that do not change the value of the number are omitted. When you format the cell in the next lesson, the zero will be displayed.*

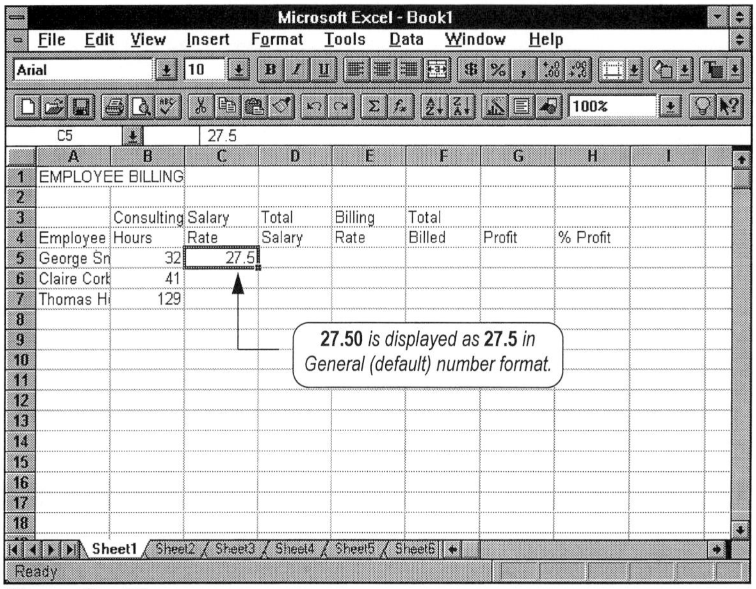

Figure 1 - 11

6. In cell **C6**, enter: **32.50**
7. In cell **C7**, enter: **42.50**
8. Select cell **E5**, and in cells **E5, E6,** and **E7**, enter the billing rates for each employee listed below:

George Snidowski	**50**
Claire Corbow	**60**
Thomas Henderson	**75**

9. Compare your worksheet with Figure 1 - 12. If any of the values on your screen are different, use one of the error correcting procedures you learned to correct the entries.

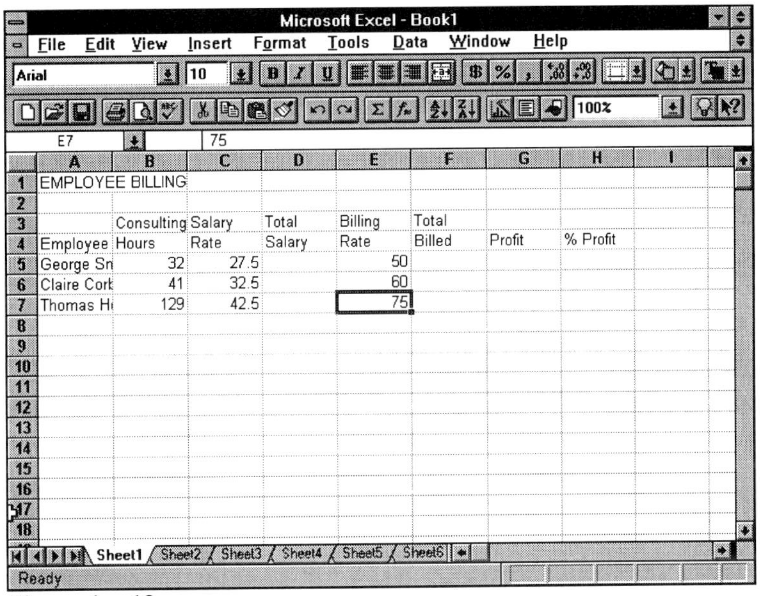

Figure 1 - 12

SAVING A WORKBOOK

While you are working on a worksheet, it is held in the *RAM* or *Random Access Memory* of your computer. RAM is the computer work area that stores work in progress until you close the file or the program.

To keep a permanent record of your work, you must *save* the workbook containing the worksheet. To save a workbook you must give it a name and tell the computer where to store it. Anything saved on a computer is saved in a *file*. Once saved a file can be accessed any time you need it.

It is important to save your work regularly (at least every 15 minutes), so that if you should make a serious mistake, or if the power should fail, you will not lose all of your work.

To save a workbook as a file:

- Choose **FILE/Save As.**

  *The **Save As** dialog box appears.*

- Type a name for your file. Your file name must follow the rules in Table 1 - 1.

RULES FOR NAMING A FILE
• The file name may have a maximum of 8 characters.
• It may NOT include spaces.
• It may NOT include any of the following symbols: , . ; : * = [ ] | / \ < > ?
• *Excel* automatically adds the extension, *.xls* to the filename, so you should not type an extension of your own.

Table 1 - 1

- If the drive which appears in the **Drives** drop-down list box is not the drive which contains your data disk, click on the arrow to the right of the box and then click on the correct drive.
- If you are saving your file on the network, make sure that the network drive is selected in the previous step. If the directory shown in the **Directories** list box is not the one to which you should store your file, double-click on the name of the correct directory.
- Click on **OK** or press **ENTER**.
- The **Summary Info** dialog box may be displayed. Enter any information that you want and then click on **OK** or press **ENTER**.

Activity 1.6: Saving Your Workbook

1. If you are saving your files on a floppy disk, put it in the disk drive.
2. Click on **FILE** on the Menu Bar.
3. Click on **Save As**.

   *You have selected the **FILE/Save As** command and the **Save As** dialog box is displayed. The default filename, **book1.xls,** is highlighted in the **File Name** box (Figure 1 - 13).*

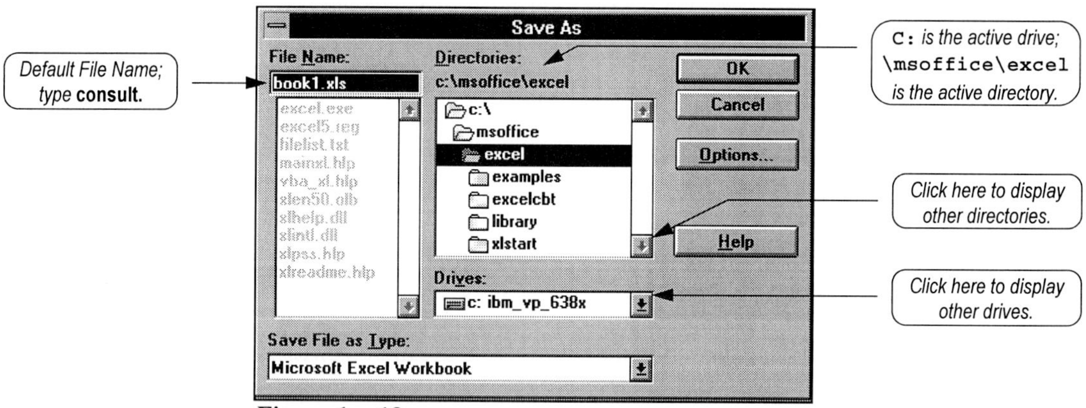

Figure 1 - 13

4. Type: **consult**

   *As soon as you begin to type, **consult** should replace **book1** in the **File Name** text box. Do <u>not</u> type the extension, **.xls**. Excel will automatically add that for you. Do <u>not</u> type a period after consult or Excel will omit the extension **.xls**.*

PROBLEM SOLVER: *If any letters remain from the old title, **book1.xls**, use the **BACKSPACE** or **DELETE** keys to remove them.*

5. Look at the drive and directory listed in the upper middle of the **Save As** dialog box (Figure 1 - 13). If the drive listed is not the one on which you are saving your file, click the arrow to the right of the **Drives** drop-down list box.
6. Click the button representing the drive containing your data disk. For floppy disks this will probably be **a:** or **b:**.
7. If you have been instructed to save your files on a network, click on the network drive. Ask your instructor for the name of the directory to which you should save your file. If that directory is not currently listed as the active directory, click on it in the **Directories** list box.

PROBLEM SOLVER: *If the directory for which you are looking is not visible, click on the ⬇ or ⬆ on the right side of the Directories list box. This will scroll the entries. When the directory you want is visible, click on it.*

8. Click on **OK** to save the file.
9. The **Summary Info** dialog box may be displayed. If it is displayed, click on **OK** to leave the screen without changing it.

   *Look at the Status Bar. The message **Saving CONSULT.XLS** will appear while the file is being saved. After the file has been saved, the Title Bar name will change to **Microsoft Excel - CONSULT.XLS**.*

PROBLEM SOLVER: *If Excel produces a warning box with the message, **Filename is not valid**, click on the **OK** button in the message box. Click in the **File Name** box and retype or delete characters until only **consult** or **consult.xls** appears in the File Name box. Click on **OK** again.*

TAKING A BREAK

You can stop any project in this book before you have completed it. Just save the worksheet and exit from *Excel*. When you are ready to continue working, open the worksheet and continue from where you stopped.

To open a previously saved workbook:

- Choose **FILE/Open** or click on the **OPEN** button on the Standard Toolbar.

  *The **Open** dialog box will appear on the screen.*
- The current drive appears in the list box labeled **Drives:**. If your file has been saved to a different drive, click on the ↓ at the right of the list box and click on the name of the drive that contains your data.
- The current directory is highlighted in the list box labeled **Directories:**. If your file has been saved in a different directory, double-click on the name of the directory containing your data.
- The file names are listed in alphabetical order in the **File Name** list box. Click on the name of the file you want to open. If the file name is not visible, click on the ↓ on the vertical scroll bar until the file name is visible and then click on it.
- Click on **OK** or press **ENTER.**

Activity 1.7: Exiting from Excel

1. Choose **FILE/Exit.**

   PROBLEM SOLVER: *If you have made any changes to* ***consult.xls*** *since you saved it, or if you have any other open, unsaved worksheets, Excel will display an alert box. Click on* ***Yes*** *to save the worksheet or click on* ***No*** *if you do not want to save the worksheet. If you don't know whether or not you want to save the worksheet, click on* ***Cancel,*** *take a look at the worksheet, and then save it if you want to.*

Activity 1.8: Returning to Excel and Your Workbook

1. If you just completed Activity 1.7, the Windows' Program Manager is probably displayed and the program group containing *Excel* is probably visible. If this is not true, switch to Program Manager and open the program group containing *Excel.*
2. Double-click the *Excel* icon.
3. Choose **FILE/Open.**

   The Open dialog box will be displayed. See Figure 1 - 14.

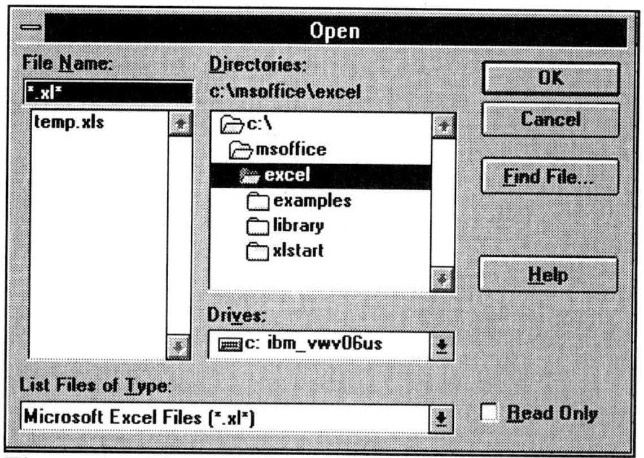

Figure 1 - 14

4. Look at the drive and directory listed in the upper middle of the **Open** dialog box (Figure 1 - 14). If the drive listed is not the one containing your file, click the arrow to the right of the **Drives** drop-down list box.
5. Click the icon representing the drive containing your data disk. For floppy disks this will probably be **a:** or **b:**.
6. If your files have been saved on a network, click on the network drive. If the directory containing your files is not currently listed as the active directory, double-click on it in the **Directories** list box.
7. Look at the list of files under the **File Name** box. If **consult.xls** is visible, click on it. If it is not visible, click on the ↓ on the file listing scroll bar until the name is visible and then choose it.

   Figure 1 - 15 shows the completed dialog box if your disk is in the ***a:*** *drive.*

8. Click on **OK** to open the file.

CAUTION: In *Excel* (and other Windows packages) you may NOT remove or switch floppy disks if any of the files on them are open. If you receive error messages like **Cannot access 'a:', The disk drive is not valid, Drive A does not exist**, etc. put the original disk back in the drive and close all files or save them to your hard drive.

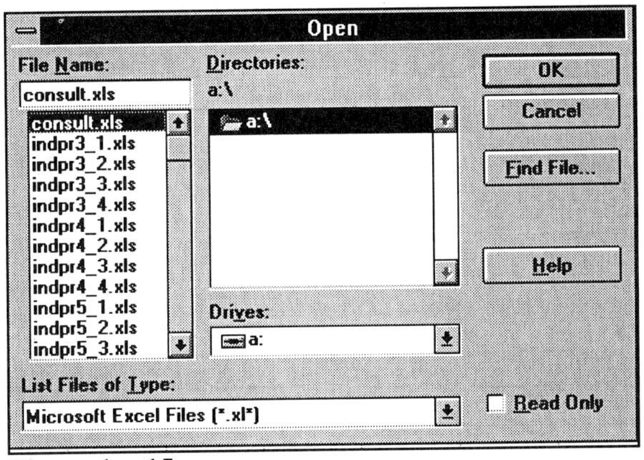

Figure 1 - 15

CHANGING COLUMN WIDTH

Excel sets a default width for all of the columns in a new worksheet. The default column width in *Excel* is 8.43. All of the employee names are too wide to fit in column **A**. Once you entered text into the adjacent cells in column **B**, the names were truncated — however, the data is still in the cell; you just can't see it. In order to view the employee names, you must increase the column width. There are several different ways that the cell width can be increased. They are summarized below.

AutoFit

Excel can automatically calculate the optimum width for a column, based on the widest entry in that column.

To use AutoFit:

- To select the entire column, click the column heading or press **CTRL+SPACEBAR**.
- Choose **FORMAT/Width, AutoFit Selection** from the menus, or double-click the right border of the column heading.

Activity 1.9: Using AutoFit to Change Column Width

Let's change the width of Column C.

1. Click on the **C** in the column headings.

   The entire column is selected (Figure 1 - 16).

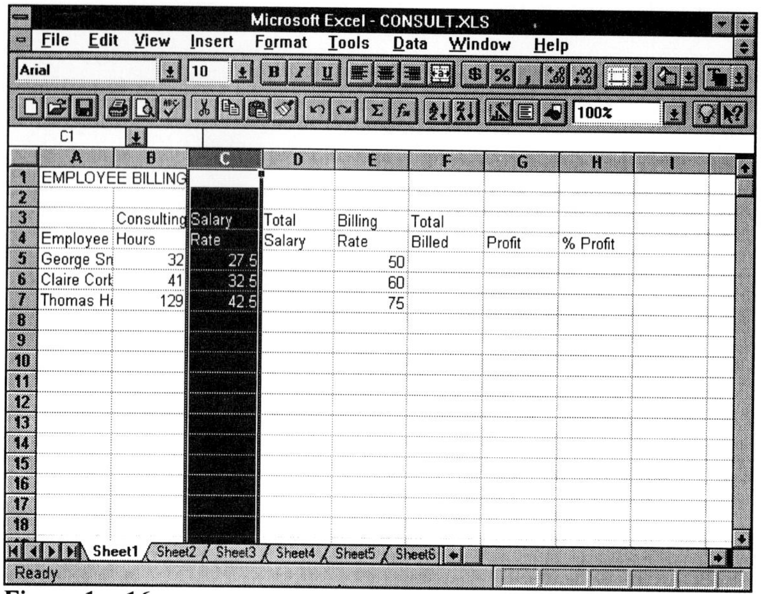

Figure 1 - 16

2. Choose the **FORMAT/Column** command by first clicking on **FORMAT** in the Menu Bar and then clicking on **Column**.

   *Since **Column** is followed by a ▸ a submenu is displayed (Figure 1 - 17).*

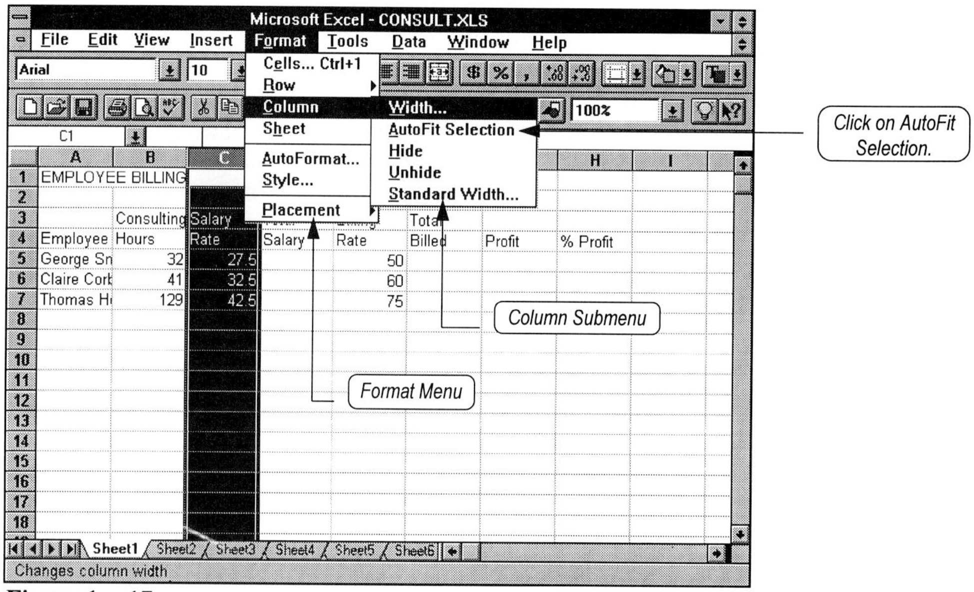

Figure 1 - 17

3. Choose **AutoFit Selection** by clicking on it in the Column submenu.

   *The Column width automatically decreases so that it is slightly wider than **Salary**, which is the widest entry in the column.*

Changing the Column Width Manually

Sometimes you want a column to have a different width than AutoFit selects. In your worksheet you cannot use AutoFit to change the width of column **A** because the worksheet title is the widest entry in column **A**, while you only want the column to be as wide as the widest employee name.

To change the column width using the menus:

- Select the column by clicking on the column name in the column heading bar or pressing **CTRL+SPACEBAR**.
- Choose **FORMAT/Column, Width** from the menus.
- Type the desired column width in the **Column Width** text box and press the **ENTER** key or click on **OK**.

To change the column width by dragging:

- Point to the line to the right of the column whose width should be changed.
- When the mouse pointer changes from an to a, click and drag until the column width appears correct.
- If the column width is narrower or wider than you wish, repeat the last step until it is the desired width.

Activity 1.10: Changing the Column Width Manually

1. Place the mouse pointer in the column **A** header and click.

   Column A is selected.

2. Choose **FORMAT/Column,AutoFit Selection**

   *The width of column A increases to accommodate **EMPLOYEE BILLING**, which is the widest entry in the column. However, you only want the column to be wide enough to fit the widest employee name.*

3. With column **A** still highlighted, choose the **FORMAT/Column** command.
4. Click on **Width** in the Column submenu.

   *The **Column Width** dialog box is displayed and the **Column Width** text box is highlighted (Figure 1 - 18). It displays the current width of column A.*

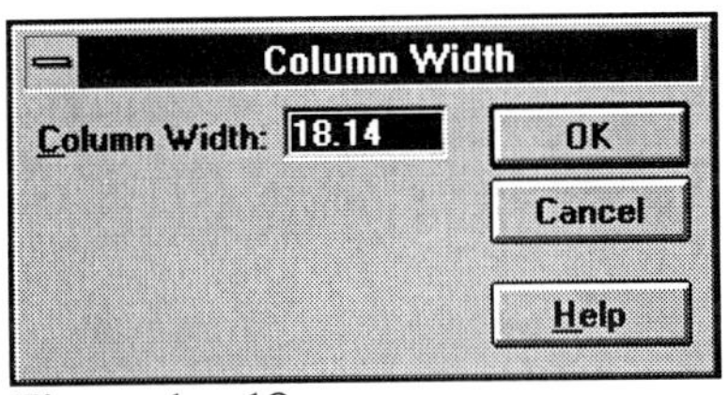

Figure 1 - 18

5. Type: **10** and click on **OK** or press the **ENTER** key.

*The column is still not wide enough to display the complete employee names. Since most people use proportional fonts, it is hard to guess how wide to make a cell. (With proportional fonts the width of each character varies, so that a "skinny" letter like **l** is narrower than a letter like **W**.)*

6. Position the mouse cursor in the column heading on the line between column **A** and column **B**.

7. When the shape of the mouse pointer changes from an to a (Figure 1 - 19), click and drag the mouse to the right until you think the cell is wide enough for all of the data. If you make the column too wide or too narrow, repeat until you can just see the complete employee names.

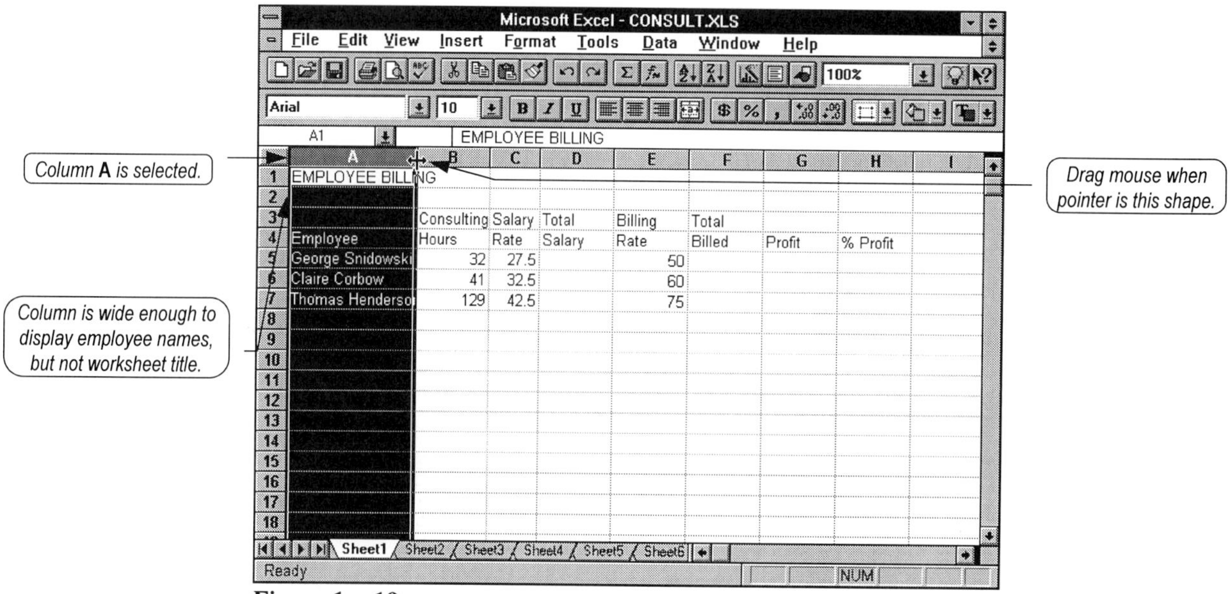

Figure 1 - 19

ENTERING FORMULAS

Formulas do the work that worksheets were designed to do—they provide the information to answer your questions. For example, you want to know George's total salary. Therefore, in cell **D5** you will to enter a formula that will multiply the number of consulting hours he worked by his salary rate. Formulas contain several components. The first component in any formula is an equal sign (=) that tells *Excel* to treat the data in the cell as a formula rather than as text. The formula may contain numbers and/or cell addresses and mathematical operators such as plus or minus signs. When the number that you want to use in a formula is on the worksheet, you always use the cell address rather than the value in the formula. That way, if the value changes, the formula will automatically recalculate and the results will still be accurate.

It is possible to enter a formula by typing the contents of the formula into the cell. However, it is preferable to type part of the formula and then *point* to the other information that you wish to include. Specifically, you will type the mathematical symbols (= and +), but *each time* a cell address should be added to the formula, you will use the mouse (or the arrow keys) to point to the cell rather than type the cell name. Pointing is better than typing because you can see exactly what data are being used in the formula and you are less likely to make an error in entering the cell address.

To enter a formula using pointing:

- Select the cell to contain the formula.
- Type an equal sign (=).
- Click on the first cell containing data that should be part of the formula.
- Type a mathematical operator. The symbols for the mathematical operators are + for addition, - for subtraction, * for multiplication, / for division, and ^ for exponentiation.
- Repeat the last two steps until the formula is complete. Do NOT type a mathematical operator after the last cell entry.
- Press the **ENTER** key or click on the **enter box.**

Activity 1.11: Creating Formulas

You will enter formulas to calculate the total salary, total billed, profit, and % profit for each employee.

1. Select cell **D5**.
2. Type: =
3. Select cell **B5** by clicking on it or pressing the left arrow (←) key twice.

   *Cell **B5** is enclosed in a moving border, and the formula =**B5** appears in the Formula Bar and in cell **D5** (Figure 1 - 20). The word, **Point,** also appears on the Status Bar because you are pointing at the cells to be included in the formula.*

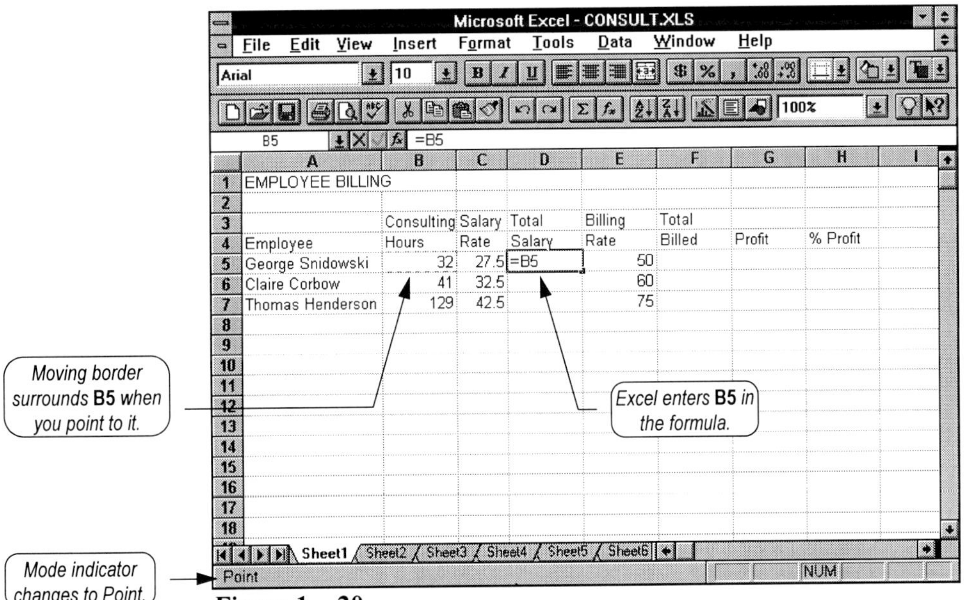

Figure 1 - 20

4. Type the multiplication operator, the asterisk (*).

   *The * indicates that you are multiplying the contents of cell **B5** by the next part of the formula. As soon as you type the asterisk, the moving border line is removed from cell **B5**.*

5. Click on cell **C5**.

*The contents of cell **D5** should now be **=B5*C5**. The formula is complete (Figure 1 - 21).*

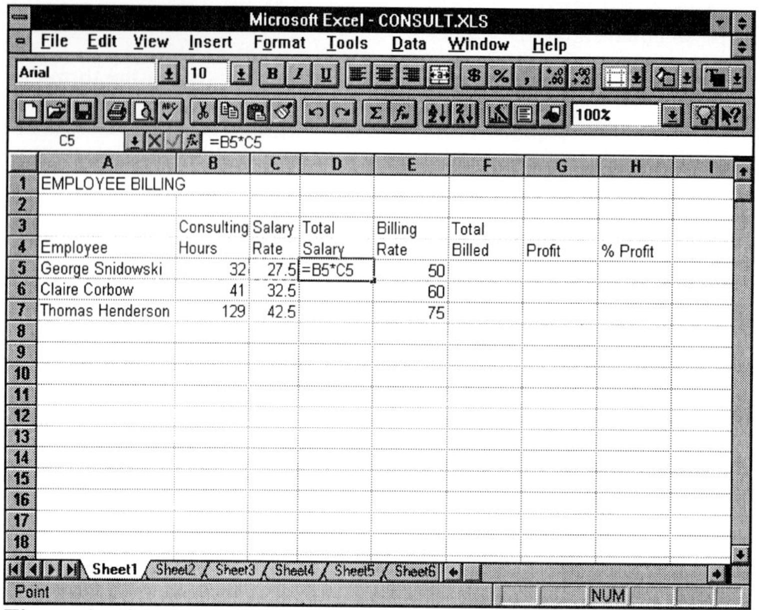

Figure 1 - 21

6. Press the **ENTER** key or click on the **enter box**.

   *When cell **D5** is selected, the formula **=B5*C5** remains visible in the Formula Bar, but the value of that formula, **880**, is inserted in the cell.*

   ***PROBLEM SOLVER:** If you have made an error in the syntax of the formula, Excel will display an error message. Read the message and click on **OK**. Excel will automatically switch to Edit mode. Compare your entry with that shown in Figure 1 - 21 and make any necessary corrections.*

7. Click on **D6**.
8. Type: =
9. Click on **B6**.
10. Type: *
11. Click on **C6**.
12. If the formula in **D6** is **=B6*C6** , press the **ENTER** key or click on the **enter box.** If it is not, press **ESC** and repeat steps 7–12.
13. The formula for cell **D7** is exactly the same as the one in cell **D6**, except that the rows are different. Therefore, you should repeat steps 7-12 using the cells in row 7 instead of row 6.

    Your worksheet should resemble Figure 1 - 22.

14. Click on cell **F5**.
15. Use pointing to enter the formula **=B5*E5** and press the **ENTER** key.

    *The value **1600** should appear in cell **F5**. If it does not, re-enter the formula. If the formula is correct, but your answer is still incorrect, check that the values in **B5** and **E5** match those shown in Figure 1 - 21.*

16. Use pointing to enter similar formulas in cells **F6** and **F7**.

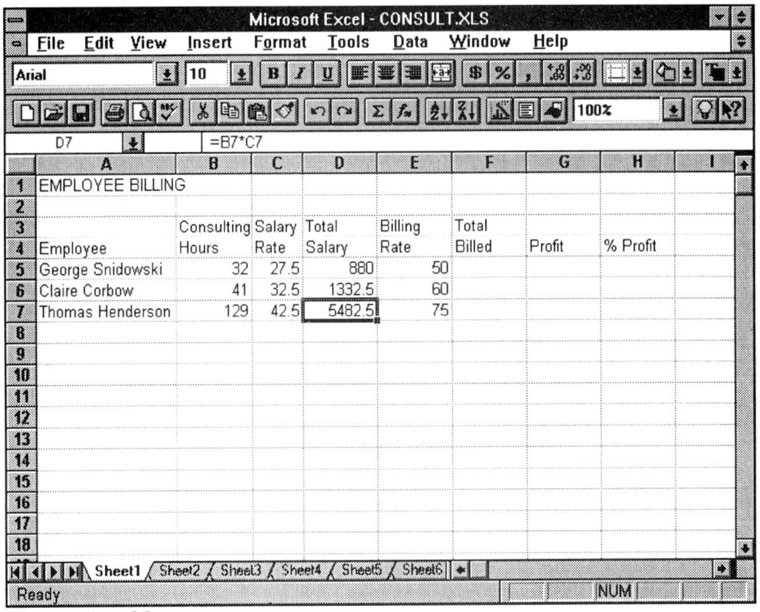

Figure 1 - 22

17. In cell **G5**, use pointing to enter the formula to calculate the profit. This formula equals the total billed for George minus his total salary.

    Your worksheet should resemble Figure 1 - 23.

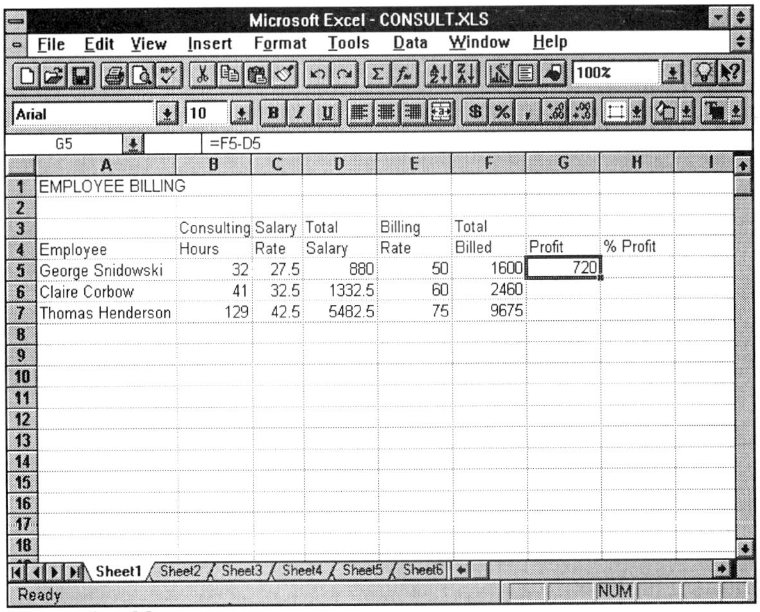

Figure 1 - 23

18. Use pointing to enter similar formulas in cells **G6** and **G7**.
19. In cell **H5**, use pointing to enter the formula to calculate the % Profit. The % Profit equals the profit divided by the total billed.
20. Use pointing to enter similar formulas in cells **H6** and **H7**.

    Your worksheet should resemble Figure 1 - 24.

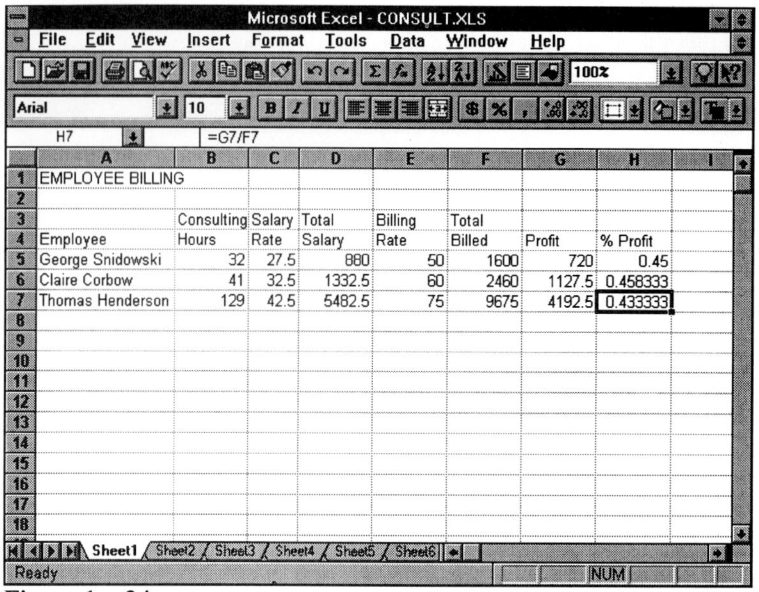

Figure 1 - 24

Activity 1.12: Letting Formulas Recalculate

One of the benefits of using formulas is that whenever any of the data in cells contained in the formula change, the value of the formula automatically changes. In looking over your worksheet, you realize that Thomas Henderson worked 29 hours not 129. You will correct this error now.

1. Position the mouse pointer on cell **B7** and double-click.

   *You should be in **Edit** Mode. (HINT: **Edit** should be on the left-side of the Status Bar.)*

2. Click immediately to the left of the **1** and press the **DELETE** key.
3. Press the **ENTER** key.
4. Compare your screen with Figure 1 - 24, which shows the worksheet before you changed Thomas Henderson's hours. Which values changed?

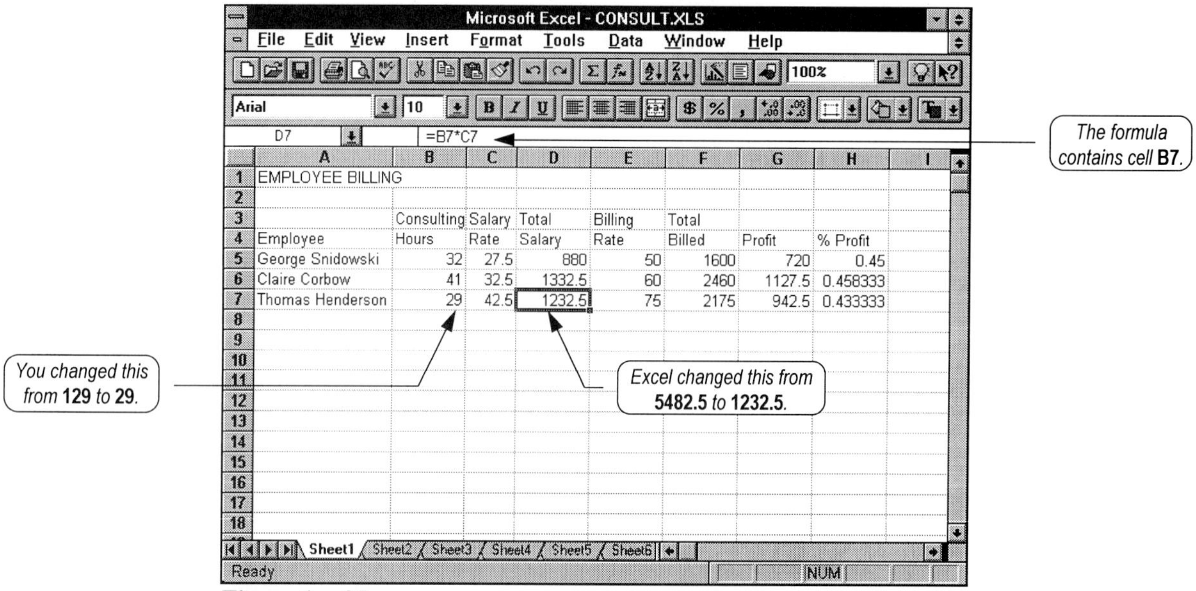

Figure 1 - 25

5. Click on each cell with a changed value and look at the Formula Bar. The formula in each of the cells should contain the address of the cell you changed, **B7**. (Figure 1 - 25 shows one of the changed cells.)

SAVING A FILE WITH THE SAME NAME

Every time you make changes to a file, you must save the file again or the changes will be lost when you close the worksheet or exit from *Excel*. When you save the file using the same name, the current version of the worksheet replaces the previously saved version.

To save a file again with the same file name:

- Choose **FILE/Save** or click the **Save** toolbar button, 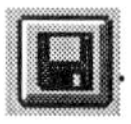.

Activity 1.13: Saving a File Again with the Same Name

This time when you save the file, you will use the toolbar instead of the menus.

1. Click on the **Save** toolbar button.

   ***Saving CONSULT.XLS** will appear on the Status Bar while the file is being saved. Depending on which disk you are saving to, and the speed of your computer, the message may only appear briefly.*

PRINTING A WORKSHEET

Typically, you want to print worksheets so that you can share the information with others. Your worksheet is complete, although its appearance is not as attractive as you would like. Let's print it now and then you will enhance its appearance in Lesson 2. You will print using the default settings. In Lesson 2 you will learn how to change the appearance of the printout.

To print a worksheet using the default settings:

- Make sure that the printer is turned on.
- Choose **FILE/Print** or click on the **Print** button.
- Click on **OK**.

Occasionally you want to have a printed copy of the formulas contained in the cells instead of the values. In the business world you can use this copy to document your worksheet, so that you and everyone else can see what formulas you used to obtain your results. If there are errors in the worksheet, a printout containing formulas can help find them. In school instructors often want a printout with formulas displayed to see what formulas were used in constructing the worksheet.

To print formulas instead of cell contents:

- Press the **CTRL** key and while keeping it depressed, press the ` (the single left quotation mark, *not* the apostrophe; the ` is usually found on the same key as the tilde (~). The location of this key varies on some keyboards but is often located to the left of the **1** on the top of the typing keyboard.)

  ***CTRL+`** not only displays formulas, but it doubles the width of the column, left-justifies all values and removes any number formatting.*

- Print the document.
- Press **CTRL+`** again to return to normal display.

Activity 1.14: Printing a Worksheet

1. Make sure that the printer is turned on.
2. Choose **FILE/Print.**

   The Print dialog box will appear. See Figure 1 - 26.

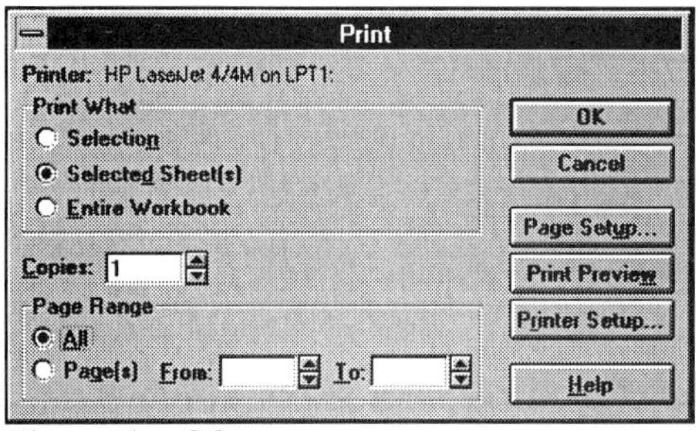

Figure 1 - 26

3. Look at the name of the printer listed. If it is not the one that you are using, click on **Printer Setup**. The **Printer Setup** dialog box will be displayed. Click on the name of the printer that you are using and then click on **OK** to return to the **Print** dialog box. If this does not work, ask your lab instructor for help.
4. In the **Print** dialog box, click on **OK** to print the worksheet.
5. Press **CTRL+`** (left single quote) to display formulas in all cells (Figure 1 - 27).

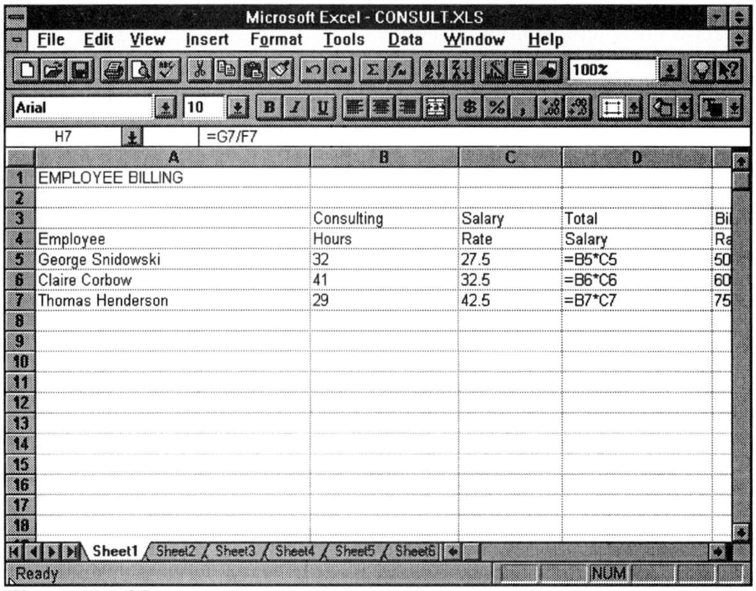

Figure 1 - 27

6. Print the worksheet again.

   The worksheet will be printed on two pages instead of one.
7. Press **CTRL+`** again to display values in all cells.
8. Choose **FILE/Close.** If asked **Save changes in 'CONSULT.XLS'?** choose **YES. FILE/Exit** *Excel* or go on to Independent Project 1.1.

SUMMARY

In this lesson, you completed the basic tasks of entering text, values, and formulas, editing cell contents, changing column widths, and saving, opening, and printing a worksheet. In Lesson 2 you will learn how to make the worksheet more attractive. In Lesson 3 you will learn some more advanced editing skills and how to use *Excel*'s various copying strategies to save you time.

KEY TERMS

Cancel Box
Cell overflow
Closing
Constants
Edit Mode
Enter Box
Enter Mode
Formulas
Insertion point
Labels
Left aligned
Opening
Point
Ready mode
Right aligned
Saving
Text entry
Values

INDEPENDENT PROJECTS

The four independent projects allow you to practice the basic skills involved in creating worksheets: entering text, values and formulas, changing data, and printing and saving the worksheet. More instructions for using **Help** are also included in Independent Project 1.1. The first two projects specificially indicate all of the tasks that you need to complete the project. Independent Project 1.3 leaves some of the worksheet design up to you. In Independent Project 1.4 you must plan the worksheet before creating it.

Independent Project 1.1: Comparing Budgets for Two Years

You have been asked to create a worksheet which compares the 1993/1994 and 1994/1995 budgets for one of the departments at your school. The worksheet will contain the budgeted amounts for four categories of expense: faculty, staff, hardware/software and research. For each category you will calculate the amount of increase in the 1994/1995 budget and the percent of the increase. The first draft of your worksheet should resemble Figure 1 - 28. The instructions for completing the project also give you more instructions on using **Help**. Use **Help** even if you can do the task, so that you are better able to use it when you need it.

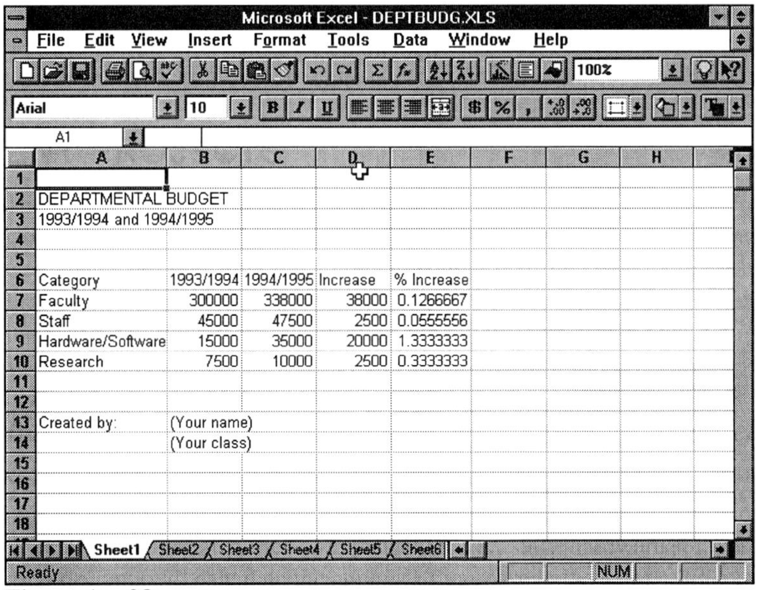

Figure 1 - 28

When you finish this project, your worksheet will be complete, but not attractive. You will enhance its appearance at the end of Lesson2.

Use Figure 1 - 28 and the following instructions to help you complete the project:

1. Start *Excel*. Maximize *Excel* and **book1** if they are not already maximized. If you start this project immediately after finishing the lesson, close all open files. If no **workbook** is open, choose **FILE/New** or click on the **New Workbook** tool.
2. Enter the worksheet title in column **A** of rows **2** and **3**.
3. Enter the column labels in row **6.**
4. Enter the budget categories (**Faculty, Staff,** etc.) in cells **A7** through **A10**.
5. Next, increase the width of column **A** so that all of the expense category labels are visible. Do not use **AutoFit Selection** because you do not want column **A** to be wide enough to include the title **DEPARTMENTAL BUDGET**. Use the instructions below so that you can see how *Excel's* **Help** system can help you change column widths.
   a. Choose **HELP/Search for Help on**.
   b. Type: **column width** in the text box at the top of the **Search** dialog box.
   c. Click on the **Show Topics** button.
   d. Four topics related to column width will appear in the bottom section of the **Search** dialog box. Click on **Adjusting column width** if it is not already highlighted.
   e. Click on the **Go To** button.
   f. The **How To** window will appear on top of the **Microsoft Excel Help** window. Click on the **On Top** button.

   g. Click on the **Control box** on the left-side of the **Microsoft Excel Help** title bar.
   h. When the **Control** menu opens, click on **Close**.
   i. Read the instructions in the **How To** window as you change the width of column **A**.
   j. When you are done, click on the **Close** button on the **How To** window.
6. If **% Increase** or any other the other column labels are too wide to fit in their columns, use **AutoFit Selection** to make the column wider.
7. Enter the values for columns **B** and **C** (shown in bold in Table 1 - 2).

Category	1993/1994	1994/1995
Faculty	**300000**	**338000**
Staff	**45000**	**47500**
Hardware/Software	**15000**	**35000**
Research	**7500**	**10000**

Table 1 - 2

8. Enter a formula in cell **D7** to calculate the increase in the faculty budget. The increase is equal to the 1994/1995 faculty budget minus the 1993/1994 faculty budget.
9. Make sure that the result in **D7** is the same as in Figure 1 - 28. Enter similar formulas in the rest of column **D** to calculate the increase for the other budget categories.
10. Next, enter a formula in **E7** that reflects the percent of increase. This is equal to the increase divided by the 1993/1994 budget amount.

11. When you are sure that the formula in **E7** is correct, enter similar formulas in the rest of the column.
12. In cell **A13**, enter: **Created by:**
13. Enter your name in cell **B13**. Don't worry if it overflows into column **C**.
14. Enter your class or any other identifying information requested by your instructor in **B14**.
15. Compare your worksheet to Figure 1 - 28 and make any editing changes necessary.
16. Save the worksheet using the file name: **deptbudg**
    Be sure that you save the file to your data disk or to the network drive to which you have been instructed to save files.
17. Print the worksheet.
18. Display formulas.
19. Print the worksheet again.
20. Re-display values.
21. The department has just received two grants for 1994/1995. The Hardware/Software budget can increase by 5000 and the Research budget by 5000. Change, the **1994/1995 Hardware/Software** budget to **40000** and the **1994/1995 Research** budget to **15000**.
22. Print your worksheet again displaying the new values.
23. Use **FILE/Save As** to save your file using the name: **dptbudg2**
24. Exit *Excel* or continue with the next project.

Independent Project 1.2: Calculating the Current Caseload

You work for a social services agency. You have been asked to create a worksheet which calculates the July caseload for each case worker. You are given the case workers' names, and each case worker's June caseload, the number of new July cases and the number of cases discharged in July. You are to calculate the final July caseload and the difference from the June caseload. The first draft of your worksheet should resemble Figure 1 - 29.

When you finish this project, your worksheet will be complete, but not attractive. You will enhance its appearance at the end of Lesson 2.

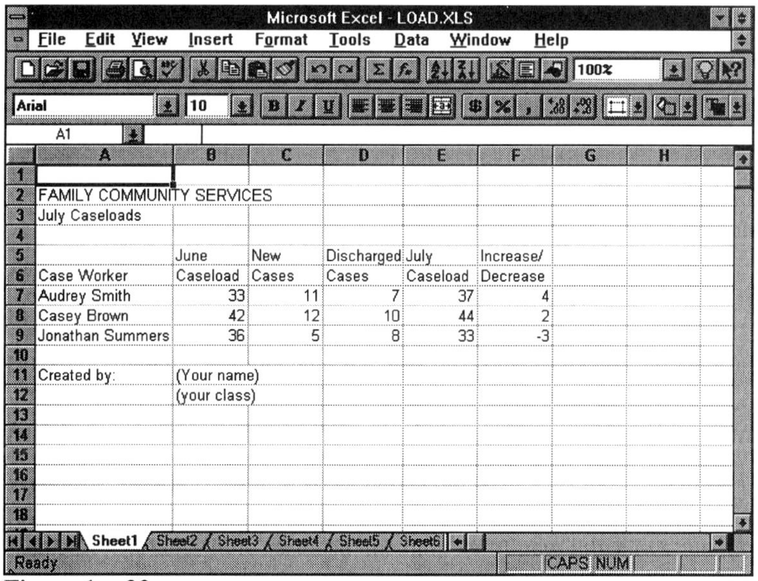

Figure 1 - 29

Use Figure 1 - 29 and the following instructions to help you create the project:

1. If you have just completed Independent Project 1.1, close it and choose **FILE/New** or the **New Workbook** tool to create a new worksheet.
2. Enter the worksheet title in cells **A2** and **A3**.
3. Enter the column labels in rows **5** and **6**.
4. Enter the case workers' names in cells **A7** through **A9**.
5. Increase column widths as necessary so that all of the labels are fully contained in their cells. The first line of the worksheet title, FAMILY COMMUNITY SERVICES, should still overflow into column **B**. If you need help increasing column widths, follow the directions for using **Help** in step 5 of Independent Project 1.1.
6. Enter the values for the **June Caseload**, **New Cases** and **Discharged Cases** as shown in Table 1 - 3.

	June	New	Discharged
Case Worker	Caseload	Cases	Cases
Audrey Smith	**33**	**11**	**7**
Casey Brown	**42**	**12**	**10**
Jonathan Summers	**36**	**5**	**8**

Table 1 - 3

7. In cells **E7** through **E9** enter the formulas to calculate the **July** Caseload**.** The **July Caseload** is the **June Caseload** plus the **New Cases** minus the **Discharged Cases.**
8. In cells **F7** through **F9** enter formulas to calculate the **Increase/Decrease**, which is equal to the **July Caseload** minus the **June Caseload.**
9. Put the information identifying who prepared this worksheet on the bottom of the worksheet as shown in Figure 1 - 29.
10. Save the worksheet using the name: **load**
11. Print the worksheet.
12. Display formulas.
13. Print the worksheet again with displayed formulas.
14. Re-display values instead of formulas.
15. You are given updated information on July caseloads. **Audrey Smith** had **1 more New Case** than initially reported and **Jonathan Summers** had **2 fewer Discharged Cases**. Change the data to reflect the new information.
16. Use **FILE/Save As** to save your worksheet using the name: **newload**
17. Print the worksheet displaying the new values.
18. Close the file.

Independent Project 1.3: Calculating Hockey Game Revenues

You are responsible for calculating the net revenue from ticket and food sales at the school hockey game. Table 1 - 4 shows the data that you have collected.

Attendance:			
	Full Price	Students	
Number Sold	178	234	
Fee	5.25	3.75	
Food:			
	Hot Dogs	Hamburgers	Soda
Number Sold	355	248	557
Unit Cost	.50	.75	.35
Sales Price	1.00	1.50	.75

Table 1 - 4

Table 1 - 5 shows the calculations that need to be made.

Result:	Calculation:
Total Number of tickets sold	Number of full price tickets plus number of student tickets sold
Total Revenue for Full Price Tickets	Number of Full Price Tickets times fee
Total Revenue for Student Tickets	Number of Student tickets times fee
Total Revenue from ticket sales	Revenue from full price tickets plus revenue from student tickets
Profit Per Item (food)	The difference between the sales price and the unit cost
Profit for Total Sales (food)	The profit per item times the number of items sold
Total Food Profit	The sum of the profit for total sales of each of the food items.
Total Hockey Game Profit	The total revenue from ticket sales plus the total food profit
Do **NOT** calculate a)the sum of the Full Price and Student Fees; b) the totals of the Number, Unit Cost, Sales Price or Profit Per Item of each of the foods sold.	

Table 1 - 5

Your worksheet may resemble Figure 1 - 30 or it may be organized differently as long as it displays all of the data.

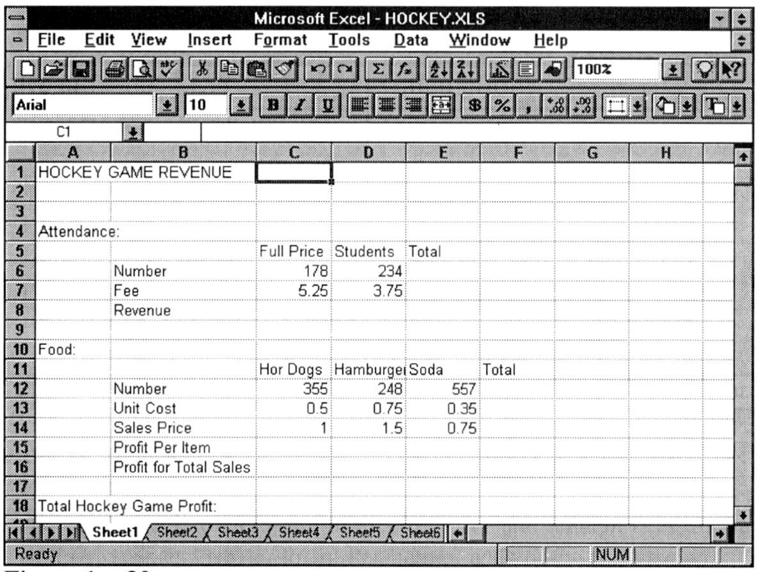

Figure 1 - 30

When you finish this project, your worksheet will be complete, but not attractive. You will enhance its appearance at the end of Lesson 2.

Use the following instructions to help your create your worksheet:

1. Plan your worksheet on a piece of paper. You may use Figure 1 - 30 as a guide for placing the values and text or you may create a design of your own.
2. Enter a worksheet title in cell **A1.**
3. Enter subtitles identifying the two parts of the worksheet (attendance and food) and column and row labels. Place them as they appear in your design; they do not need to be placed as they are in Figure 1 - 30.
4. Change column widths as necessary.
5. Enter the values shown in Table 1 - 4.
6. Enter formulas to perform the calculations indicated in Table 1 - 5.
7. Enter your name and any other required identifying information a few rows below the last row used in the worksheet.
8. Save your worksheet using the name: **hockey**
9. Print your worksheet displaying values.
10. Print your worksheet displaying formulas.
11. Replace the existing data with the following new data:

Number of Full Price Tickets Sold:	**182**
Number of Student Tickets Sold:	**236**
Number of Sodas Sold:	**580**
Unit Cost of Soda:	**.32**

12. Save your revised worksheet as: **hockey2**
13. Print your worksheet displaying the new values. Close the worksheet.

Independent Project 1.4: Planning a Budget

You are responsible for determining the **total amount of money** that should be budgeted for purchase of additional sporting goods for a community athletic program. You need to purchase **shirts** (which will serve as team uniforms for the soccer and hockey teams), **soccer balls** and **field hockey sticks**.

Unlike the previous projects, in this project you will perform all of the steps in planning the worksheet. Then you will create the worksheet using test data. Use your own figures for the **number of each item** bought and for the **costs of each item**. Don't worry about the accuracy of the numbers that you include.

When you finish this project, your worksheet will be complete, but not attractive. You will enhance its appearance at the end of Lesson 2.

The completed project should include:

1. A statement of the general objectives of the worksheet (see the section on **PLANNING A WORKSHEET** in the beginning of this lesson).
2. A statement of the specific results you want the worksheet to provide.
3. A statement of the data needed to obtain the results.
4. A statement of the calculations to be performed on the data

5. A handwritten design of what the worksheet will look like.
6. A printout of the worksheet showing values.
7. A printout of the worksheet showing formulas.
8. Save your worksheet using the name: **sports**

Lesson 2 Enhancing a Worksheet

Objectives

In this lesson you will learn how to:

- Select a range of cells
- Change the format of value entries
- Change the alignment of labels
- Change fonts and font sizes
- Add bold, italics, and underlining
- Add borders to cells
- Enhance printouts by changing the page setup
- Check Spelling

PROJECT DESCRIPTION

In Lesson 1 you created a simple worksheet **consult.xls**. The information it contains is correct, but it is hard to read and not very attractive. For example, the numbers in each column have a differing number of decimal places, don't have commas separating thousands, and lack the formatting symbols that indicate if they are dollars or percents. Similarly, the labels are not aligned over the numbers in the same column, the title isn't centered, and there is no variety in the font. In this lesson you will enhance **consult.xls**, so that it is more attractive and more clearly conveys the information it contains. When you are finished, your worksheet will resemble Figure 2 - 1.

EMPLOYEE BILLING

Employee	Consulting Hours	Salary Rate	Total Salary	Billing Rate	Total Billed	Profit	% Profit
George Snidowski	32	$ 27.50	$ 880.00	$ 50	$ 1,600.00	$ 720.00	45.0%
Claire Corbow	41	$ 32.50	$ 1,332.50	$ 60	$ 2,460.00	$ 1,127.50	45.8%
Thomas Henderson	29	$ 42.50	$ 1,232.50	$ 75	$ 2,175.00	$ 942.50	43.3%

Figure 2 - 1

RANGES

Most of the changes that you want to make affect groups of cells. Therefore, instead of changing the format of each cell individually, you will apply most changes to a *range* of cells. In a worksheet a *range* refers to a rectangular block of cells that has been selected to be operated on as a whole (Figure 2 - 2). The range is selected first, and then the operation affecting the entire range is specified. The range remains selected until another cell or range is selected. Therefore, you may apply more than one command to a range without selecting it again.

There are many ways to select a range. The two most basic techniques are described below.

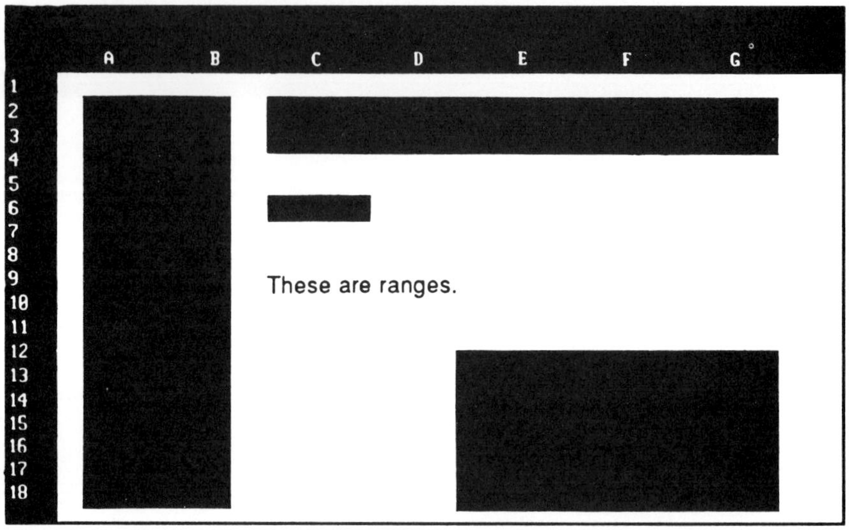

Figure 2 - 2

To select a range of cells:

- To use the mouse, point to the cell at one corner of the range, click and drag the mouse until the highlight extends to the diagonally opposite corner of the range, *or*
- To use the keyboard, select the first cell of the range, hold down the **SHIFT** key and, keeping **SHIFT** depressed, use the **ARROW** keys to extend the highlight.

  *Ranges are named by the upper left and bottom right cells in the range, separated by a colon (:). For example, the range that starts in **A3** and ends in **G7** is **A3:G7**.*

! **CAUTION:** The mouse pointer **must** be a ✥ when you begin highlighting cells to select a range. If the mouse pointer is an ↖, you are pointing to the cell frame and will **move** the cell contents. If the mouse pointer is a +, you are pointing at the fill handle and will **copy** the cell contents.

SELECTING MULTIPLE COLUMNS

In Lesson 1 you changed the width of individual columns. If you want to make the same change to more than one column you must select the range of columns first.

To select more than one adjacent column:

- Point to the first column heading. Make sure the mouse pointer is a ✥. Click and drag the mouse until all columns are highlighted. Release the mouse button.

FORMATTING CELLS

Making formatting changes is such a frequent activity that in the default setup the Formatting Toolbar (Figure 2 - 3) is displayed in addition to the Standard Toolbar. All of the formatting changes that you wish to make can be made using this toolbar. They also can be made by selecting **FORMAT/Cells** from the menu. You will use both of these approaches in this lesson.

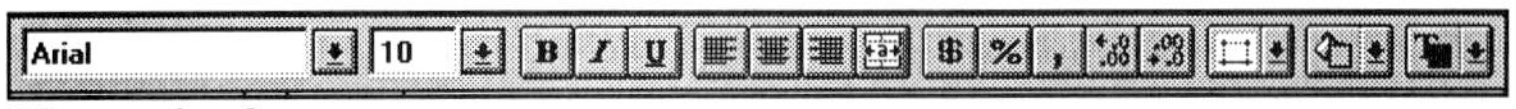

Figure 2 - 3

Activity 2.1: Becoming Familiar with the Formatting Toolbar

1. Start *Excel*. Maximize the *Excel* window if it is not already maximized.
2. If the Formatting Toolbar (Figure 2 - 3) is NOT displayed, use **VIEW/Toolbars** to display it. (See Activity I.4 in the Introduction.)

   The Formatting Toolbar is normally displayed near the top of the worksheet. However, it may be displayed at the bottom or sides of the worksheet (or as a block anywhere on the worksheet).
3. With the mouse, point to each of the buttons on the Formatting Toolbar and read the name that appears below the toolbar and the description that appears on the Status Bar.

Most of the formatting changes that you want to make can be applied to both values and text. Before you look at those, you will look at changes that can only be applied to values.

Formatting Numbers

When numbers are typed into a cell, they appear exactly as entered, except that any zeroes that do not change the value of the number are dropped. This is the *general number format.* You want to format the numbers on the worksheet so that they contain a specified number of decimal places, commas to separate thousands, and dollar or percent signs, if appropriate. The three most common number formats can be accessed from the Formatting Toolbar. Each one displays the currently defined style for the selected format. If the style definitions have not been changed in your copy of *Excel*, the styles are:

- Currency style — commas to separate thousands, two decimal places, and a dollar sign ($); the dollar sign is on the *left side of the cell*
- Percent style — multiplies the number in the cell by 100, and displays a percent sign and no decimal places
- Comma style — displays commas to separate thousands and two decimal places

In all of the formats, the value that appears on the worksheet is rounded to the specified number of decimal places. However, the actual value is kept by *Excel* and used in all calculations. This can make your worksheet appear to be incorrect when it is really correct. For example if *2.4, 3.4*, and *4.4* are all formatted for zero decimal places they would appear as *2, 3*, and *4*. If these three cells are added, and the sum formatted for zero decimal places, the sum would be *10* (short for *10.2*). Therefore, your worksheet would be correct, but would appear to say *2+3+4=10*!

To use the Toolbar to format a number:

- Select the cell or range of cells to be formatted.
- Click on the **Currency** , **Percent** , or **Comma**  button.

- If you want to change the number of decimals displayed, click on the **Increase Decimal**  or **Decrease Decimal**  button.

Activity 2.2: Using Number Formats

In this activity, you will use the toolbar to format parts of your worksheet for currency with two decimal places or percent with one decimal place.

1. Open **consult.xls**. Remember, you may need to make changes to the drive or directory in the **Open** dialog box so that *Excel* specifies the location of your data files.
2. Maximize **CONSULT.XLS** if it is not already maximized.
3. To select the range **C5:D7,** point to **C5,** click and drag the mouse across and down to cell **D7;** when the range **C5:D7** is highlighted, release the mouse button. Make sure that the mouse pointer is always this shape .

PROBLEM SOLVER: *If you release the mouse button before the correct range is selected, use the* ***SHIFT+ARROW*** *keys to extend or contract the range. You cannot use the mouse unless you select the entire range again.*

The range ***C5:D7*** *will be highlighted (Figure 2 - 4).* ***C5*** *is in the* ***name box (****left-side of the Formula Bar) and has a white background while the rest of the range has a black background.* ***C5*** *is the active cell. If you were to begin typing, the data would be entered in* ***C5****. Any commands you choose will affect the entire range,* ***C5:D7****.*

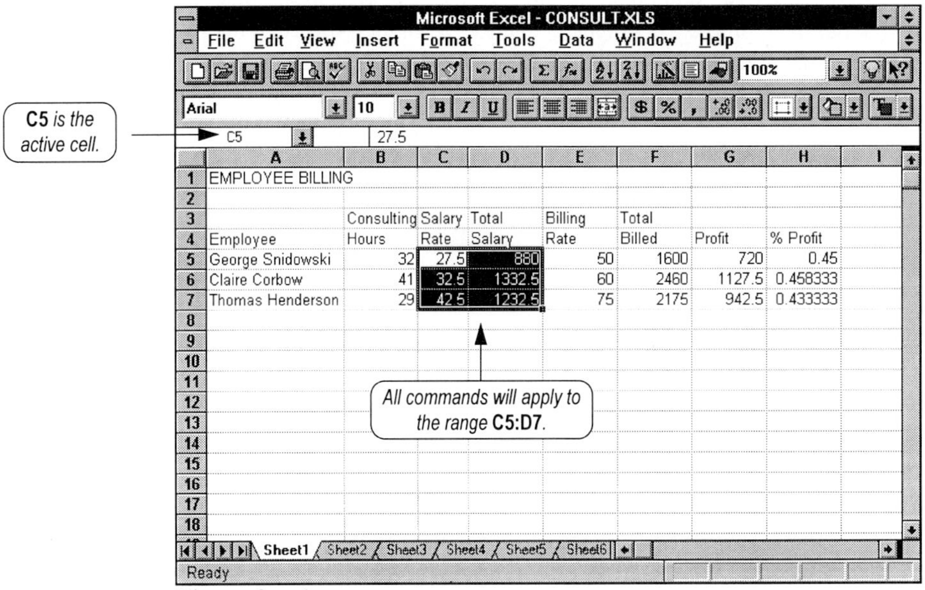

Figure 2 - 4

4. Click on the **Currency Style** button on the toolbar.

   Are you surprised at what happened? All of the cells, except for the one containing George Snidowski's total salary are filled with ##### (Figure 2 - 5). As you saw in Lesson 1, when a label is too wide to fit in a cell, it is truncated. However, when a number is too wide to fit in a cell, the entire cell is filled with ###. To correct this you must widen the column. The easiest way to do this is to use the ***AutoFit*** *feature that you learned in Lesson 1.*

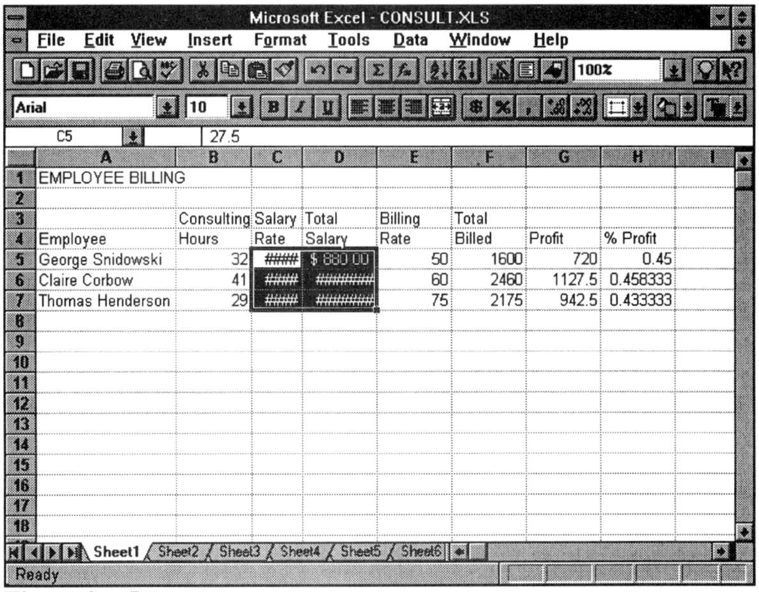

Figure 2 - 5

5. To select both columns **C** and **D**, point to **C** in the column header, click and drag the highlight one column to the right, until columns **C** and **D** are highlighted, and release the mouse button.

   *Both columns **C** and **D** are selected (Figure 2 - 6).*

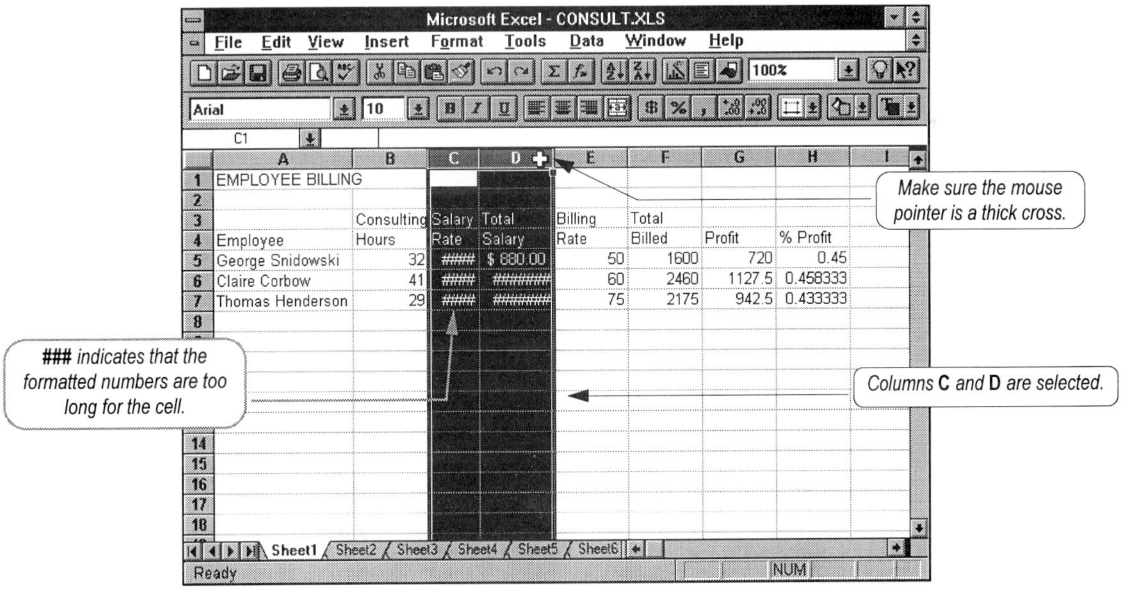

Figure 2 - 6

6. Choose **FORMAT/Column, AutoFit Selection.**

   *Columns **C** and **D** have increased in width so that all of the cell entries are visible. All of the numbers contain two decimal places even if they are zeroes. Dollar signs and commas also appear.*

7. To select the range **F5:G7,** point to cell **F5,** click and drag the highlight to the right and down to cell **G7**.

8. Click on the **Currency Style** toolbar button.
9. Point to the **F** in the column header, and click and drag to highlight columns **F** and **G.**
10. Choose **FORMAT/Column, AutoFit Selection.** Unless someone has changed the default setting, the dollar signs will line up at the left edge of the cell (Figure 2 - 7).

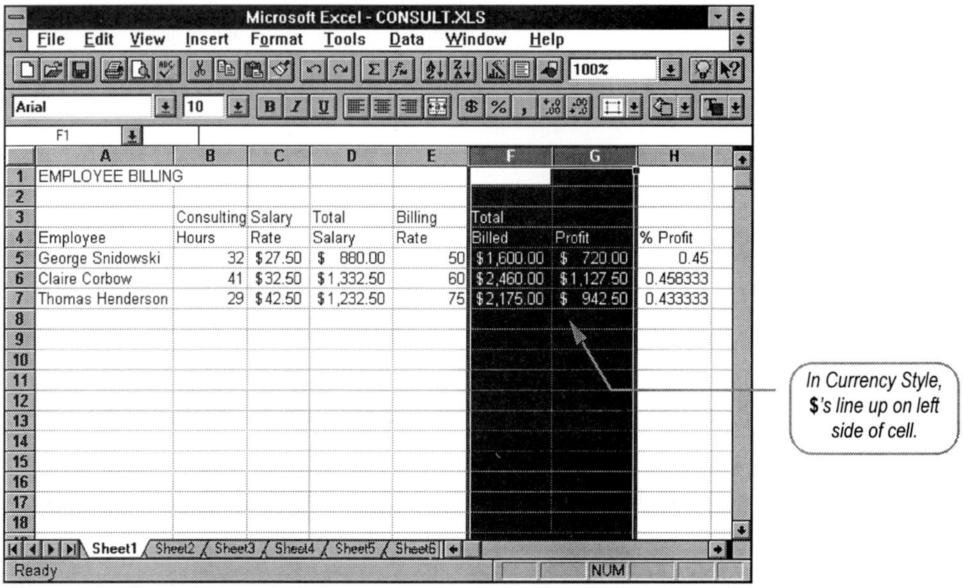

Figure 2 - 7

11. Use the mouse to select the range **H5:H7.**

12. Click on the **Percent Style** button.

The cells containing the % Profit are formatted for percent with zero decimal places. All of these values are displayed because they fit within the column (Figure 2 - 8).

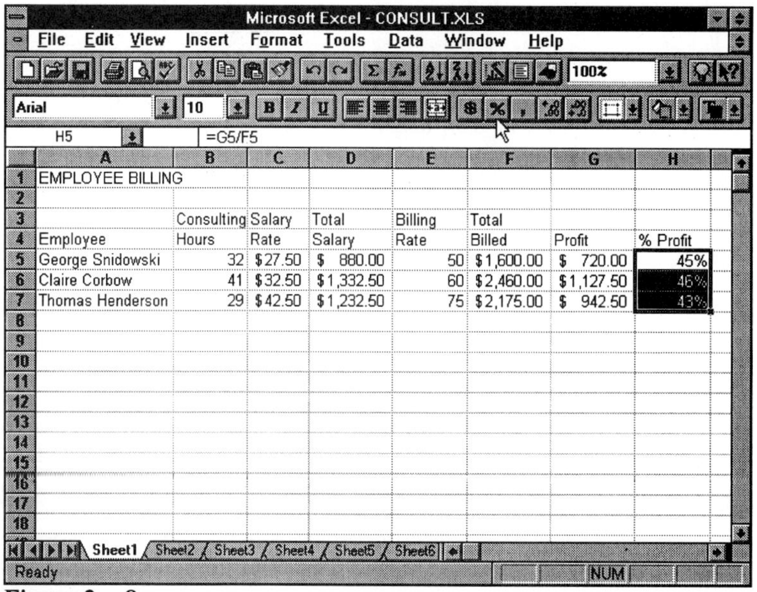

Figure 2 - 8

13. Cells **H5:H7** should still be highlighted. To display the percents with one decimal place, click on the **Increase Decimals** toolbar button once.

    One decimal place will be displayed for each of the percent profits.

14. Format **E5:E7** for **Currency Style**. **Decrease Decimals** twice.

Changing Cell Alignment

You are going to change the *horizontal alignment* of the labels in the cell. The alignment determines if the text is displayed aligned with the left or right side of the cell or centered within the cell. In addition, if a range of cells is selected and text is contained only in the leftmost cell(s) in the range, that text may be centered across the entire range.

It is possible to change the horizontal alignment of values, but this is NOT good to do. Values should always be right-aligned in a cell. Do you know why?

To change the horizontal alignment of text:

- Select the cell or range of cells containing the labels to be aligned. If you want to align a title over a range of cells, the title must be in the leftmost cell in the range.
- Click on the **Align Right** , **Center** , **Align Left** , or **Center Across Columns** buttons on the Formatting Toolbar.

Activity 2.3: Changing Text Alignment

Since text is left-aligned and values are right-aligned automatically when they are entered, the column labels for columns containing values are not aligned with the numbers underneath them. In addition, the title of the worksheet, EMPLOYEE BILLING, is not centered over the rest of the worksheet. You will change these alignments.

1. Select the range **B3:H4** (Figure 2 - 9).

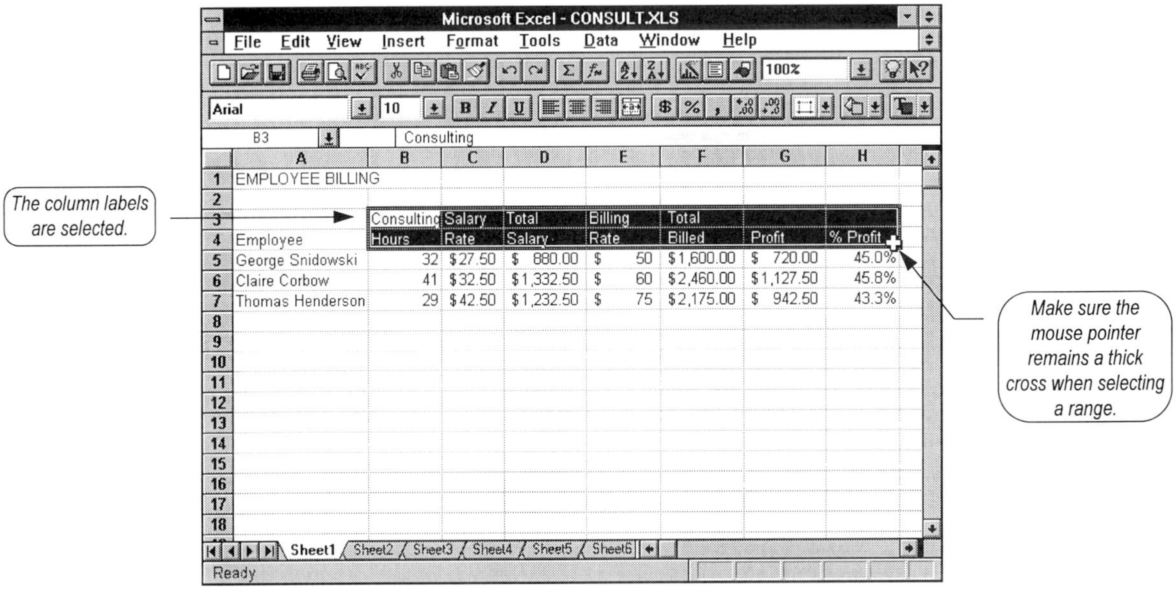

Figure 2 - 9

2. Click on the **Align Right** toolbar button.

*The labels in columns **B** through **H** are right-aligned. In columns **C:G**, the labels are closer to the right side of the cell than are the numbers under them (See Figure 2 - 10). Those numbers are formatted for Currency Style which displays negative numbers enclosed in right parentheses. Therefore, if the number is positive, the rightmost space in the cell is empty.*

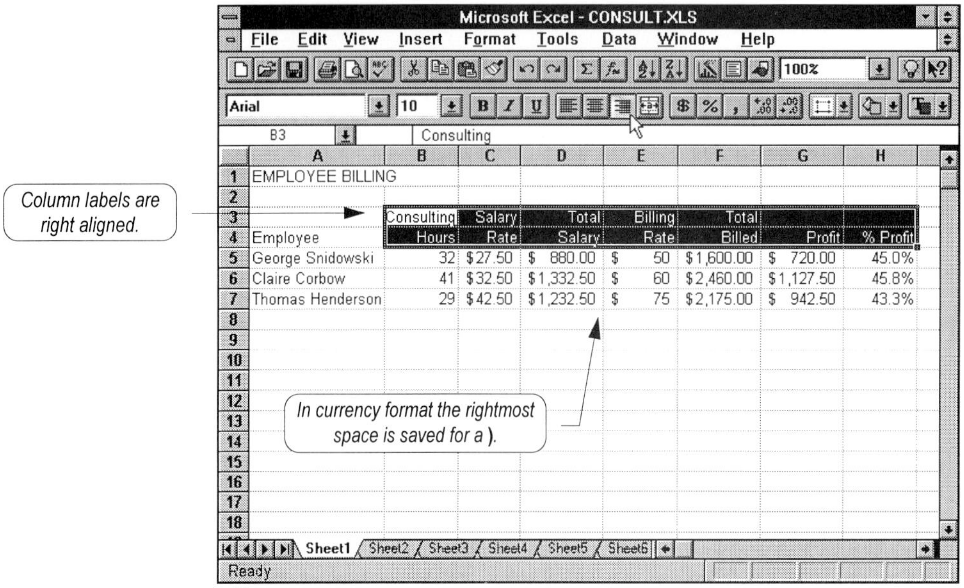

Figure 2 - 10

3. Select the range **A1:H1**.

   ***EMPLOYEE BILLING** is in cell **A1**. The rest of the range is blank.*

4. Click on the **Center Across Columns** toolbar button.

   ***EMPLOYEE BILLING** is centered across columns **A:H**. The vertical gridlines in Row **1** in the selected range have been removed. **EMPLOYEE BILLING** also appears in the Formula Bar.*

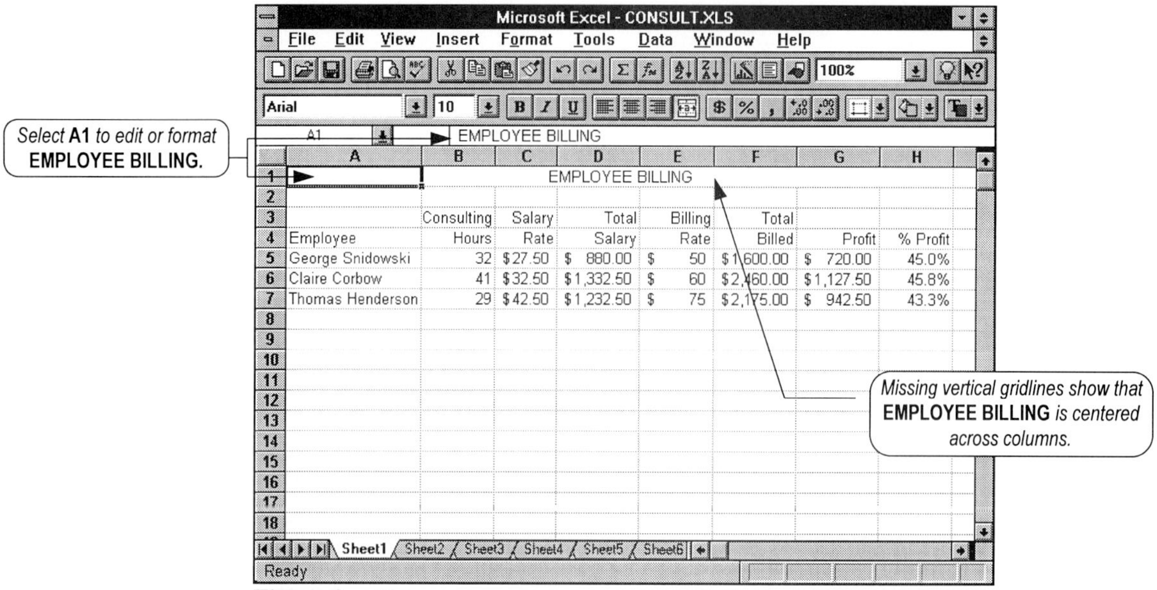

Figure 2 - 11

PROBLEM SOLVER: *If no gridlines are displayed anywhere on the worksheet, select* ***TOOLS/Options.*** *Click on the* ***View*** *tab. Click on the* ***Gridlines*** *check box if it is not already marked.*

5. Click on cell **D1** and look at the Formula Bar.

   The Formula Bar is empty.

6. Click on **A1** and look at the Formula Bar (Figure 2 - 11).

   EMPLOYEE BILLING *is displayed in the Formula Bar. If you want to edit or apply any other commands to* ***EMPLOYEE BILLING****, you must select* ***A1****.*

Let's save your file now, so that you won't lose any of your work.

Activity 2.4: Saving a File Using a New Name

1. To save the file to a new file name, select **FILE/Save As**.

   The ***Save As*** *dialog box should be displayed. The* ***File Name*** *text box should contain the highlight (Figure 2 - 12).*

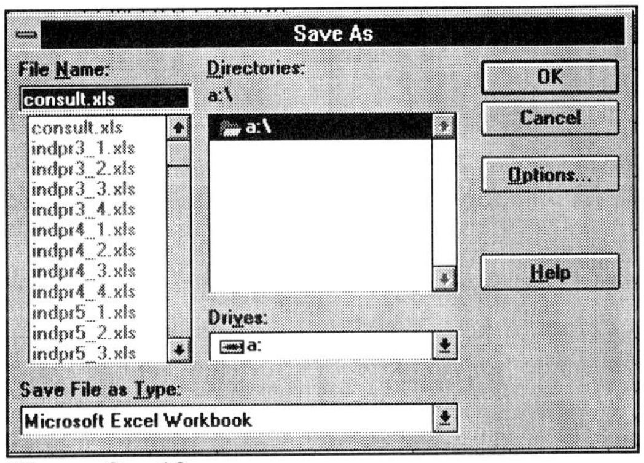

Figure 2 - 12

2. Type the new **file name: consult2** and click on **OK**.
3. If the **Summary Info** dialog box appears, click on **OK**.

   The *Status Bar will indicate that the file is being saved. When the save is complete, the Title Bar will say,* ***Microsoft Excel - CONSULT2.XLS****.*

   Remember, anytime that you want to take a break, save your worksheet and exit Excel. Start Excel and open the worksheet when you are ready to continue working.

Changing Font, Font Size, and Font Style

The font is the design or typeface of the characters. Font sizes are typically measured in *points*, where each point is 1/72 of an inch. Point sizes between 10 and 12 are commonly used for the body of the worksheet, with larger fonts used for titles. Each font can be displayed in a variety of sizes and styles. The font styles are regular, **bold**, and *italics*. Bold and italics are usually used to emphasize the characters. Underlining can also be used for emphasis. The default *Excel* font is Arial, 10 point.

Windows comes with a set of fonts called TrueType fonts. These should be installed in Windows and then are available for all Windows applications to use regardless of the printer you are using. These fonts are also displayed on your screen as they will be displayed when they are printed. In this book we will limit our choices to TrueType fonts.

The five leftmost buttons on the Formatting Toolbar control the font, font size, and font style (bold, italics, and underline) enhancements. In addition, the font, font size, and font style can be changed using the **FORMAT/Cells** command. An advantage of **FORMAT/Cells** is that you can see what the fonts will look like before you select them. **FORMAT/Cells** can also be used to change alignment and number format and to add borders around cells.

To change font, font size, and font style using menus:

- Select the cell or range of cells to be formatted.
- Choose **FORMAT/Cells.**
- When the **Format Cells** dialog box is displayed, click on the **Font** tab.
- Use the **Font, Font Style,** and **Size** list boxes to make your changes. Use the **Underline** list box to add underlining.
- Click on **OK** to apply the format changes.

To change font, font size, and font style using the Formatting Toolbar:

- Select the cell or range of cells to be formatted.
- To change the font style click on the **Bold** B, **Italic** I, or **Underline** U button.
- To change **Font Name** Arial, or **Font Size** 10, click on the ↓ to the right of the button, and click on your selection.

Activity 2.5: Changing Font, Font Size and Font Style

You will use **FORMAT/Cells, Font** to change the font, font size, and font style of the employee data to Times New Roman, 10 point regular and the column headings to Arial, 12 point bold. You will then use the toolbar to change **EMPLOYEE BILLING** to Arial, 14 point, bold italics.

1. Select the range **A5:H7**.
2. Choose **FORMAT/Cells.**

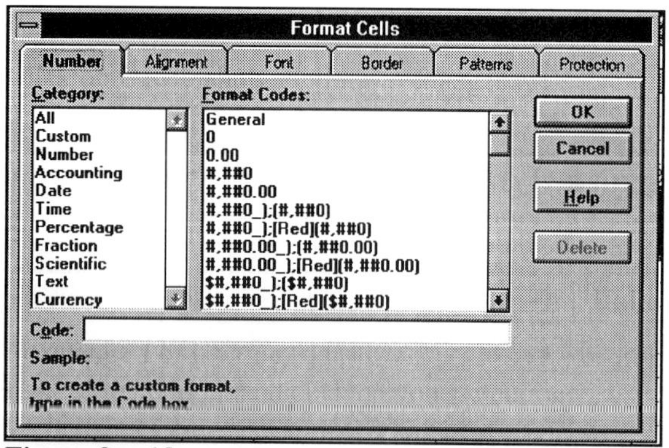

Figure 2 - 13

*The **Format Cells** dialog box will be displayed. **Format Cells** is a **tabbed** dialog box, which means that it contains a number of related sheets. In Figure 2 - 13, the **Number** tab is highlighted and the number formatting options are displayed. A different tab may be displayed on your screen.*

3. Click on the **Font** tab.

   The font formatting choices will be displayed (Figure 2 - 14).

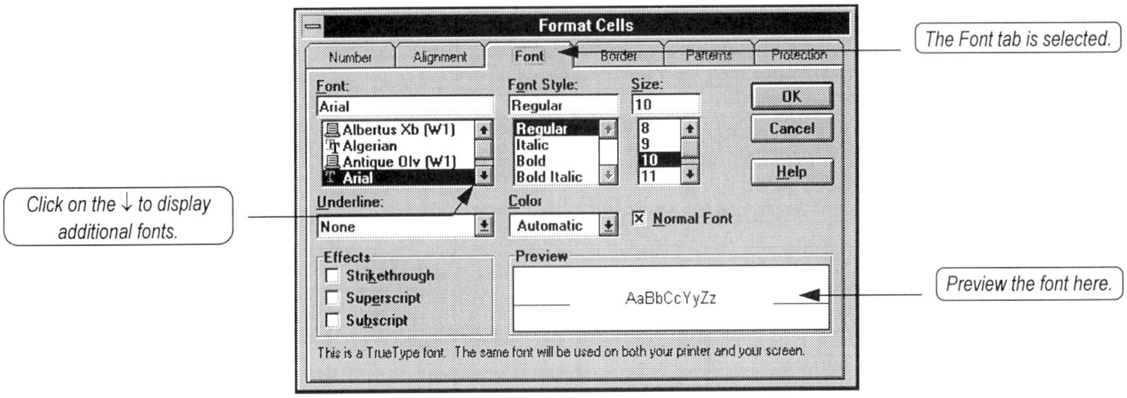

Figure 2 - 14

4. In the **Font** list box, click on **Arial**, which should already be selected (see Figure 2 - 14). Press the **DOWN ARROW** key on the keyboard. As each new font is selected, you will be able to preview it in the **Preview** area of the dialog box.
5. After previewing the fonts, use the arrow keys to select the **Times New Roman** TrueType font.
6. Click on **Regular** in the **Font Style** list box and **10** in the **Size** box (Figure 2 - 15) if they are not already selected.

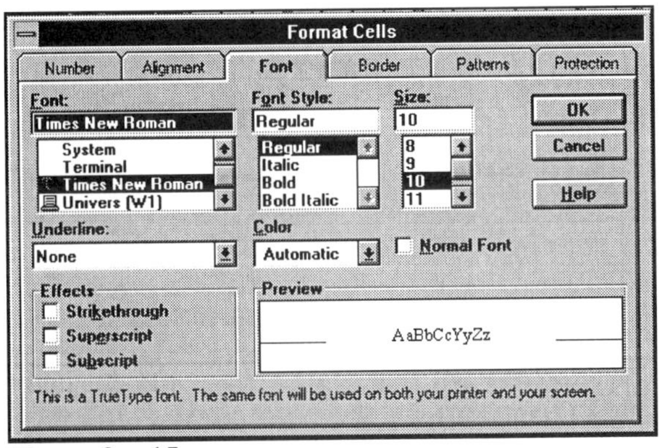

Figure 2 - 15

7. When the **Format Cells** dialog box resembles Figure 2 - 15, click on **OK** or press the **ENTER** key.

   *Your screen should resemble Figure 2 - 16. Even though you changed the font using a menu command, the **Font** toolbar button changes to reflect the new font.*

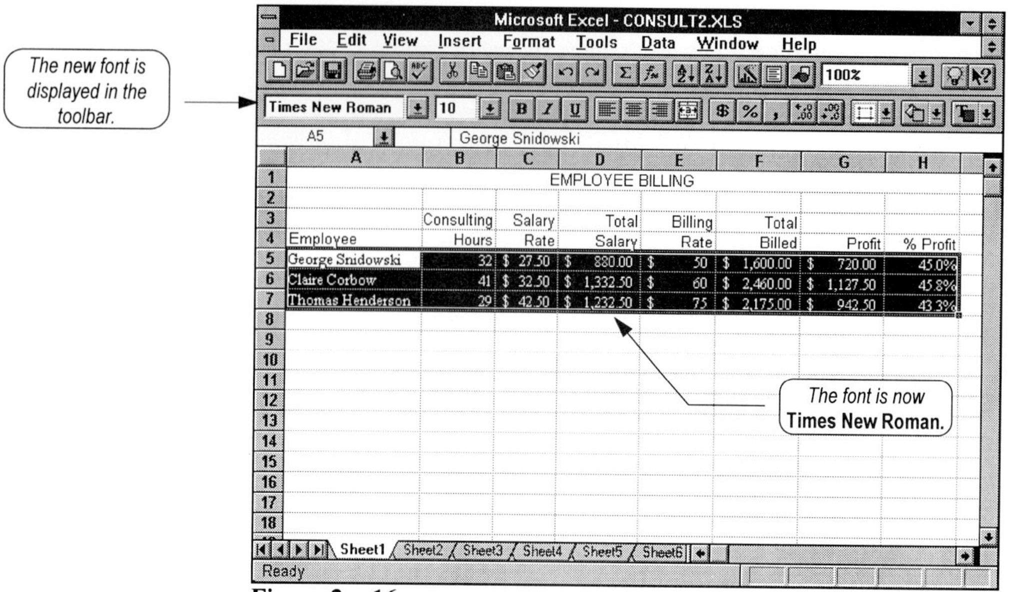

Figure 2 - 16

8. Select the range **A3:H4**.

   *Ranges must be rectangles. So you must include **A3** in the range even though it is blank.*

9. Choose **FORMAT/Cells**.

   *The **Font** tab should be displayed as Excel displays the last tab used.*

10. Change the font size to **12** and the font style to **Bold**. Click on **OK**.

    ***Problem Solver:** If the **12** is not visible in the **Size** list box, click on the ↓ on the scroll bar until the **12** is visible.*

    ***Consulting** is now too wide to fit in column **B**. Since it is right-aligned, it overflows into **A3**, the cell to its left (Figure 2 - 17).*

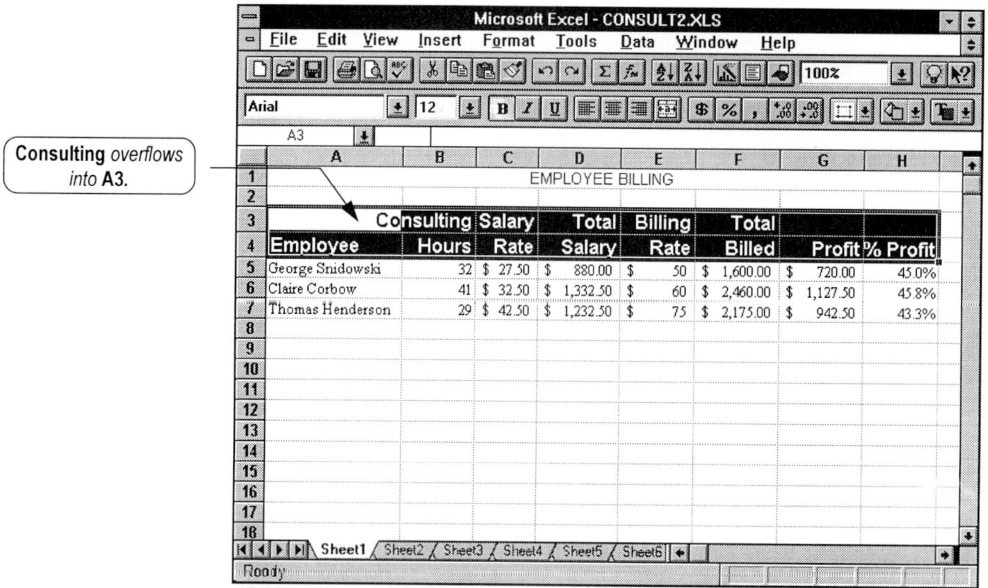

Figure 2 - 17

11. Use **AutoFit** to make column **B** wide enough for all entries. ***Hint:** If you forget the steps involved, see Activity 2.2, steps 5 and 6.*

MOUSE SHORTCUT: *To use the mouse to invoke* ***AutoFit****, point to the line to the right of* ***B*** *in the column header. When the mouse pointer changes to a ✥ double-click.*

12. To change the font size for the worksheet title, click on cell **A1**.

13. To use the toolbar to change font size, click on the ↓ to the right of the **Font Size** button on the Formatting Toolbar.

    A list of font sizes is displayed (Figure 2 - 18).

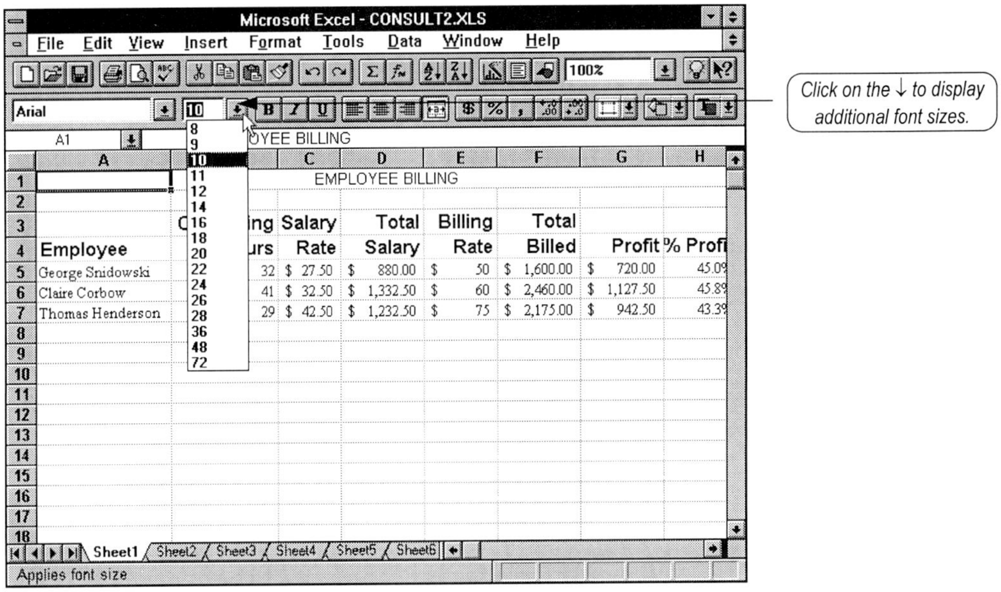

Figure 2 - 18

14. Click on **14**.

    Notice that the height of the row automatically increases to fit the larger font size.

15. With your cursor still in **A1**, click on the **Bold** toolbar button.

16. Click on the **Italic** toolbar button. (Figure 2 - 19).

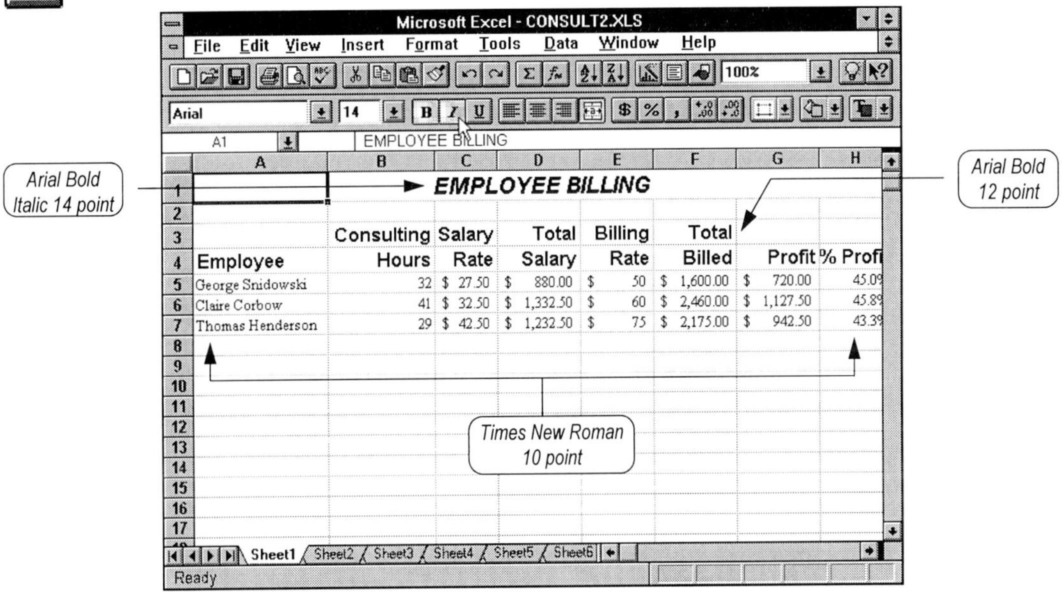

Figure 2 - 19

Adding Cell Borders

Often you want to draw a line under or around certain cells. In your worksheet, you would like a line under the column labels so that they are separated from the data. In order to do this you want to add a border to the bottom of the cells containing the column labels. You can do this using the **FORMAT/Cells, Borders** dialog box or by using the **Borders** toolbar button.

To add cell borders using the toolbar:

- Select the cell or range of cells.
- If the **Borders** Toolbar button shows the border you want to use, click on the button. If it does not:
  - Click on the ↓ at the right side of the button.
  - Click on the icon displaying the border of your choice.

Activity 2.6: Adding a Bottom Border

1. Select the range, **A4:H4**. (Hint: If **H4** is only partially visible on the screen, stop dragging the mouse as soon as **H4** is highlighted and before touching the right border of the window.)

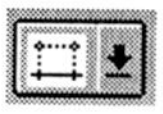

2. Click on the ↓ to the right of the **Borders** button.

   Twelve border choices will be displayed (Figure 2 - 20).

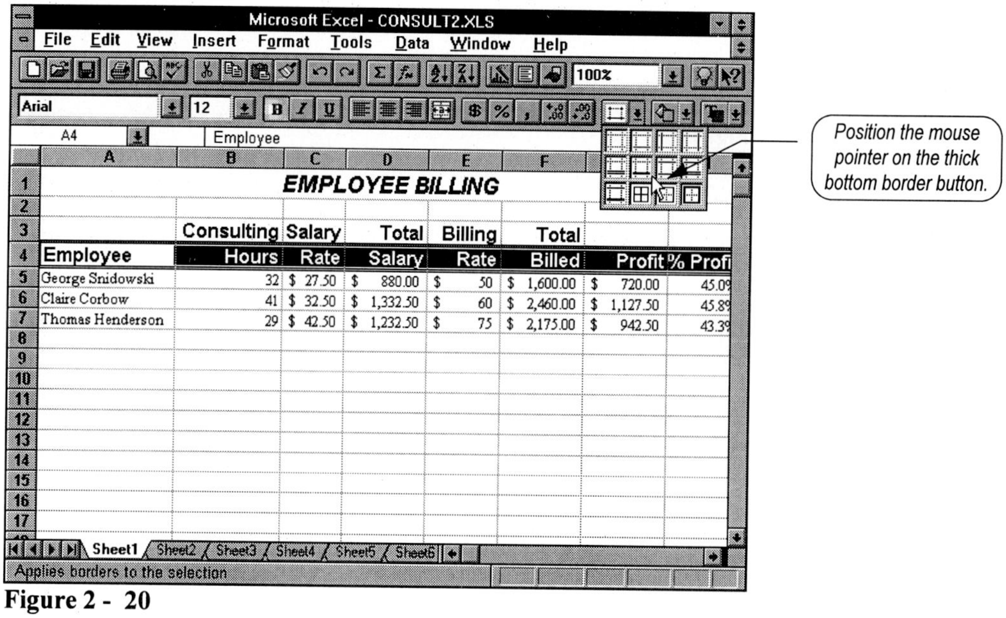

Figure 2 - 20

3. Click on the thick bottom underline border shown in Figure 2 - 20.

4. Click on the **Save** toolbar button to save your worksheet again using the existing file name and location.
5. Click on any cell in the worksheet to remove the highlight from cells **A4:H4**.

MORE PRINTING

In Lesson 1 you printed your worksheet using the default page setup. However, parts of the printout — like the headers and footers and gridlines — made the printout less attractive than it could have been. In this lesson you will learn to change the appearance of the printout. The print options are changed using the **Page Setup** command. **Page Setup** can be reached directly from the **FILE** menu or from the **FILE/Print Preview** dialog box.

Previewing a Document

Previewing a document lets you decide if you like the way it will look before you print it out. If you don't, you can change it before printing.

To preview a document:

Choose **FILE/Print Preview** or click the **Print Preview** button  on the Standard toolbar. The Status Bar on the bottom of the Preview Window (Figure 2 - 21) indicates the current page and the total number of pages in the printout. The screen does not contain any menus. However, it has eight buttons which can be used to work with the document:

- **Next** – displays the next page of a multipage printout
- **Previous** — displays the previous page of a multipage printout
- **Zoom** — switches between a magnified view and a full page view
- **Print** — displays the **Print** dialog box
- **Setup** — displays the **Page Setup** dialog box
- **Margins** — turns on or off "handles," which can be dragged to change margins
- **Close** — closes the Preview window and displays the active worksheet
- **Help** — displays a help screen

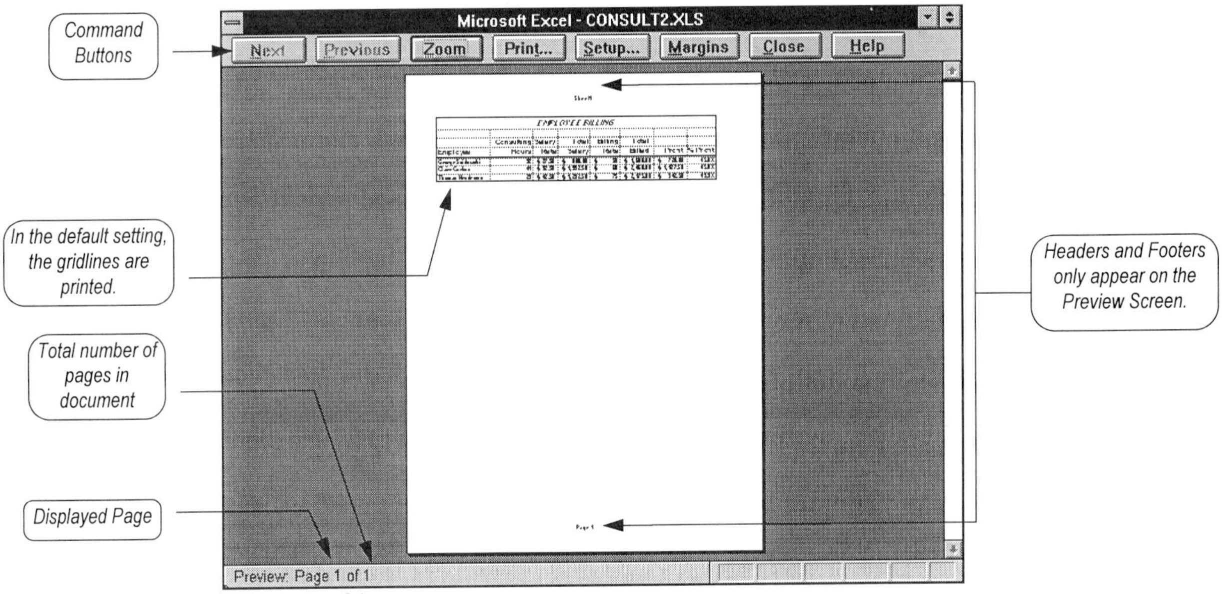

Figure 2 - 21

Activity 2.7: Previewing the Printout

1. Choose **FILE/Print Preview** or click on the **Print Preview** toolbar button.

   *The **Print Preview** screen will be displayed (Figure 2 - 21). Notice that the gridlines appear. The preview also shows two lines of text that did not appear on the worksheet but will appear* *on each page of the printout: a header that will appear on the top of each page; and a footer that will appear on the bottom of each page.*

PROBLEM SOLVER: *If the Status Bar indicates that there are two pages (e.g. Preview: Page 1 of 2), click on the* ***Close*** *button. The worksheet will re-appear. Make Column* ***A*** *narrower. The worksheet should now fit on one page. Choose* ***FILE/Print Preview****.*

2. Click on the **Zoom** button.
3. Click on the ↑ and ↓ on the vertical scroll bar to view all of the worksheet.
4. Click on **Zoom** again to return to full page view.

Changing the Page Setup

The **Page Setup** dialog box is used to change the appearance of the printout. It does not change the appearance of the worksheet itself.

To change the appearance of a printout:

- Choose **FILE/Page Setup** or choose **FILE/Print Preview** and then click on the **Setup** button.
- Make the desired changes in the **Page Setup** dialog box and click on **OK**.

Activity 2.8: Changing the Page Setup

1. If the Preview Window is no longer displayed, choose **PRINT/Preview.**
2. Click on the **Setup** button.

   The ***Page Setup*** *dialog box appears. Like the* ***Font*** *dialog box,* ***Page Setup*** *contains multiple tabs.*

3. Click on the **Sheet** tab to make that tab active (Figure 2 - 22).

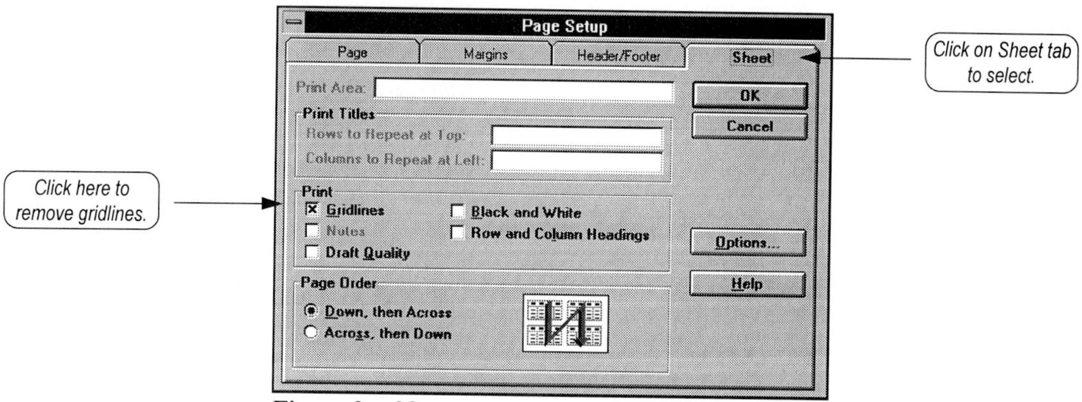

Figure 2 - 22

4. Click on the **Gridlines** check box to remove the check.
5. Click on the **Header/Footer** tab.

   The ***Header/Footer*** *tab options are displayed (Figure 2 - 23). You will delete the current header and create a custom footer to replace the current one.*

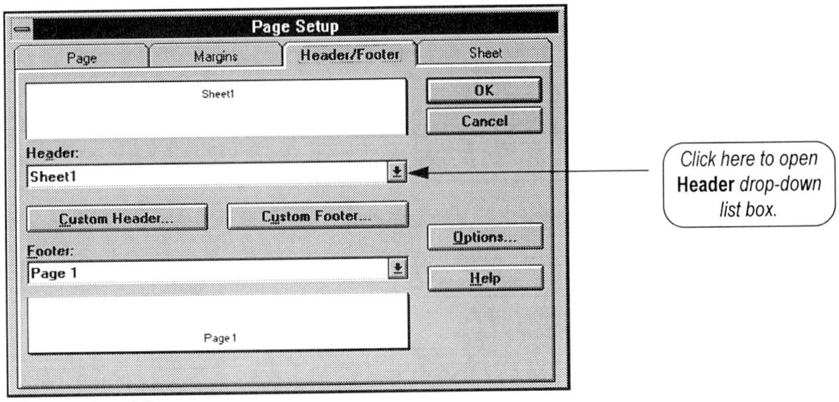

Figure 2 - 23

6. Click on the ↓ on the right side of the **Header** pull-down list box.

   The list contains built-in headers created by Excel.

7. Click on the ↑ scroll arrow until the first item, **None**, is displayed (Figure 2 - 24). Click on **None** to select it.

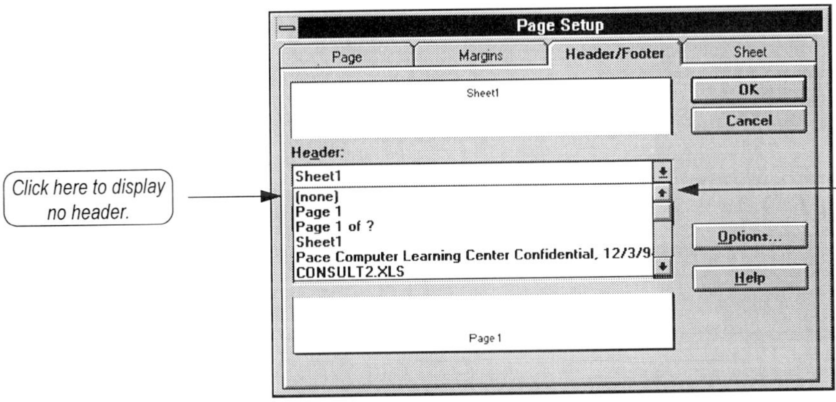

Figure 2 - 24

8. Click on the **Custom Footer** button.

   *The **Footer** dialog box is displayed.*

9. Point to **Page &[Page]** in the **Center Section:** text box. Click and drag the mouse across **Page &[Page]** until it is highlighted (Figure 2 - 25).

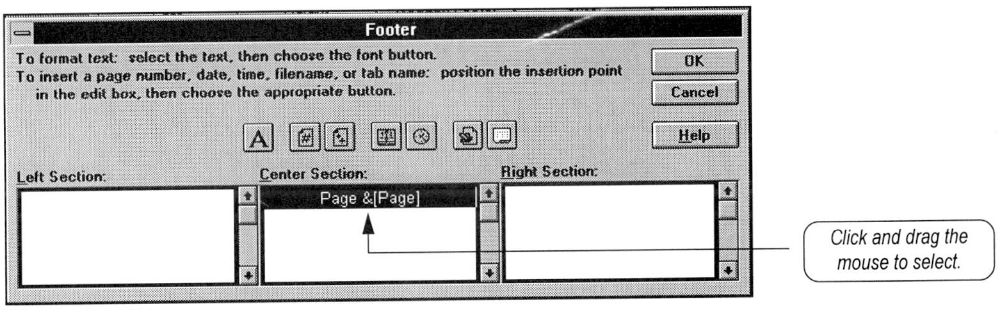

Figure 2 - 25

10. Type: **Created by (your name)**

    Created by (your name) *will replace* ***Page &[Page]*** *in the center section. If your name is long* ***Excel*** *will move it to a second line.*

11. Click on **OK** to leave the **Footer** dialog box.

    The ***Page Setup*** *dialog box will reappear on the screen. The Footer* ***Created by (your name)*** *will be in the* ***Footer*** *text box.*

12. Click on **OK** to return to the Preview window.

    The gridlines and original header should not be displayed (Figure 2 - 26). To read the ***Footer****, click on* ***Zoom*** *and then scroll to the bottom of the page.*

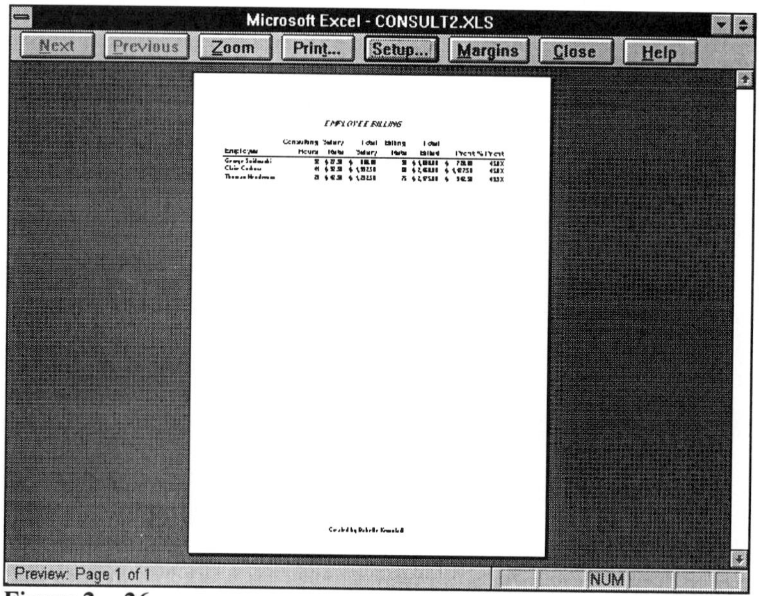

Figure 2 - 26

13. Click on the **Print** button.

    The same ***Print*** *dialog box that you saw in Lesson 1 will be displayed.*

14. Click on **OK** to print your worksheet.
15. Choose **FILE/Close.**

    An alert box will be displayed asking if you want to save your worksheet.

16. Click on **Yes** to save your worksheet again. If you do <u>not</u> save the worksheet, the page setup changes will not be saved.

SUMMARY

In this lesson you learned how to use formatting and page setup commands to enhance the appearance of your worksheet. The **CONSULT2.XLS** worksheet is now complete. However, in Lesson 6 we will add a pie chart to the worksheet so that your data can also be presented pictorially. The Independent projects will give you practice formatting, and will introduce a new skill, spell checking.

KEY TERMS

Align Left
Align Right
Borders
Center
Center Across Columns
Comma Style
Currency Style
Font
Font Size
Font Style
Footers
Format
Formatting Toolbar
General Number Format
Gridlines
Headers
Increase Decimals
Label Alignment
Number Style
Page Setup
Percent Style
Point
Preview
Range

INDEPENDENT PROJECTS

The four independent projects allow you to practice using ranges and enhancing the worksheets that you created in the independent projects in Lesson 1. You will review formatting of value entries, changing label alignments, changing fonts, font sizes and font styles and adding borders to cells. You will also review the use of **Page Setup** to change the appearance of your printouts and learn a few page setup changes not introduced in this lesson. You will also learn how to check the spelling of your worksheet. You will find the spell checking procedure very similar to that used in Windows word processors, particularly *Microsoft Word for Windows*.

Independent Project 2.1: Enhancing Your Department Budget

In Independent Project 1.1 you created a department budget. In this project your will format the budget so that it is easier to read and more attractive. When you are finished your worksheet should resemble Figure 2 - 27.

		DEPARTMENTAL BUDGET		
		1993/1994 and 1994/1995		
Category	**1993/1994**	**1994/1995**	**Increase**	**% Increase**
Faculty	$ 300,000	$338,000	$ 38,000	12.7%
Staff	$ 45,000	$ 47,500	$ 2,500	5.6%
Hardware/Software	$ 15,000	$ 40,000	$ 25,000	166.7%
Research	$ 7,500	$ 15,000	$ 7,500	100.0%
Created by:	*(Your name)*			
	(Your class)			

Figure 2 - 27

Use Figure 2 - 27 and the following instructions to enhance dptbudg2.xls:

1. Open **dptbudg2.xls** that you created in Independent Project 1.1. If you did not complete this project, do it now using the instructions in Lesson 1.
2. **Center** the titles, **DEPARTMENTAL BUDGET** and **1993/1994 and 1994/1995 across columns A:E**.
3. Make both titles **bold**.

4. Increase the **font size** of **DEPARTMENTAL BUDGET** to **12** points. (**HINT:** Remember that the title is in cell **A2.**)
5. Increase the **font size** of **1993/1994 and 1994/1995** to **11** points.
6. **Right align** the column labels, **1993/1994, 1994/1995, Increase** and **% Increase.**
7. Make the column headings in cells **A6:E6, bold.**
8. Place a thin bottom **border** under the column labels in cells **A6:E6,**
9. Format **B7:D10** using **currency style. Decrease decimal** places until none are displayed.
10. Use **AutoFit Selection** to increase column widths for any columns containing values which have been replaced by ######.
11. Format **E7:E10** using **percent style. Increase decimal** places until one is displayed.
12. Make your name and other identifying information (cells **B13:B14**) **italic.**
13. **Save** the file **As: enhbudg**
14. To check the spelling of the document:

   a. Select a single cell.
   b. Choose **TOOLS/Spelling** or click on the **Spelling** button on the Standard Toolbar. If a word shows as misspelled, click on the **Help** button in the **Spelling** dialog box for instructions. Do NOT use the Add button. If you need further help, scroll to the bottom of the Help screen and choose the jump term, **Check Spelling.**
15. Preview the printout.
16. Use **Setup, Sheet** to turn off **Gridlines.**
17. Use the **Margins** tab in the **Page Setup** dialog box to **Center on Page Horizontally** and **Vertically.**
18. Change the **Header** and the **Footer** to **None.**
19. Print the worksheet.
20. **Save** the worksheet again using the current name.

Independent Project 2.2: Enhancing Your Caseload Worksheet

In Independent Project 1.2 you created a worksheet that calculated each case worker's current caseload based on the previous month's caseload and new and closed cases within the month. In this project your will format the worksheet so that it is easier to read and more attractive. When you are finished your worksheet should resemble Figure 2 - 28.

FAMILY COMMUNITY SERVICES
July Caseloads

Case Worker	*June Caseload*	*New Cases*	*Discharged Cases*	*July Caseload*	*Increase/ Decrease*
Audrey Smith	33	12	7	38	5
Casey Brown	42	12	10	44	2
Jonathan Summers	36	5	6	35	-1

Figure 2 - 28

Use Figure 2 - 28 and the following instructions to enhance newload.xls:

1. Open **newload.xls** that you created in Independent Project 1.2. If you did not complete this project, do it now using the instructions in Lesson 1.

2. **Center** the titles, **FAMILY COMMUNITY SERVICES** and **July Caseloads across columns A:F**.
3. Increase the **Font Size** of **FAMILY COMMUNITY SERVICES** to **14** points and make it **bold. (HINT:** Remember that the title is in cell **A2**.)
4. Increase the **Font Size** of **July Caseloads** to **12** points and make it **bold**.
5. **Right align** all of the column labels except for **Case Worker**.
6. Make the column labels in cells **A5:F6 bold, italic, 11** point.
7. Use **AutoFit Selection** to increase column widths as necessary.
8. Place a thick bottom **border** under the column labels in cells **A6:F6**.
9. Clear your name and other identifying information (cells **A11:B12**). Spellcheck.
10. **Save** the file **As: enhload**
11. Use **Page Setup** to turn off **Gridlines**.
12. While still in **Page Setup** change the **Header** to **None**.
13. Create a **Custom Footer** that says: **Created by (your name)** in the **Left Section**. Delete the code **Page &[Page]** from the **Center Section**. In the **Right Section** insert the current date by clicking in the **Right Section** text box and then clicking on the **Date** button in the middle of the **Footer** dialog box.

    If you don't know which button to select to enter the date, click on the ***Help*** *button. Choose the* ***Footer dialog box*** *jump term from the first help screen. Choose the* ***header or footer code*** *jump term from the* ***Header and Footer Dialog Boxes*** *help screen. When you find the correct button, choose* ***FILE/Exit*** *from the Microsoft Excel Help menu and finish your custom footer.*
14. Print the worksheet.
15. **Save** the worksheet again using the current name.

Independent Project 2.3: Enhancing Your Hockey Revenues Worksheet

In Independent Project 1.3 you created a worksheet that calculated the revenue from ticket and food sales at the school hockey game. In this project you will format the worksheet so that it is easier to read and more attractive. Figure 2 - 29 shows the enhanced hockey worksheet without formulas. Your worksheet may look different as you may have used a different design.

HOCKEY GAME REVENUE					
Attendance:					
		Full Price	**Students**	**Total**	
	Number	182	236		
	Fee	$ 5.25	$ 3.75		
	Revenue				
Food:					
		Hot Dogs	**Hamburgers**	**Soda**	**Total**
	Number	355	248	580	
	Unit Cost	$ 0.50	$ 0.75	$ 0.32	
	Sales Price	$ 1.00	$ 1.50	$ 0.75	
	Profit Per Item				
	Profit for Total Sales				
Total Hockey Game Profit:					
Created by:	*Jessica Gabriel*				
	Introduction to Computers				

Figure 2 - 29

Use Figure 2 - 29 and the following instructions to enhance hockey2.xls:

1. Open **hockey2.xls** that you created in Independent Project 1.3. If you did not complete this project, do it now using the instructions in Lesson 1.
2. Center the title, **HOCKEY GAME REVENUE** across all of the columns used in the worksheet.
3. Make the title **bold** and change the **font** to **14** points.
4. Make the subtitles, **Attendance** and **Food** and the label for **Total Hockey Game Profit, bold** and **12** points. Leave them in column **A** or center them across the columns in the section.
5. Change the **font** and **font size** for the rest of the worksheet to **Times New Roman, 11** point.
6. **Right align** all column labels for columns of numbers, and make all column labels **bold.**
7. Format all values which represent currency with **currency style** (2 decimal places).
8. Widen any columns that are not wide enough to display their full contents.
9. Format your name and any other identifying information that you put on the worksheet as **italics**. Spell check the worksheet.
10. **Save** the worksheet **As**: **enhockey**
11. Use **Page Setup** to:
    a) Remove **Gridlines**.
    b) Remove the **Header**.
    c) Create a **Custom Footer** that contains only the **Date** in the **Center Section**.
12. Print the worksheet.
13. **Save** the worksheet again using the current name.

Independent Project 2.4: Enhancing Your Sports Budget

In Independent Project 1.4 you planned and created a budget for the purchase of additional sporting goods for a community athletic program (**sports.xls**). In this project you will use the skills learned in Lesson 2 to enhance the worksheet so that values are formatted correctly, labels aligned appropriately and font, font sizes and font styles are applied to the worksheet title and column labels.

Enhancements to your worksheet should include:

1. Changing the font, font size and/or font style so that the worksheet title is emphasized.
2. Changing the alignment of the column labels so that they are centered or right aligned over columns of values. Use font, font size, or font style to enhance the column labels.
3. Adding borders as you wish.
4. Formatting totals which represent currency for currency. Format other values appropriately.
5. Spell checking the worksheet.
6. Save your worksheet using the name: **enhsport**
7. Before printing the worksheet, preview the worksheet. Remove gridlines, change the header and/or footer as you wish and make any other desired changes to the page setup.
8. Print your worksheet.

Lesson 3 Copying and Rearranging Worksheets

Objectives

In this lesson you will learn how to:

- Move around a worksheet
- Use the AutoSum button to add the contents of a range of cells
- Copy cell contents to one or more adjacent cells
- Copy cell contents to nonadjacent cells
- Select nonadjacent cells
- Insert and delete rows and columns
- Move cell contents
- Activate the shortcut menus

PROJECT DESCRIPTION

Nationwide Sporting Goods is a national corporation selling a variety of sports products. The file **lesson3.xls** contains a partially completed worksheet that summarizes 1994 sales by product and region. In this project you are going to calculate the total sales by product and region and create a separate part of the worksheet that compares the sales to previous and projected sales.

The worksheet you will complete in this project is larger than the one you used in Lessons 1 and 2. Therefore, you will learn to scroll the window to see parts of the worksheet that are not visible. In addition you will learn several shortcuts that speed up worksheet design — copying, moving, and functions. Finally you will learn how to insert and delete columns and rows so that you can modify your initial worksheet design.

In the process of completing the worksheet, you will also review:

- Entering values
- Entering formulas
- Centering titles across columns
- Formatting numbers
- Increasing column widths to display all values in the column
- Using Page Setup to remove grid lines and change headers and footers
- Printing the worksheet

When completed, your worksheet will resemble Figure 3 - 1.

Nationwide Sporting Goods
1994 Regional Sales Summary

Sales in Thousands of Dollars

PRODUCT	Eastern	Western	Northern	Southern	Totals
Baseball Bats	$ 8,056	$ 2,297	$ 1,768	$ 4,807	$ 16,928
Olympic Frisbees	6,017	6,647	6,926	1,474	21,064
Golf Club Sets	4,663	8,717	8,458	7,536	29,374
Athletic Wear	10,325	2,234	1,823	9,236	23,618
Kayaks	4,328	4,773	3,572	1,160	13,833
Camping Equipment	6,147	2,543	3,420	11,222	23,332
Football Pads	7,968	9,584	6,489	6,210	30,251
Boxing Gloves	1,569	2,884	3,607	1,310	9,370
Totals	$ 49,073	$ 39,679	$ 36,063	$ 42,955	$167,770

Projected Vs. Actual Sales

DOLLAR VOLUME SOLD

PRODUCT	1993 Sales	Projected	Actual	Variance	% Variance
Baseball Bats	$ 14,345	$ 16,000	$ 16,928	$ 928	5.5%
Olympic Frisbees	20,567	22,000	21,064	(936)	-4.4%
Golf Club Sets	28,567	30,000	29,374	(626)	-2.1%
Athletic Wear	23,145	25,000	23,618	(1,382)	-5.9%
Kayaks	10,111	12,000	13,833	1,833	13.3%
Camping Equipment	24,536	25,000	23,332	(1,668)	-7.1%
Football Pads	26,000	28,000	30,251	2,251	7.4%
Boxing Gloves	9,328	10,000	9,370	(630)	-6.7%
Totals	$156,599	$168,000	$167,770	$ (230)	-0.1%

Figure 3 - 1

MOVING AROUND THE WORKSHEET

In Lessons 1 and 2, you used a very small worksheet. The cells you wanted to go to were always visible and you could move around the worksheet by pressing the **ARROW** keys or clicking on the next cell. In this lesson the worksheet data will not all be visible on the screen at one time. Therefore, you must move, or *scroll*, the window to see different parts of the worksheet. Tables 3-1 and 3-2 describe shortcuts for moving around the screen using the mouse and the keyboard.

Key	Cell Selected	Screen Movement
↑, ↓, ←, →	The adjacent cell in the direction of the arrow	One cell in direction of arrow, only if necessary to display the selected cell
HOME	The cell in column **A** of the current row	As necessary to display column **A**
CTRL+HOME	**A1**	As necessary to display **A1**
CTRL+END	The cell at the intersection of the last row and the last column containing any data	As necessary to display cell
PAGE DOWN	The cell one window down from the active cell	Down one screen
PAGE UP	The cell one window up from the active cell	Up one screen
ALT+PAGE DOWN	The cell one window right from the active cell	Right one screen
ALT+PAGE UP	The cell one window left from the active cell	Left one screen

Table 3 - 1 - Using Keys to Scroll the Screen

Mouse Action (On Scroll Bars)	**Screen Movement** (The scroll bar changes the part of the screen displayed, but does not change the selected cell.)
Click the arrow at the end of the bar	One row or column in the direction of the arrow
Click the bar above, below, to the right or to the left of the scroll boxes	One window above, below, or to the right or left
Drag the scroll box	To the position in the worksheet matching the position of the scroll box in the scroll bar

Table 3 - 2 - Using the Mouse to Scroll the Screen

Activity 3.1: Scrolling the Screen to See the Full Worksheet

In this activity you will open the worksheet **lesson3.xls** and scroll the window to see all parts of the worksheet.

1. Start *Excel.*

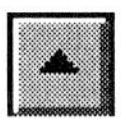

2. Open **lesson3.xls**. If *Excel* is not maximized, click on the **Maximize** button on the right side of the *Excel* Title Bar.

3. If **LESSON3.XLS** is not maximized, click on the **Maximize** button on the right side of the **LESSON3.XLS** Title Bar.

   *The worksheet shows the sales figures for the products in each of four regions. Cell **A1** is the active cell (Figure 3 - 2).*

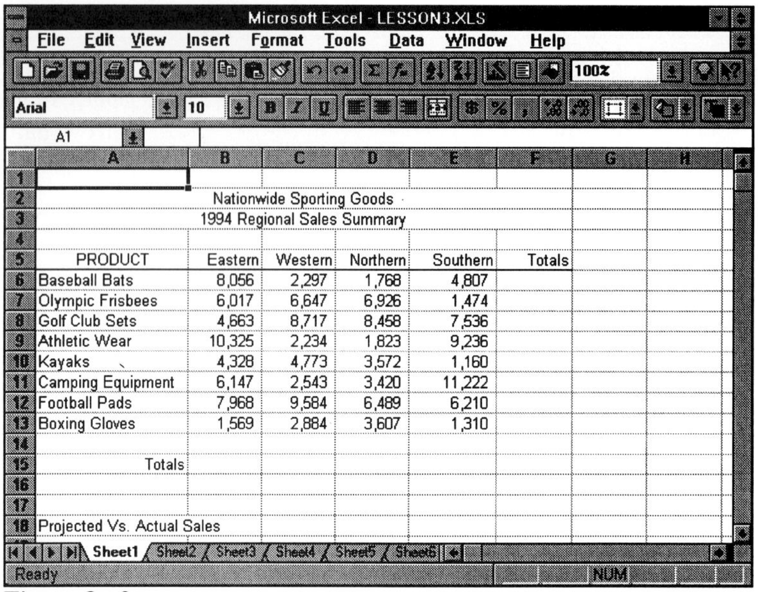

Figure 3 - 2

4. Write down the number of the last row visible in the **LESSON3.XLS** worksheet. Press the **PAGE DOWN** key.

   The row one below the number you wrote down is now the first visible row of the worksheet. The cell one window down from the previous active cell is now active. A partially completed section of the worksheet, which will be used to compare projected and actual sales, is displayed (Figure 3 - 3).

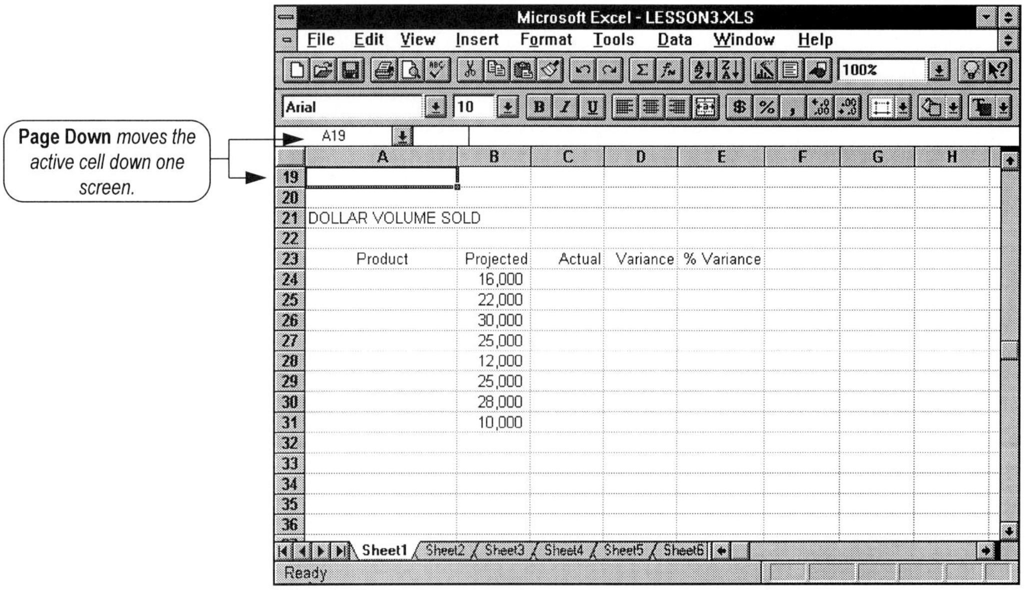

Figure 3 - 3

5. Press **CTRL+HOME** to jump back to the home position and make **A1** the active cell again.

6. Click on the ⬇ on the vertical scroll bar until row **33** is the last row on the screen.

   The Projected vs. Actual part of the worksheet is displayed, but the selected cell is not visible. As the name box (on the left side of the Formula Bar) indicates, the active cell remains ***A1*** *(Figure 3 - 4)****.***

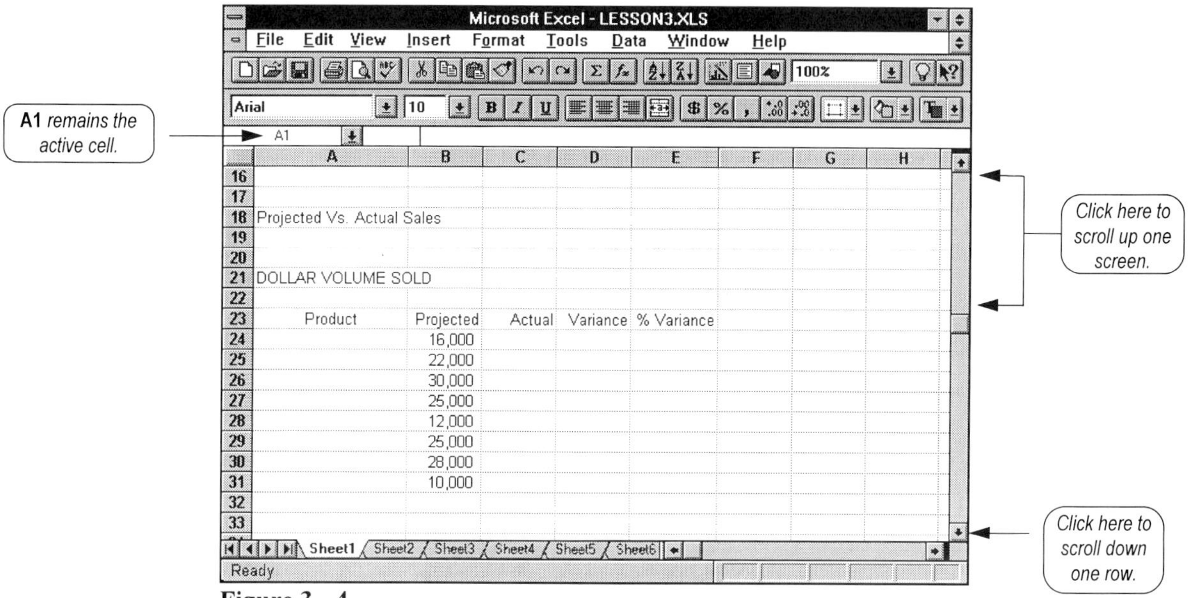

Figure 3 - 4

7. Click anywhere in the area on the scroll bar above the scroll box (Figure 3 - 4) to scroll the window up one screen.

   The top part of the worksheet is displayed (as in Figure 3 - 2).

THE SUM FUNCTION

In Lesson 1 you created formulas to perform calculations. *Excel* already contains hundreds of built-in formulas that perform many calculations for you. To use a function, you enter the name of the function and the cells that contain the data needed by the function, and *Excel* performs the calculation. This process is even easier for the sum function. The sum function is used to add a range of cells. This task is performed so often in worksheets that there is a special button on the toolbar that automatically enters the sum function and even suggests the range containing the cells that you wish to add.

To use the AutoSum button:

- Select the cell to contain the function.
- Click on the **AutoSum** Σ button.
- Look at the range that *Excel* has entered in the function. If it is correct, click on the **AutoSum** button again or press **ENTER**. If it is incorrect, select the correct range and then enter the function.

You will learn to use other functions in Lesson 4.

Activity 3.2: Entering Sums with the AutoSum Button

1. Select **B15**.
2. Click the **AutoSum** button.

   *The function =**SUM(B6:B14)** is displayed in **B15** and in the Formula Bar and the range **B6:B14** is enclosed in a moving border. When AutoSum is used, Excel automatically selects a group of filled cells above or to the left of the selected cell (Figure 3 - 5). If the cell immediately above or to the left of the selected cell is blank, it is included in the range, since an empty cell will not change the total. Therefore, in this example, Excel selected the range **B6:B14**.*

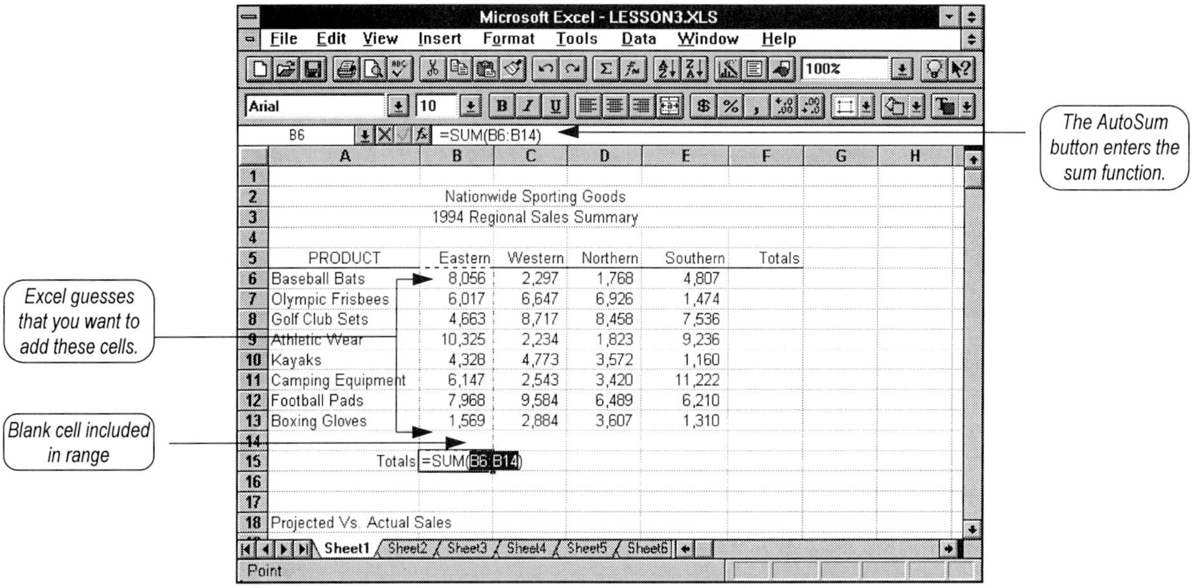

Figure 3 - 5

3. Since *Excel* has correctly selected the cells that you want to add, click on the **AutoSum** button again or click on the **enter box**.

   *The total, **49073,** is entered in **B15**, while the function =**SUM(B6:B14)** remains in the Formula bar.*

4. Select cell **F6**.
5. Click on the **AutoSum** button.
6. Since *Excel* has selected the cells that you want to add (**B6:E6**), click on the **AutoSum** button again or click on the **enter box** (Figure 3 - 6).
7. Select **F7**.
8. Click the **AutoSum** button, make sure the range is correct, and click again.

   *The value **21064** should be displayed in **F7**. You could continue to enter the **SUM** function in the rest of the column, but as you will see in the next section, there is a quicker way to sum.*

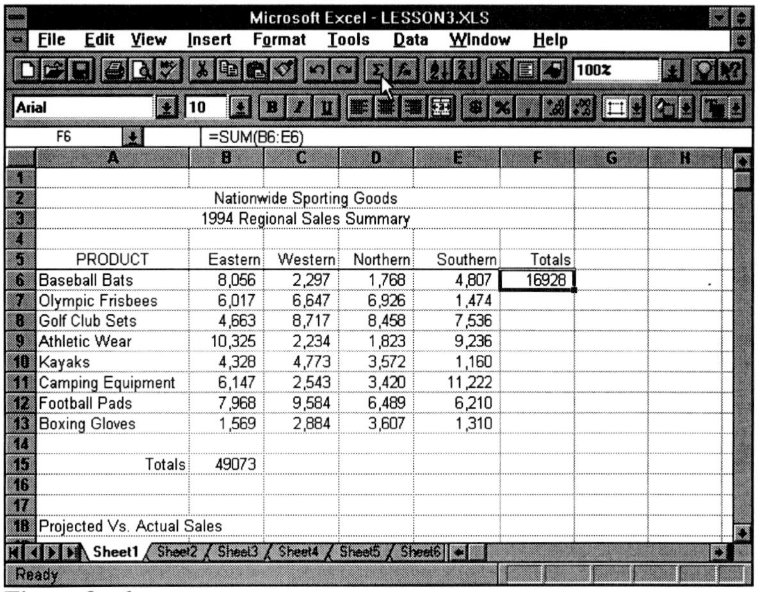

Figure 3 - 6

COPYING

Relative Cell Adjustment

Often you develop one formula and then discover that it will work quite well for the rest of the relationships in a specific row or column. For example, the formulas in cells **F6** and **F7** are almost the same. The only difference is that the formula has been *adjusted* to reflect the actual **row** that it is in. (The formula in cell **F6** is **=SUM(B6:E6)** while the formula in **F7** is **=SUM(B7:E7).**)

If the contents of the cell to be copied is a formula or function, *Excel* automatically adjusts the column or row reference so that the same relationship is maintained between the cell containing the formula and the cells to which it refers. In Lesson 5 you will learn how to create a formula that should not be adjusted as it is copied.

Copying to Adjacent Cells

Excel has a special command that allows you to copy to adjacent cells in the same column or row.

To copy cell contents to adjacent cells in the same column or row:

- Select the cell containing the information to be copied and all of the cells in the same column or row to which you want to copy.
- Choose **EDIT/Fill**.
- From the submenu, choose **Down, Right, Up,** or **Left**.

!

The contents and format of the initial cell will be copied to the other cell(s).

CAUTION: *Any existing contents in the cells you fill will be replaced.*

Activity 3.3: Copying Cell Contents to Adjacent Cells

1. Select the range **F7:F13**, by clicking on **F7** and dragging the mouse down until the range **F7:F13** is highlighted.
2. Choose **EDIT/Fill.**

   *The **Fill** submenu is displayed (Figure 3 - 7).*

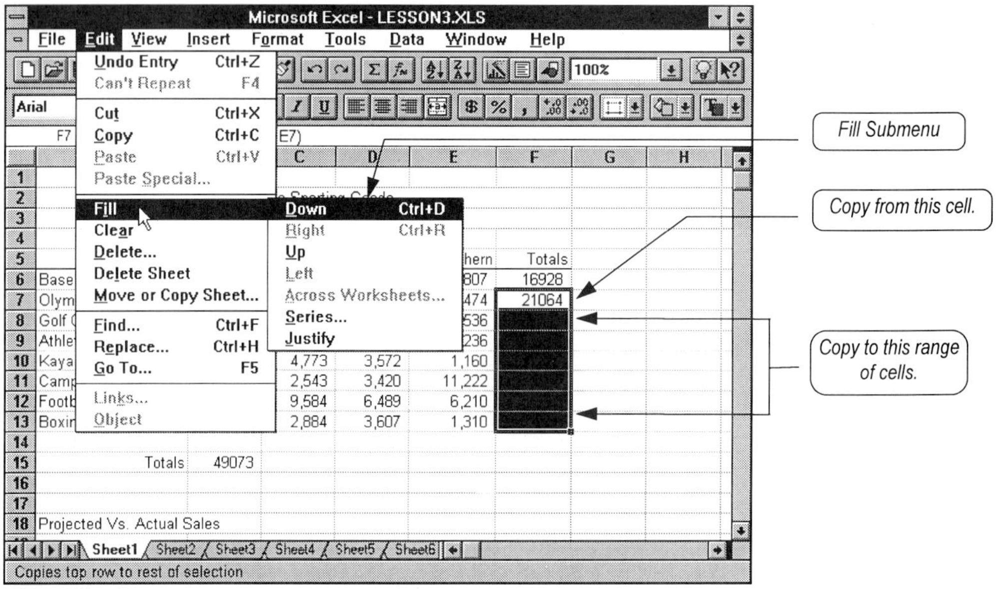

Figure 3 - 7

3. Click on **Down.**
4. Click on cell **F7**. Read the Formula Bar entry. It should say **=SUM(B7:E7).**

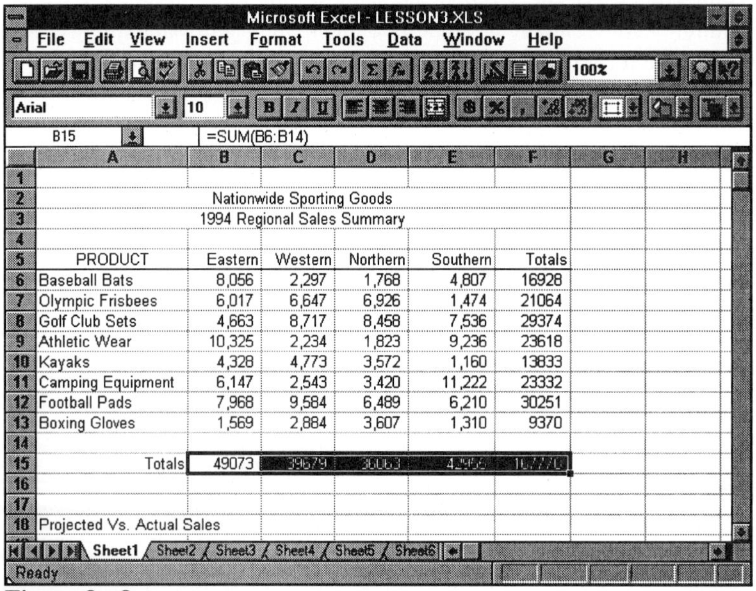

Figure 3 - 8

5. Click on cell **F8**.

   =SUM(B8:E8) *appears in the Formula Bar. When the formula was copied, the row numbers of the cells contained in the formula increased by one (from* ***7*** *to* ***8****) as the row number of the cell containing the formula increased by one.*

6. Select the range **B15:F15**.

7. Choose **EDIT/Fill**.

8. When the **Fill** submenu is displayed, choose **Right**.

   The function in cell ***B15*** *will be copied across the row (Figure 3 - 8).*

9. Click, one at a time, on cells **B15** through **F15.** As you select each cell, compare the contents of the Formula Bar with Table 3-3. Note how the formulas adjust as they are copied.

Cell	Cell Entry	What the formula does
B15	=SUM(B6:B14)	Adds the values in the cells 1, 2, 3, 4, 5, 6, 7, 8, and 9 rows above **B15.**
C15	=SUM(C6:C14)	Adds the values in the cells 1, 2, 3, 4, 5, 6, 7, 8, and 9 rows above **C15.**
D15	=SUM(D6:D14)	Adds the values in the cells 1, 2, 3, 4, 5, 6, 7, 8, and 9 rows above **D15.**
E15	=SUM(E6:E14)	Adds the values in the cells 1, 2, 3, 4, 5, 6, 7, 8, and 9 rows above **E15.**
F15	=SUM(F6:F14)	Adds the values in the cells 1, 2, 3, 4, 5, 6, 7, 8, and 9 rows above **F15.**

Table 3 - 3: The Effects of Relative Cell Adjustment

10. Choose **FILE/Save As**. Save the file using the new File Name: **natnwide**

Copying to Nonadjacent Cells

Sometimes worksheet contents can be reused in a part of the worksheet that is not adjacent to the current location. *Excel* uses the **EDIT/Copy** command to start the copying process. When you choose **EDIT/Copy** the highlighted range is copied to the Windows clipboard where it remains until somthing else is cut or copied. The cells are then said to be *pasted* to the new location. The cell contents can be pasted anywhere in the worksheet or even to other sheets in the workbook or to other programs. As with **EDIT/Fill** the cell contents and format are copied and formulas are adjusted relatively.

To copy cell contents to nonadjacent locations:

- Select the cell(s) to be copied.
- Choose **EDIT/Copy** or click the **Copy** button on the Standard Toolbar.

  The range to be copied is surrounded by a moving border.

- Select the upper-left cell of the range to which the cell contents are to be copied.
- Press **ENTER** to copy the cell contents and remove the moving border.

  ALTERNATE METHOD: If you want to paste the cell contents in more than one location, choose **EDIT/Paste** or click the **Paste** button instead of pressing **ENTER**. After you have copied the data for the last time, press **ESC** to remove the moving border.

Activity 3.4: Copying to Nonadjacent Cells

In this activity you will copy the product names from the top part of the worksheet to the **Projected vs. Actual Sales** section.

1. Select the range **A6:A15**.

2. Click on the **Copy** button or choose **EDIT/Copy.**

   *A moving border should appear around cells **A6:A15**. The message **Select destination and press ENTER or choose Paste** appears on the Status Bar.*

3. Press **PAGE DOWN** or scroll down until row **A24** is visible.
4. Select **A24** if it is not already the active cell.
5. Press **ENTER**.

   *The product names and **Totals** should be copied to cells **A24:A33** (Figure 3 - 9). **Totals** is right aligned because the copy command copies cell formats as well as cell contents.*

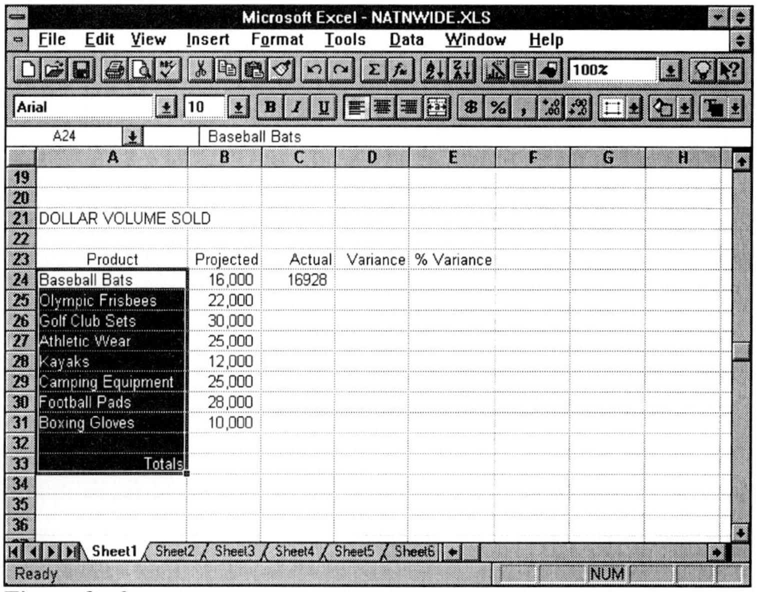

Figure 3 - 9

A MOUSE SHORTCUT FOR THE EDIT/FILL COMMAND

EDIT/Fill,Down and **EDIT/Fill,Right** are so commonly used that there is a mouse shortcut for them. When a cell or range of cells is selected, the lower-right corner of the heavy border around the cell or range of cells has a small square, which is called the ***fill handle***. Dragging the fill handle copies the data in the selected cell or range.

To use the fill handle in copying:

- Select the cell or range of cells containing the data to be copied.
- Point to the **fill handle**. The mouse pointer will change to a cross-hair +.
- Making sure the pointer remains a +, drag the **fill handle** across the cells you want to fill and then release the mouse button.

CAUTION: *Dragging the* ***fill handle*** *back over the selected cells erases the cell contents. If this happens immediately choose* ***EDIT/Undo*** *or click on the* ***UNDO*** *button.*

Activity 3.5: Reviewing Entering and Copying Formulas and Functions

In this activity you will enter the formulas needed for the bottom section of the worksheet and copy them to the appropriate cells.

1. Select cell **C24**.
2. The **Actual** value of the **Baseball Bats** sales is equal to the total **Baseball Bat** sales at the top of the worksheet. To enter this as a formula:
   a. Begin the formula by typing: =
   b. Click the [↑] on the scroll bar until **F6** is visible and select the cell containing total baseball sales, **F6**.
   c. Click on the **enter box** or press **ENTER**.

   The screen scrolls down to display row 24. The value of baseball bats' total sales, ***16928****, appears in* ***C24*** *(Figure 3 - 10).*

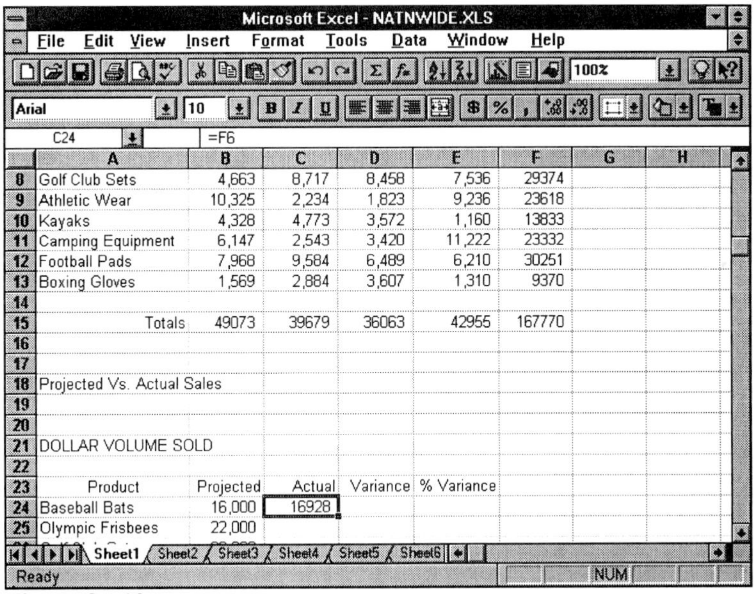

Figure 3 - 10

3. Select **D24**. Use pointing to enter a formula for the **Variance**. The **Variance** is equal to the **Actual** sales minus the **Projected** sales.
4. In **E24** enter a formula for the **% Variance**. The **% Variance** is equal to the **Variance** divided by the **Actual** sales.

   Cell ***D24*** *should contain the value* ***928****; cell* ***E24*** *should contain* ***0.0548204****.*
5. To copy all three formulas at one time, select the range **C24:E31**.

HINT: *Point to* ***C24****, click and drag the mouse across row* ***24*** *and down to row* ***31****. As the highlight hits the bottom edge of the window, the screen will scroll. If you have trouble selecting the entire area, release the mouse button. Use* ***SHIFT+ARROW*** *keys to extend or contract the selected area.*

6. Choose **EDIT/Fill, Down.**

   If cells in more than one column are selected, ***EDIT/Fill, Down*** *copies the contents of the first cell in each column to the other cells in the same column (Figure 3 - 11).*

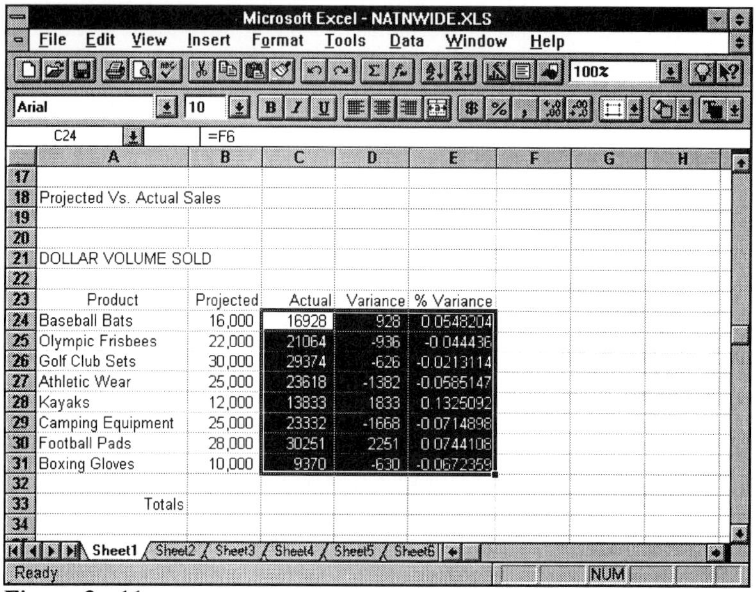

Figure 3 - 11

7. If row **33** is not displayed, click on the [scroll down arrow] on the vertical scroll bar until row **33** is displayed.
8. Select **B33** and use the **AutoSum** button to create a total of the **Projected** sales.
9. Point to the **fill handle**. When the mouse pointer changes to a +, drag the **fill handle** (Figure 3 - 12) to copy the function to cells **C33** and **D33**. Do NOT copy the function to **E33.**

   The contents of ***B33*** *(the* ***SUM*** *function) and its format are copied to the other cells.*

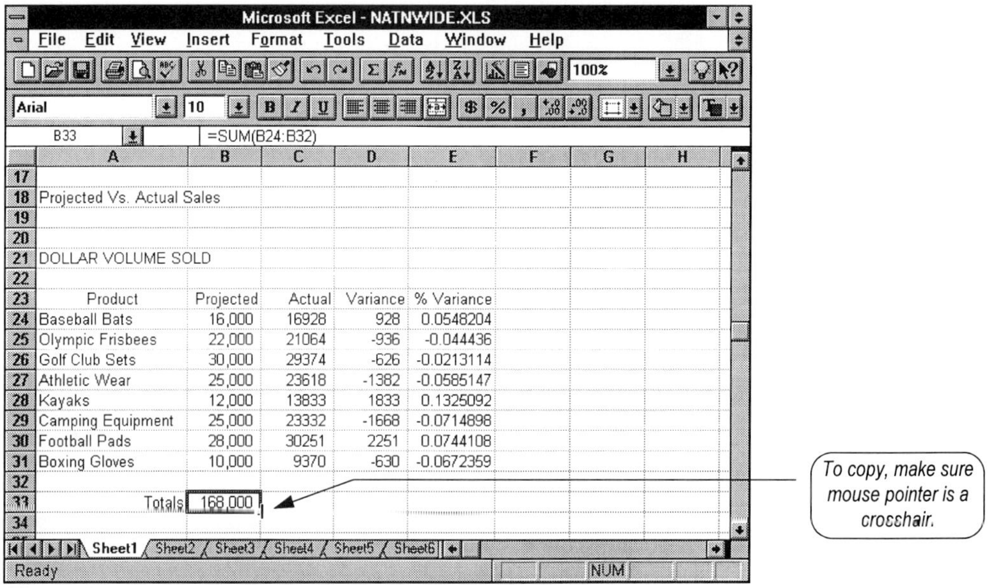

Figure 3 - 12

10. Use **EDIT/Copy** or the **Copy** tool to copy the variance formula from **E31** to **E33.**

    Your worksheet should resemble Figure 3 - 13.

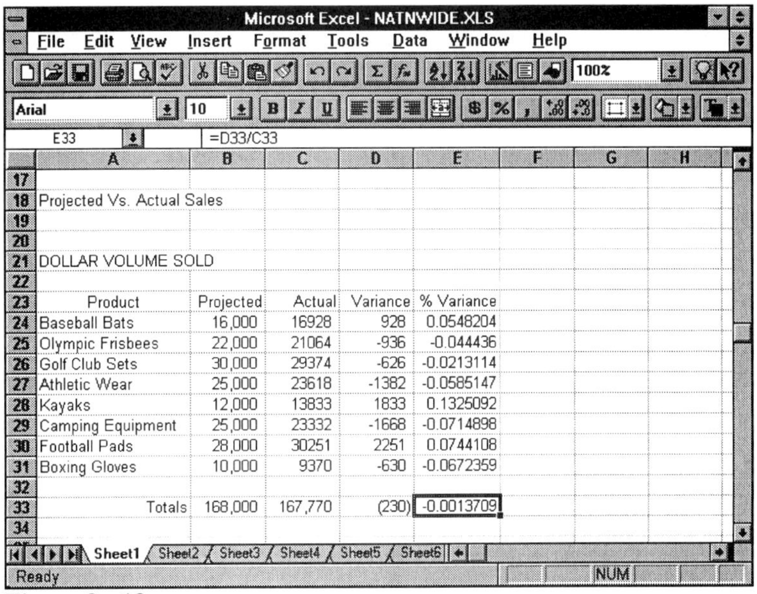

Figure 3 - 13

SELECTING NONADJACENT RANGES

As worksheets get larger, you often want to apply the same command to groups of cells that are not next to each other.

To select nonadjacent ranges:

- Select the first block of cells.
- Press the **CTRL** key and <u>while keeping it depressed</u> use the mouse to select the second range.
- Keep the **CTRL** key depressed and select any other blocks of cells to which you want to apply the command. Release the **CTRL** key when all blocks are selected.

Activity 3.6: Formatting

In this activity you will use the number formatting skills you learned in Lesson 2 to format the worksheet.

1. Select **C24:D31**.
2. Use the **Comma Style** button to format the range.

   Remember if any of the formatted numbers are too wide to fit in the cell they will be replaced by ###. You will fix this in a moment.
3. Use the **Decrease Decimal** button to display the numbers with no decimal places.
4. Use the **Percent Style** and **Increase Decimal** buttons to format **E24:E33** for **Percent** with one decimal place.

The comma and decimal styles use parenthesis to indicate negative numbers; the percent style uses the minus sign (Figure 3 - 14).

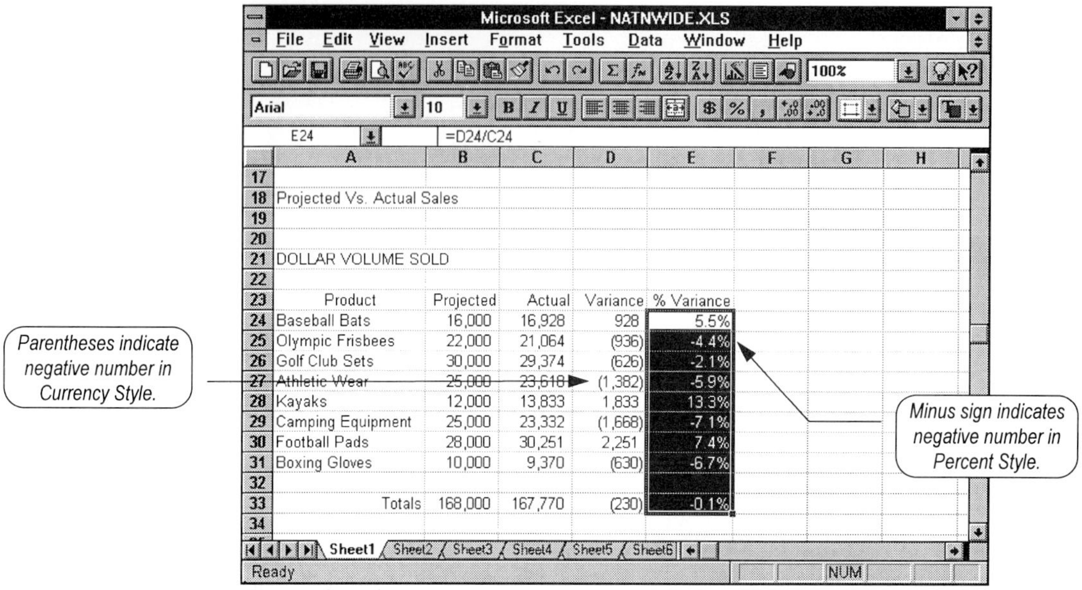

Figure 3 - 14

5. To format **B24:D24** and **B33:D33** for currency with no decimal places.
   a. Select **B24:D24**.
   b. Press the **CTRL** key and while keeping it depressed, use the mouse to select **B33:D33**.
   c. Release the **CTRL** key and click the **Currency Style** button; then click the **Decrease Decimal** button twice.

6. If any of the columns are too narrow to display the formatted cell contents, use **FORMAT/Column,AutoFit** to increase the column width.

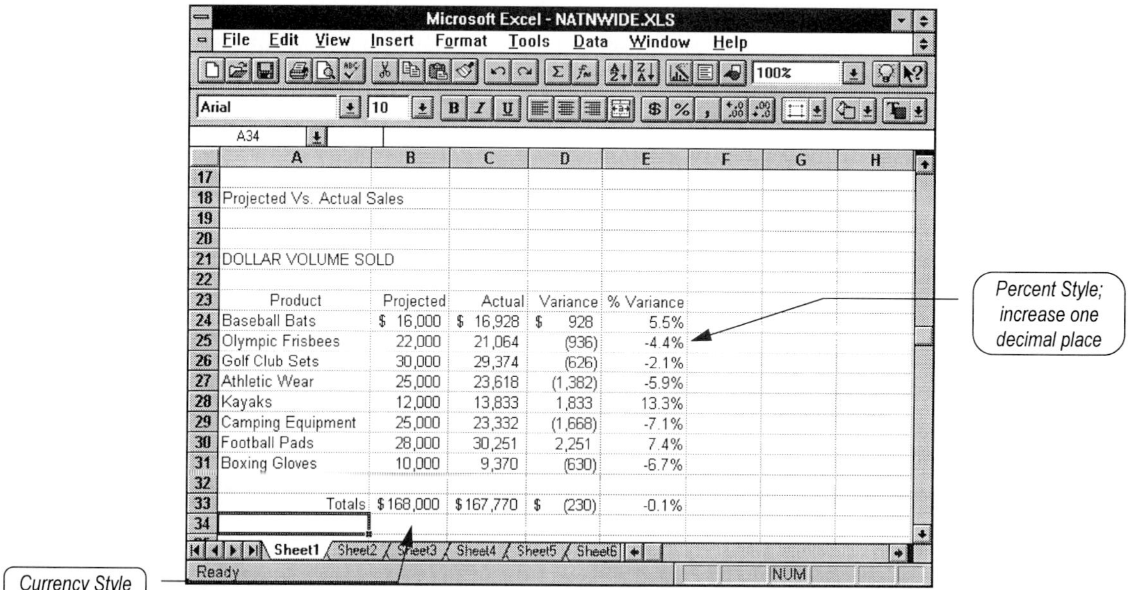

Figure 3 - 15

7. Compare the **Projected Vs Actual Sales** part of the worksheet with Figure 3 - 15 and make any formatting changes necessary to match the figure.
8. Press the **PAGE UP** key to move up one screen.
9. Format **B6:F6** and **B15:F15** using **Currency Style** with no decimal places.
10. Format **F7:F13** using **Comma Style** with no decimal places.
11. Increase column widths as necessary.

   Use Figure 3 - 16 to make sure that you made all of the formatting changes.

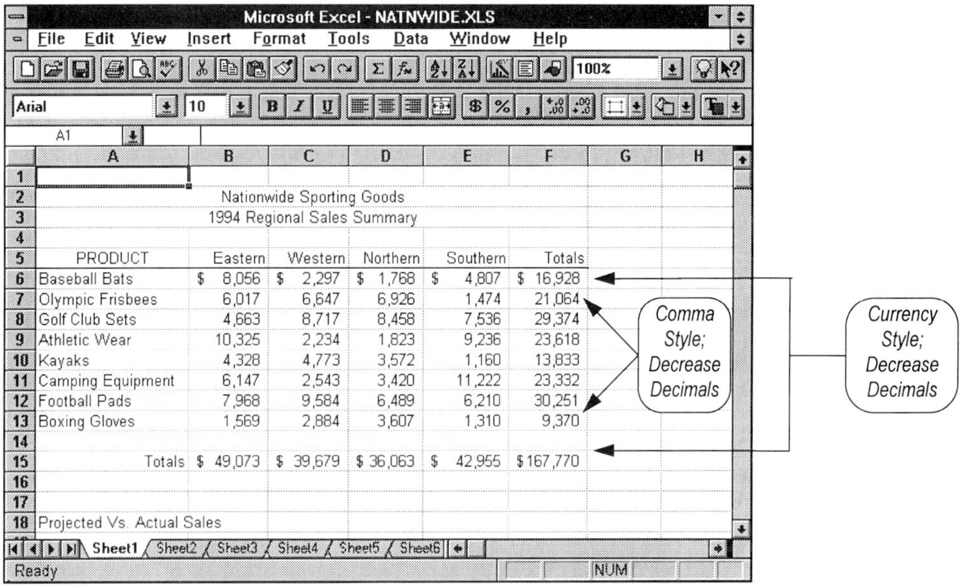

Figure 3 - 16

You've worked long enough. It's time to save the document, but let's use a new name so that you still have the original if you need to go back to it.

12. Choose **FILE/Save As**.
13. In the **File Name** box, type the new filename: **natn2** and click on **OK**.

REARRANGING A WORKSHEET BY DELETING AND INSERTING

Inserting and Deleting Rows

Sometimes after you have designed a worksheet you find that you want to add information that should be included in its own row or delete blank rows or rows that contain information. The easiest way to insert or delete rows is to use the *shortcut menus*. A *shortcut menu* is a list of commands relevant to a particular item. The contents of the shortcut menu depends on what actions you have just taken and what part of the screen you are working with. Therefore, you display one shortcut menu if the mouse pointer is pointing at a toolbar, another if it is pointing to a range that you have just selected, etc. Shortcut menus are activated using the **right** mouse button instead of the left button.

To insert a row:

- Select the entire row below the one to be inserted by clicking on the row header.

- Point anywhere in the selected row and click the **right** mouse button.
- Choose **Insert** from the shortcut menu.

ALTERNATE METHOD: *After selecting the row, choose **INSERT/ Row** from the regular menus in the menu bar.*

To delete a row:

- Select the entire row to be deleted by clicking on the row header.
- Point anywhere in the selected row and click the **right** mouse button.
- Choose **Delete** from the shortcut menu.

ALTERNATE METHOD: *After selecting the row, choose **EDIT/Delete Row** from the regular menus in the menu bar.*

CAUTION: *A row is deleted for the entire width of the worksheet, including parts that are not currently visible on the screen. Make sure that the row does not contain any information that you want to keep.*

Activity 3.7: Inserting and Deleting Rows

In this activity you want to insert a row for an extra title line and delete several blank lines. When rows are inserted or deleted, *Excel* automatically adjusts all cell references in formulas which refer to data which now have new cell addresses.

1. Click on cell **B15**. It contains the formula =**SUM(B6:B14)**.
2. Point to row heading **5**. Make sure the mouse pointer is a and click the mouse button to select the entire row (Figure 3 - 17).

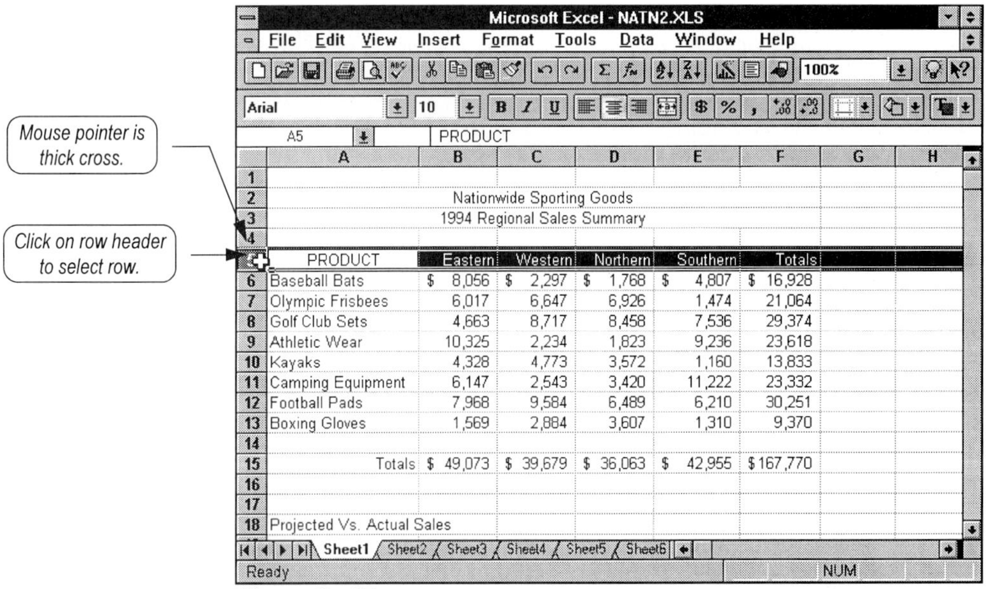

Figure 3 - 17

3. Continue to point at the row **5** header and click the **right** mouse button.

The shortcut menu listing activities that are commonly used with selected rows is displayed (Figure 3 - 18).

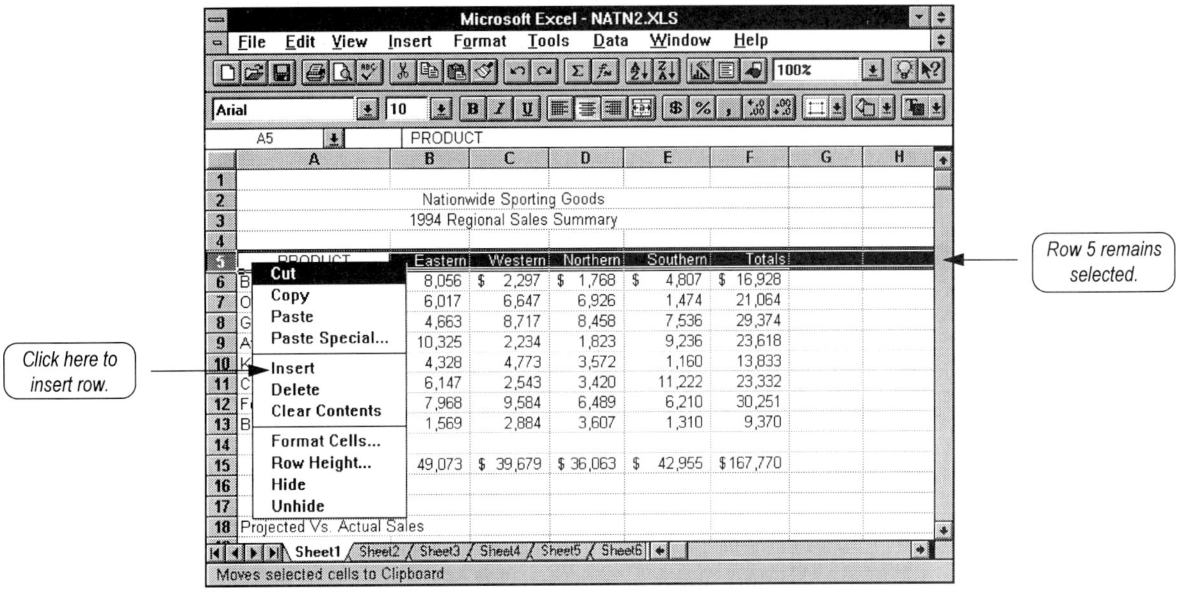

Figure 3 - 18

4. Click on **Insert.**

   *A new blank row is now labeled row **5** and the original row **5** is now row **6** (Figure 3 - 19).*

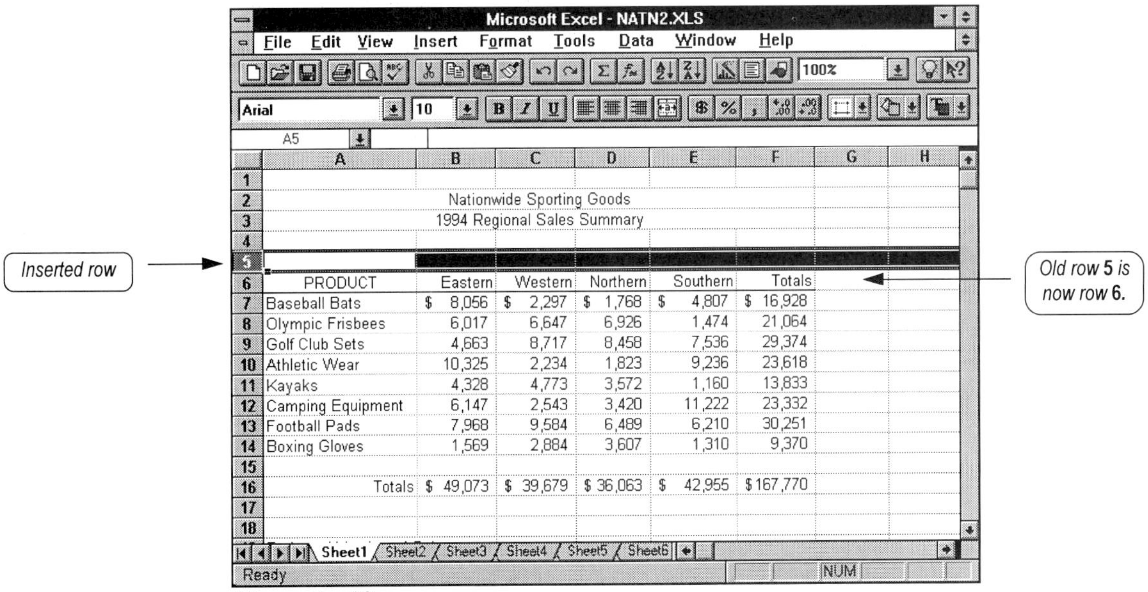

Figure 3 - 19

5. Click on the cell **B16**. The names of the cells it sums have changed, so the formula now reads **=SUM(B7:B15)**.

6. Select **B5** and enter: **Sales in Thousands of Dollars**

7. Select the range **B5:F5** and click on the **Center Across Columns** button.

8. Scroll the screen until row **21** is visible.
9. Click on the row heading **21** to select the entire row. Row **21** should be blank.
10. While still pointing at the row, click the **right** mouse button.
11. Choose **Delete** from the shortcut menu.

    *The previous row **21** is deleted. The row containing **DOLLAR VOLUME SOLD** is now row **21** (Figure 3 - 20).*

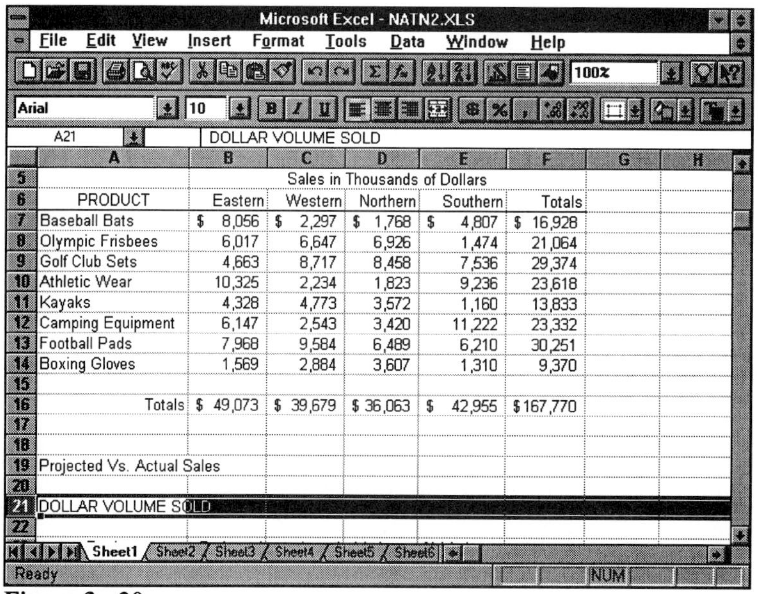

Figure 3 - 20

Inserting and Deleting Columns

The same procedure is used to insert and delete columns, except that the column heading is selected instead of the row heading.

To insert or delete multiple columns or rows, click on the first column or row heading and drag the highlight across the other column or row headings. When inserting columns, one column is inserted for each highlighted column. The columns are inserted to the left of the first highlighted column.

REARRANGING A WORKSHEET BY MOVING CELL CONTENTS

When you insert rows or columns, the row or column is added for the full width or length of the worksheet. Sometimes, you want to add a new column of data in one part of your worksheet without disturbing the rest of the worksheet. In this case, you must move the existing cell contents. The procedure for moving cells is similar to that for copying cells but the effect is very different. When cells are moved the original location becomes blank. In addition if the cell contains a formula, it is not adjusted in the same way that copied cells are.

To move cell contents:

- Select the cell(s) containing the information to be moved.
- Choose **EDIT/Cut** or click the **Cut** button on the Standard Toolbar.

The range to be moved is surrounded by a moving border.

- Choose the upper-left cell of the range to which the cell contents are to be moved.
- Press **ENTER** to move the cell contents. The original cells will be empty.

CAUTION: *When the cut cells are pasted in their new location, they will overwrite any existing cell contents.*

Activity 3.8: Adding New Data to Part of the Worksheet

After you have completed your worksheet, you are told that the 1993 actual sales figures should also be included in the **Projected vs. Actual Sales** part of your worksheet. You want to include the **1993 Sales** figures between the **Product** names and the **Projected** 1994 figures. You cannot add a new column, because the column would also be added to the top part of the worksheet. Therefore, you must move the existing cell contents to make room for the new data.

1. Select **B33.** Look at the Formula Bar. It should say =**SUM(B24:B32)**.
2. Select **B23:E33**.
3. Choose **EDIT/Cut** or click the **Cut** button.

   *A moving border surrounds cells **B23:E33** (Figure 3 - 21).*

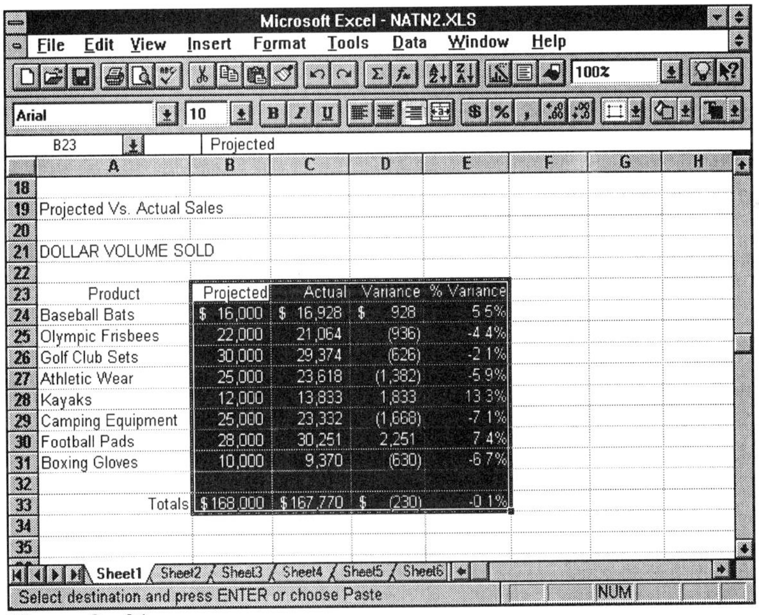

Figure 3 - 21

4. Select the top left cell of the new range, **C23**.
5. Press **ENTER**.

   *The selected range is moved to **C23:F33**. Some numbers may be replaced by ### because they are wider than the column they are now it.*

6. Increase column widths if necessary to display cell contents.
7. Select **C33** and look at the Formula Bar.

*When a formula and the cells referenced in the formula are both moved, the formula adjusts to reflect the new locations of the referenced cells (Figure 3 - 22). Therefore, the formula is now =**SUM(C24:C32)** instead of =**SUM(B24:B32)**.*

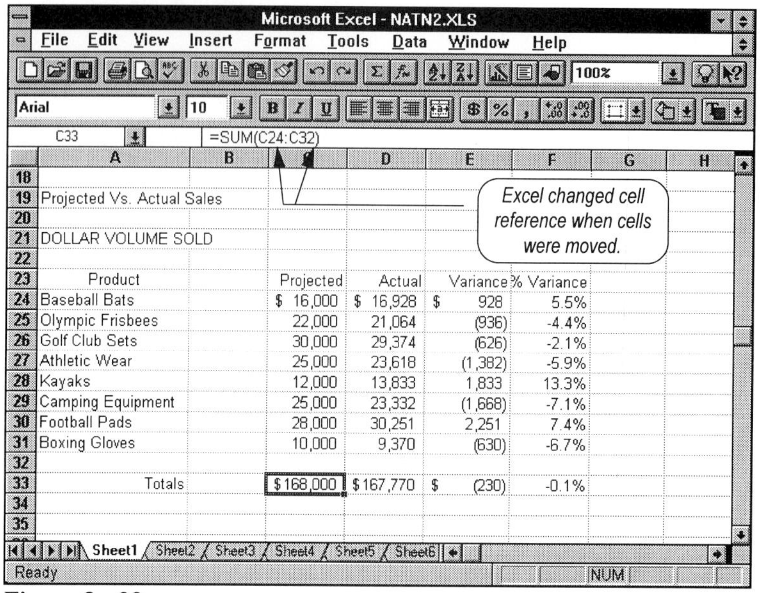

Figure 3 - 22

8. In **B23** enter the label for the new column: **1993 Sales**
9. In cells **B24:E31** enter the data below. Only type the numbers in **bold**. The row labels are only included to keep you from getting lost while entering the data.

Existing Row Headings	***Data to enter:***
Baseball Bats	**14345**
Olympic Frisbees	**20567**
Golf Club Sets	**28567**
Athletic Wear	**23145**
Kayaks	**10111**
Camping Equipment	**24536**
Football Pads	**26000**
Boxing Gloves	**9328**

*Notice that the new numbers are not formatted. **EDIT/Cut** and **Paste** move cell formatting along with cell contents. The original cells revert back to general format.*

10. In cell **B33** enter the **SUM** function to add up the 1993 sales.

*The value **156599** should appear in **B33**. If your sum is different, check that you entered the correct values for **1993 Sales**.*

Activity 3.9: Finishing Touches

1. Format **B24:B33** to match **C24:C33**.

2. Center **Projected Vs. Actual Sales** and **DOLLAR VOLUME SOLD** over columns **A:F.** (**HINT:** Select **A19:F21** and then click on the **Center Across Columns** button).
3. Select **A23:F23** and use the **Borders** button to add a thin line as a bottom border (i.e. the border should match the one under row **6** at the top of the worksheet).

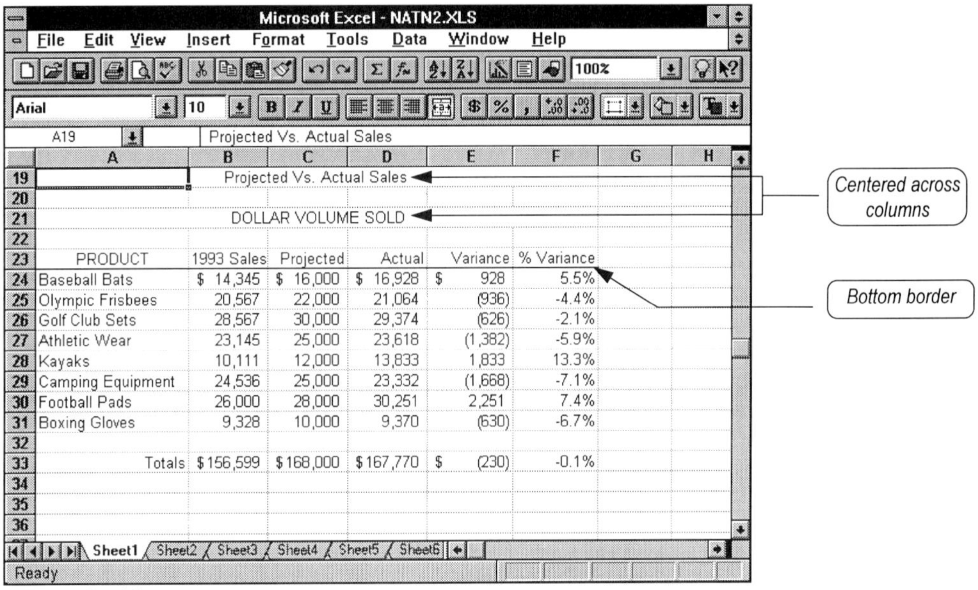

Figure 3 - 23

4. Edit cell **A23** so that **Product** is in uppercase as on the top of the worksheet.
5. When your screen resembles Figure 3 - 23 use the **Save** button to save the file again using the existing name.
6. Choose **FILE/Page Setup**.
7. Choose the **Sheet** tab and remove the mark from the **Gridlines** check box.
8. Choose the **Header/Footer** tab and choose **None** from the **Header** drop-down list.
9. Choose the **Print** button from the **Page Setup** dialog box. When the **Print** dialog box appears, click on **OK** to print the document.
10. Press **CTRL+`** to display formulas.
11. Use **FILE/Print** to print the worksheet again with formulas displayed.
12. Press **CTRL+`** to reset the worksheet to display values.
13. **Save** the file again to save the page setup changes. Close the file.

SUMMARY

In this lesson you have learned to use copying to automate worksheet creation. Although it is important to plan a worksheet before you create it, you often need to change your original design. The ability to move data and insert and delete rows makes worksheet modification much easier. In Lesson 6 you will further modify this project by adding a chart to represent part of the worksheet visually.

KEY TERMS

AutoSum
Clipboard
Copy
Cut
Deleting rows
Fill Down
Fill handle
Fill Right
Function
Inserting rows
Paste
Relative cell adjustment
Scroll
Shortcut menu

INDEPENDENT PROJECTS

Independent Project 3.1: Completing a Sales Worksheet

You work for a mail order company. You have been given a worksheet that lists a number of invoices, the amount of each sale and the shipping cost. You need to add the formulas to compute the tax and the total due, and to sum the total sales, tax, shipping and amount due. In addition you find that some of the clients have two-part invoices, but only one part has been entered. You need to insert rows and add the new data.

When you finish this project, your worksheet should resemble Figure 3 - 24.

SALES					
Invoice Number	**Name**	**Amount of Sale**	**Tax (6.75%)**	**Shipping**	**Total Due**
00115	Peter Lynch	842.40	56.86	5.00	904.26
00116	Nancy Smith	597.78	40.35	5.00	643.13
00117	Jacklyn Jones	779.33	52.60	5.00	836.93
00117a	Jacklyn Jones	112.65	7.60	4.00	124.25
00118	Barry Turko	997.41	67.32	5.00	1,069.73
00119	Samuel Patter	647.03	43.67	5.00	695.71
00119a	Samuel Patter	98.53	6.65	3.00	108.18
00120	Jerry Gerald	181.65	12.26	3.00	196.91
00121	Kurry Hirray	22.37	1.51	3.00	26.88
00122	Nurnak Rumold	758.20	51.18	5.00	814.38
00122a	Nurnak Rumold	89.60	6.05	4.00	99.65
00123	Stan Williams	293.73	19.83	3.00	316.56
00124	Jennifer Lewis	75.48	5.10	3.00	83.58
00125	Sharon Jeeves	975.94	65.88	5.00	1,046.82
00126	Willie White	152.04	10.26	3.00	165.31
	Totals	6,624.15	447.13	61.00	7,132.28

Figure 3 - 24

Use Figure 3 - 24 and the following instructions to help you complete the project:

1. Open **indpr3_1.xls**.
2. In cell **D4** enter a formula to compute the tax. The formula should multiply the **Amount of Sale** by **6.75%**.
3. Check the result of your formula with Figure 3 - 24. If it is correct, use the **fill handle** or **EDIT/Fill down** to copy the formula down column **D** through row **15**.
4. While **D4:D15** is still selected, format the values using **Comma Style**, two decimal places.

5. In cell **F4**, enter a formula to calculate the sum of the **Amount of Sale, Tax** and **Shipping** for the first invoice. You may use a formula which adds the three amounts or you may use the **AutoSum** button to let *Excel* insert the **sum** function.
6. Copy the formula down column **F** to row **15**.
7. Add a **Bottom Border** to cells **A15:F15**.
8. In cell **B16** add the label: **Totals**
9. Right align and bold **Totals**.
10. In cell **C16** use **AutoSum** to total the sale amounts.

    Your total will not agree with the total shown in Figure 3 - 24. You will be adding data in the next few steps.
11. Copy the function across row **16.**
12. Save the worksheet using the name: **sales1**
13. To add the second part of the invoice for **Jacklyn Jones**:
    a. Insert a row between rows **6** and **7**.
    b. Add the following data in the correct columns:

Invoice Number	**0117a**
Name:	**Jacklyn Jones**
Amount of Sale:	**112.65**
Shipping:	**4.00**

    c. Copy the formulas for the **Tax** and **Total Due** from cells **D6** and **F6.**
14. Add the second part of the invoices for **Samuel Patter** and **Nurnak Rumold** in an inserted row beneath each of their current invoices. Copy the appropriate formulas from the preceding row. Use the following data:

Invoice Number:	**00119a**	**00122a**
Name:	**Samuel Patter**	**Nurnak Rumold**
Amount of Sale:	**98.53**	**89.60**
Shipping:	**3.00**	**4.00**

    Your totals should now agree with those shown in Figure 3 - 24.
15. Use **Page Setup** to remove gridlines. Delete the header and create a custom footer which includes your name, course name and the current date. Print the worksheet.
16. Save the file again using the current name.
17. Print the worksheet again displaying formulas. Close the worksheet.

Independent Project 3.2: Re-arranging Data by Country

You have been given a worksheet which analyzes sales of several American, British, German and Japanese cars in 7 states. Currently the sales for each country's cars are presented next to each other. You have been asked to reorganize the worksheet so that the sales for each country's cars are separated. Once this is completed you will also add totals for each state and for the total number of each car sold in the included states.

When you finish this project, your worksheet should resemble Figure 3 - 25 except for font size and column spacing.

1			**AUTO SALES BY STATE**		
2					
3			American Manufacturers		
4	State:	Ford	GM	Chrysler	Totals
5	Florida	12,349	78,924	13,454	104,727
6	Georgia	45,675	12,372	24,344	82,391
7	S. Carolina	89,017	87,459	2,345	178,821
8	N. Carolina	23,453	34,250	14,548	72,251
9	Pennsylvania	56,786	67,337	14,456	138,579
10	New Jersey	87,658	123,395	45,665	256,718
11	New York	15,230	64,544	45,660	125,434
12	Totals	330,168	468,281	160,472	958,921
13					
14					

15		UK Manufacturers		
16	State:	Jaguar	Rolls Royce	Totals
17	Florida	1,257	5,668	6,925
18	Georgia	89	3,000	3,089
19	S. Carolina	154	569	723
20	N. Carolina	887	1,220	2,107
21	Pennsylvania	2,167	0	2,167
22	New Jersey	980	3,453	4,433
23	New York	1,336	12,909	14,245
24	Totals	6,870	26,819	33,689
25				
26				

27			German Manufacturers		
28	State:	BMW	Mercedes	Volkswagen	Totals
29	Florida	2,267	5,512	1,229	9,008
30	Georgia	984	983	5,403	7,370
31	S. Carolina	127	3,380	4,812	8,319
32	N. Carolina	1,176	2,945	8,882	13,003
33	Pennsylvania	2,365	1,287	22,445	26,097
34	New Jersey	4,002	5,005	8,110	17,117
35	New York	5,910	12,760	23,800	42,470
36	Totals	16,831	31,872	74,681	123,384
37					
38					

39			Japanese Manufacturers			
40	State:	Honda	Toyota	Mazda	Nissan	Totals
41	Florida	52,378	5,436	3,429	1,355	62,598
42	Georgia	5,572	23,234	559	3,452	32,817
43	S. Carolina	9,030	4,564	4,312	2,356	20,262
44	N. Carolina	12,988	5,673	6,780	5,664	31,105
45	Pennsylvania	66,800	7,855	23,678	23,445	121,778
46	New Jersey	43,811	3,453	36,890	4,534	88,688
47	New York	59,802	34,532	12,765	34,555	141,654
48	Totals	250,381	84,747	88,413	75,361	498,902

Figure 3 - 25

Use Figure 3 - 25 and the following instructions to help you complete the project:

1. Open **indpr3_2.xls**.
2. Move the data on the **UK Manufacturers** from **E3:F11** to an area of the worksheet beginning in cell **B15**.
3. Move the data on the **German Manufacturers** from **G3:I11** to an area of the worksheet beginning in cell **B27**.
4. Move the data on the **Japanese Manufacturers** to an area of the worksheet beginning in cell **B39**.
5. You need labels for the UK, German, and Japanese cars. Copy the **State** names from **A4:A11** to areas beginning in cell **A16, A28,** and **A40**.
6. In **E4** enter the column label: **Totals**
7. Right align **Totals** and add a thick bottom border to the cell.
8. In **E5** use **AutoSum** to total the **Florida** sales for the three American Manufacturers. Copy the formula down the column.
9. Enter the same labels and totals for the other three countries.
10. In cell **A12** enter the row label: **Totals** and **right-align** it.
11. In cell **B12** use **AutoSum** to total the sales for **Ford**. Copy the formula across the row through column **E**.
12. Enter the same labels and totals for the other three countries.
13. Add a thick **Bottom Border** to the row above all of the totals lines. Increase any column widths for columns where all of the values or labels are not displayed. Make any other formatting changes necessary so that your worksheet resembles Figure 3 - 25.
14. Save your file as: **auto2**
15. Preview the worksheet. In preparation to print your document, remove gridlines, and create a custom header which contains only your name, class and the current date.
16. Print the worksheet.
17. Save the worksheet using the current name so that you save your page setup.
18. Print the worksheet again displaying formulas. Close the worksheet without saving.

Independent Project 3.3: Re-arranging Data to Facilitate Projections

The travel agency that you work for has a simple worksheet which analyzes the sales of its special vacation packages to five different locations. The travel agency wants you to compare sales in the peak summer season, June through August, with the two bordering periods, spring (April/May) and autumn (September/October) so that you can make projections for next year's sales.. You decide that it would be easier for you to do this if you separate the current worksheet into three sections — one for each of the time periods. Then you will total the sales figures for each destination and each month in each time period.

Use Figure 3 - 26 as a general guide to completing your worksheet, but your worksheet need not be an exact copy. (Font sizes and spacing differs from your worksheet.)

THE BEST TRAVEL AGENCY IN THE UNITED STATES

Summer Vacation Package Sales

Destination	June	July	August	Totals
New York	125	165	154	444
Disney World	653	754	558	1,965
Alaska	425	552	425	1,402
Yellowstone National Park	332	425	411	1,168
LA/San Francisco	199	210	205	614
Totals	1,734	2,106	1,753	5,593

Spring Vacation Package Sales

Destination	April	May	Totals
New York	85	60	145
Disney World	500	335	835
Alaska	100	200	300
Yellowstone National Park	175	160	335
LA/San Francisco	150	130	280
Totals	1,010	885	1,895

Autumn Vacation Package Sales

Destination	September	October	Totals
New York	135	86	221
Disney World	350	290	640
Alaska	225	65	290
Yellowstone National Park	190	123	313
LA/San Francisco	175	148	323
Totals	1,075	712	1,787

Figure 3 - 26

Use Figure 3 - 26 and the following instructions to help you complete the project:

1. Open the file **indpr3_3.xls**.
2. To begin the part of the worksheet that will look at spring sales, add the title, **Spring Vacation Package Sales**, in column **A** a few rows below the current filled cells.
3. Move the labels and values which deal with **April** and **May** sales to the new section of your worksheet. Remember to leave a blank column for the destination names.
4. Label a section for autumn sales and move **September** and **October** data to this section.
5. Copy the destinations for your vacation packages from the original section of the worksheet to the two new sections.
6. Move the remaining summer months next to the destinations.
7. Label the remains of the first part of your worksheet: **Summer Vacation Package Sales.**
8. For each section of the worksheet total the sales for each destination and each month. Format the labels to match existing labels. Format all values for comma with no decimal places. Separate the bottom row of totals from the values above it with a line.
9. Format the names of the sections anyway you wish, as long as you use a different font, font size or font style from the rest of the labels on the worksheet.

10. Center titles across columns if you wish.
11. Save the file as: **vacation**
12. Preview your file. Remove gridlines, change the header to include identifying information about you, and make any other formatting changes to the printout that you wish.
13. Print the worksheet.
14. Save the file again using the current name.
15. Print the worksheet with formulas displayed.

Independent Project 3.4: Creating a Payroll

ECAP Corporation has decided to computerize their payroll. As the first step in the process, they have given you a worksheet which contains the raw data for last week's payroll. You have been asked to add all of the necessary formulas to the worksheet and do some basic formatting. You have also been asked to separate the exempt and hourly employees.

Use the following guidelines while completing your project:

1. Open the file **indpr3_4.xls**.
2. Separate the sections for hourly and exempt employees. You can create the second section by moving the data on each exempt employee to a row under those of all of the hourly employees. The section should have a label and each of the columns should have the same labels as already included in the worksheet. Figure 3 - 27 shows you the organization of the worksheet after it has been divided into two sections and step 3 has been completed (some of the exempt employees are not shown). Use moving and copying to reorganize the worksheet or use the shortcut directions which follow.

			ECAP CORPORATION				
Hourly Employees							
		Hourly	Gross		Taxes		Net
Employee	Hours	Wage	Pay	FICA	State	Federal	Pay
Albert, Joel	80	6.5					
Boyenga, Gladys	80	5					
Dodd, Doris	78	3.8					
Eisenberg, Sun-Wong	80	5.5					
Harrison, Wilbert	80	4.5					
King, John	76	5.5					
Raymond, Frank	80	4.5					
Stoddard, James	80	6.5					
Thompson, Frederic	75	7					
Exempt Employees							
	Gross		Taxes		Net		
Employee	Pay	FICA	State	Federal	Pay		
Cruz, Elinor	636						
Farrell, Dudley	1650						
Glass, Cynthia	1850						
Major, John	1200						
Nelson, Charles	580						
Paige, Carol	750						
Wagner, George	1800						
Zandonetta, Bjorn	2000						

Figure 3 - 27

SHORTCUT: *It is hard to move all of the data on the exempt employees, because these employees are scattered throughout the employee list. A shortcut involves the use of the* ***Sort Ascending*** *button* , *one of the data features that is not covered in this book. To use* ***Sort Ascending:***

a. Select **B6**, one of the cells in the column which includes the word **exempt**.

b. Click on the **Sort Ascending** button on the Standard Toolbar. *Excel* automatically selects all of your data and puts it in order according to the entries in the **Hours** column. The exempt workers are at the end because values are sorted before labels.

c. Insert **4** rows before the first exempt worker.

d. Copy the existing column labels to the two rows immediately above the first exempt employee.

e. To alphabetize the names of the hourly employees, select a cell containing a name of an hourly employee and click on the **Sort Ascending** button.

f. To alphabetize the names of the exempt employees, select a cell containing a name of an exempt employee and click on the **Sort Ascending** button.

*For further information on sorting use **Help**.*

3. The exempt employee part of the worksheet should not include the **Hours** or **Hourly Wage** columns (as indicated in Figure 3 - 27).

4. Include formulas for the **Gross Pay** for the hourly (nonexempt) workers, and **FICA, State** and **Federal** taxes and the **Net Pay** for all workers. In order to compute these values, we will use the following simplified assumptions:

   Gross Pay (for hourly workers) equals hours times hourly wages
   FICA equals 7.65% of gross pay
   State taxes equal 4.5% of gross pay
   Federal Taxes equal 28% of gross pay
   Net pay equals gross pay minus FICA, state and local taxes

5. Total the **Gross Pay** and **Net Pay** for the hourly employees and for the exempt employees.

6. Format the worksheet appropriately.

7. Save the worksheet using the name: **payroll**

8. Print the worksheet using a page setup which does not display gridlines and which includes identifying information about you in the header or footer.

9. Print the worksheet with formulas displayed.

Lesson 4 More Formulas and Functions

Objectives

In this lesson you will learn how to:

- Let *Excel* help you create a series
- Adjust column widths to fit part of a column
- Create more complex formulas
- Change the range inserted by the **AutoSum** button
- Create multi-line labels in one cell
- Use the statistical functions, **AVERAGE, MIN, MAX**
- Use the **TODAY** function to enter the current date
- Use the **Function Wizard** to enter functions
- Use nonadjacent cells in a function

PROJECT DESCRIPTION

In this lesson you will create an expense report. While on your business trip, you used your Notebook computer to enter your expenses quickly. In this project you will finish entering data and then calculate your daily expenditures in each category to determine the amount that you should be reimbursed. In addition, your company, ECAP Corporation, is reconsidering its expense account guidelines for meals. Therefore, it has requested that you analyze your meal expenses. When finished, your worksheet will resemble Figure 4 - 1.

The focus of this lesson is to increase your ability to use formulas and functions. However, you will also review the formatting skills learned in Lesson 2 and learn about an extension of *Excel's* **Fill** command—**Fill Series.**

CREATING A SERIES

In Lesson 3 you used the **fill handle** or **EDIT/Fill** to copy a cell or range of cells to adjacent cells. However, if the filled cell contains a day of the week, a month, a date, or other data that *Excel* recognizes as the beginning of a *series* (see Table 4-1), *Excel* assumes that you want to create a series of entries rather than make an exact copy of the cell contents.

CONTENTS OF CELL(S) TO BE COPIED	NEXT TWO VALUES OF SERIES
January	February, March
Nov	Dec, Jan
Tue	Wed, Thu
1/1/95	1/2/95, 1/3/95
Division 1	Division 2, Division 3
1/1/95, 1/8/95	1/15/95, 1/22/95

Table 4 - 1 Results of Filling a Series

ECAP Corporation Travel Expense Report

Submitted by: Jessica Gabriel
Date: 2/10/95

Categories	**2/1/95**	**2/2/95**	**2/3/95**	**2/4/95**	**2/5/95**	**Total**
Breakfast		7.89	8.99	6.50	4.50	27.88
Dinner		15.50	20.00	22.75	12.00	70.25
Tips		4.21	5.22	5.27	2.97	17.66
Air Fare	358.00					358.00
Car Rental	49.00	49.00	49.00	49.00		196.00
Hotel	119.00	119.00	119.00	119.00		476.00
Miscellaneous	5.00	3.50	8.00	2.75	15.00	34.25
Daily Total	$ 531.00	$ 199.10	$ 210.21	$ 205.27	$ 34.47	$ 1,180.04

Expense	**Minimum Spent**	**Maximum Spent**	**Average Spent**
Breakfast	4.50	8.99	6.97
Dinner	12.00	22.75	17.56
Total	$ 16.50	$ 31.74	$ 24.53

Figure 4 - 1

To create a series:

- Enter a day, a month, a date, or other data that implies a series.
- Select the cell(s) containing the series starting point(s).
- Drag the **fill handle** to fill adjacent cells with the next entries in the series.

*ALTERNATE METHOD: **EDIT/Fill,Series** can also be used to fill a range with a series. More customized series can also be created with this command. Click on the **Help** button in the **Series** dialog box for further instructions.*

Activity 4.1: Creating a Series of Days

In this activity you will use the **fill handle** to help you replace the column labels Day 1 through Day 5 with the actual dates. Then you will use the **fill handle** to copy the daily hotel and car rental fees to the rest of the week.

1. Start *Excel* and open **lesson4.xls**. If necessary, maximize *Excel* and **LESSON4.XLS** (Figure 4 - 2).

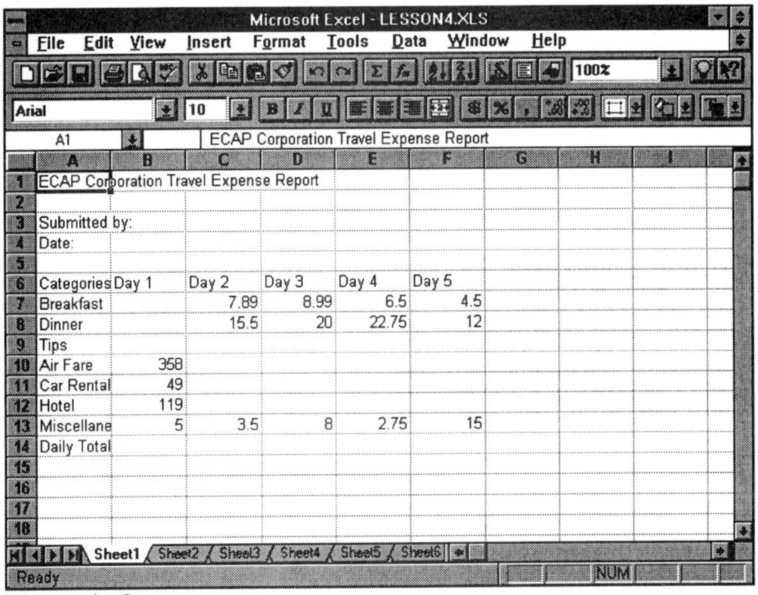

Figure 4 - 2

2. Select cell **B6** and enter the date: **2/1/95**

   *2/1/95 will replace **Day 1** as soon as you click on the **enter box**.*

3. Point to the **fill handle**. When the mouse pointer changes to a +, press the left mouse button and slowly drag to the right to select cells **B6:F6.** Before you release the mouse button, look at the **name box** in the Formula Bar. It will say **2/5/95**. Release the left mouse button.

   Excel automatically fills the range with the series of dates that follow 2/1/95 (Figure 4 - 3).

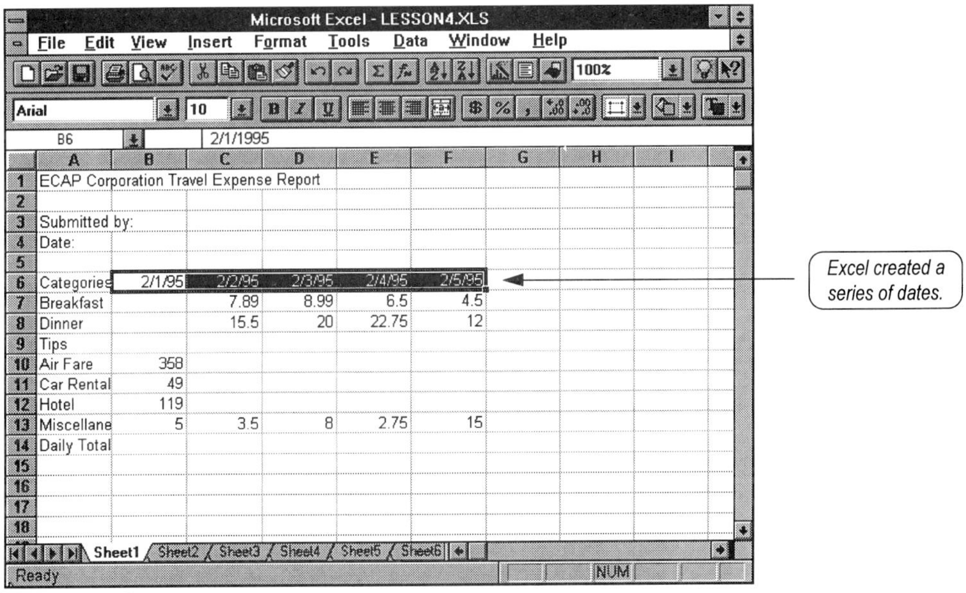

Figure 4 - 3

4. Select the range **B11:B12**.
5. To copy the daily car rental and hotel charges to the rest of the row, drag the **fill handle** to **E12**. Look at the **name box** in the Formula Bar as you drag the mouse. The number **49** remains in the **name box** because that number is being copied instead of incremented. When the range **B11:E12** is highlighted, release the left mouse button (Figure 4 - 4).

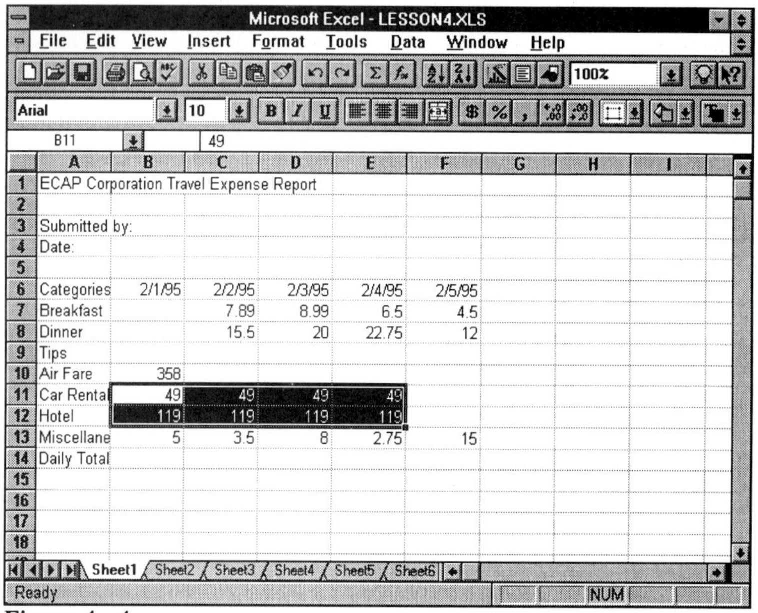

Figure 4 - 4

AUTOMATICALLY ADJUSTING COLUMN WIDTHS FOR PART OF A COLUMN

As you saw briefly in Lesson 3, occasionally you want *Excel* to adjust the column width to fit some, but not all, of the entries in a column. This is most often used when the column contains titles for the worksheet or a section of the worksheet.

To adjust the column width to fit some of the entries in a column:

- Select the cells containing the data that you want to be fully displayed within the column.
- Choose **FORMAT/Column,AutoFit Selection.**

Activity 4.2: Changing Column Widths

In this activity you will change the width of column **A** to accommodate the expense categories. Since you do not want the column width to accommodate the worksheet title, you will select the expense categories before applying **AutoFit Selection**.

1. Select the part of column **A** to which you want to adjust the column, **A6:A14**.
2. Choose **FORMAT/Column,AutoFit Selection** (Figure 4 - 5).

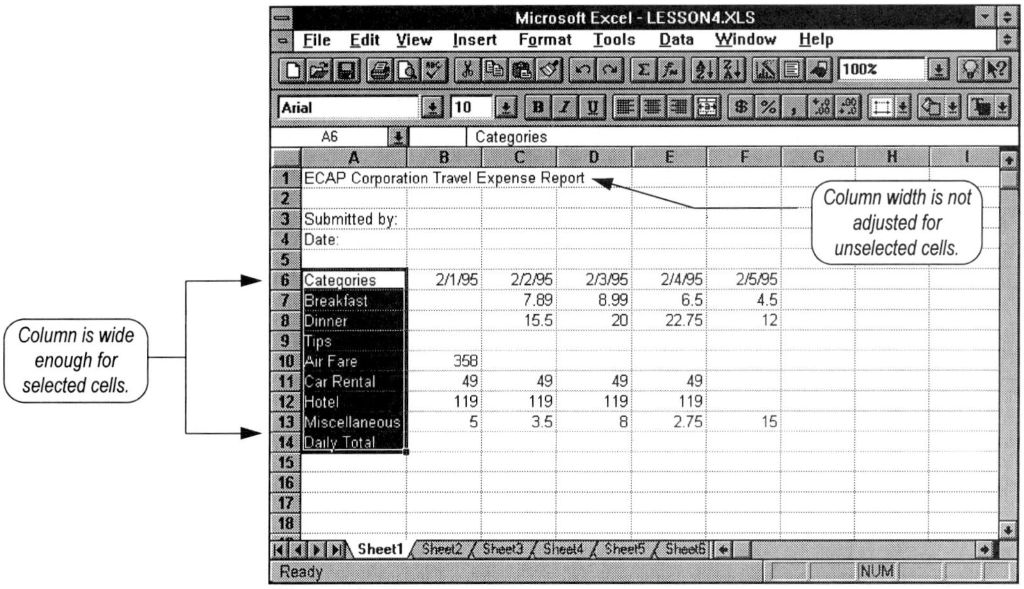

Figure 4 - 5

ORDER OF OPERATIONS IN FORMULAS

In Lessons 1 and 3 you created simple formulas that contained only one mathematical operator in each formula. When a formula contains more than one operator, *Excel* must decide which operation to perform first. You probably learned rules for the *order of operations* when you took Algebra. *Excel* follows these same rules. In a formula, *Excel* moves from left to right, first performing all operations contained within parentheses, then performing all exponentiation (^), then all multiplications (*) and divisions (/), and finally additions (+) and subtractions (-). You must use parentheses to change the normal order of operations. See Table 4 - 2 for examples of how this works.

Formula	Order of Operations	Result (Assuming A1=3, B1=4, C1=5 and D1=6)
=2*A1+B1	Multiply 2 times A1(3); Then add B1 (4)	=6+4 =10
=2*(A1+B1)	Add A1 (3) and B1 (4); Then multiply the sum by 2	=2*7 =14
=A1+B1*C1	Multiply B1 (4) by C1 (5); Then add A1 (3)	=3+20 =23
=A1+B1*C1+D1	Multiply B1 (4) by C1 (5); Then add A1 (3); Then add D1 (6)	=3+20+6 =23+6 =29
=(A1+B1)*(C1+D1)	Add A1 (3) and B1 (4); then add C1 (5) and D1 (6); Then multiply the two sums	=7*11 =77

Table 4 - 2 Order of Operations

Activity 4.3: Using Parentheses to Change Order of Operations

In this activity you will create a formula to calculate the allowable tip. For expense account purposes, ECAP defines the tip as 18% of the total amount paid for breakfast and dinner.

1. To enter a formula to calculate 18% of the total spent on breakfast and dinner:

   a. Select **C9**.

   b. Type: **=18%*(**

      You may type ***18 percent*** *as* ***.18*** *or as* ***18%.*** *If you type* ***18%,*** *Excel automatically divides 18 by 100 and uses .18 in the calculations.*

   d. Click on cell **C7.**

   e. Type: +

   f. Click on cell **C8**.

   g. Type: **)** and press **ENTER** or click on the **enter box**.

      Excel calculates .18 (18%) times the sum of (7.89+15.5) and enters the result, ***4.2102*** *in* ***C9*** *(Figure 4 - 6). Don't worry about the appearance of the number; you'll format it later.*

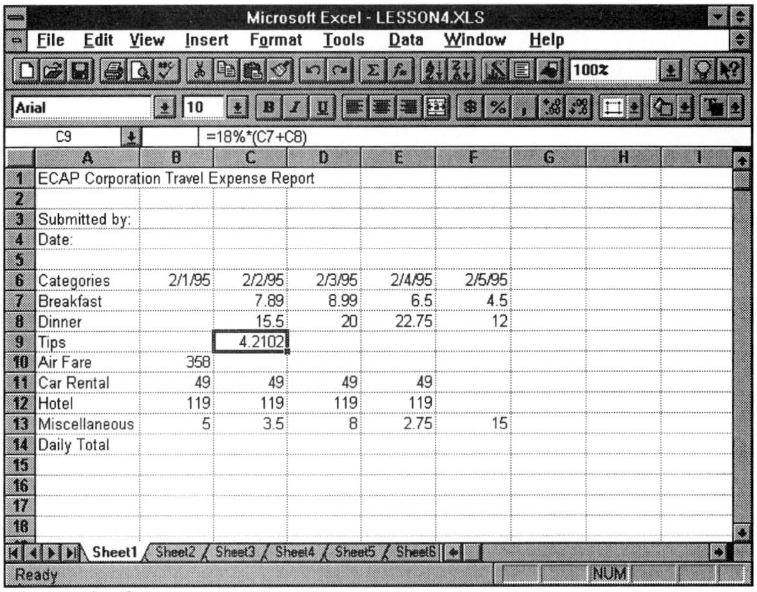

Figure 4 - 6

2. Use the **fill handle** to copy the formula to cells **D9:F9**.

Activity 4.4: Changing the Range Inserted by the AutoSum Button

Next, you want to calculate the totals for each category and for each day. The easiest way to do this is to use the **AutoSum** tool that you used in Lesson 3.

1. In **G6** enter the column label: **Total**
2. Select cell **G7**.
3. Click the **AutoSum** button once.

*The function =**SUM(C7:F7)** will be entered (Figure 4 - 7). Excel did not include **B7** in the range because it is empty. Since you want to copy the function down column **G**, you must include **B7** in the function. Even though **B7** is empty, column **B** does contain data in the other rows to which you will copy the function.*

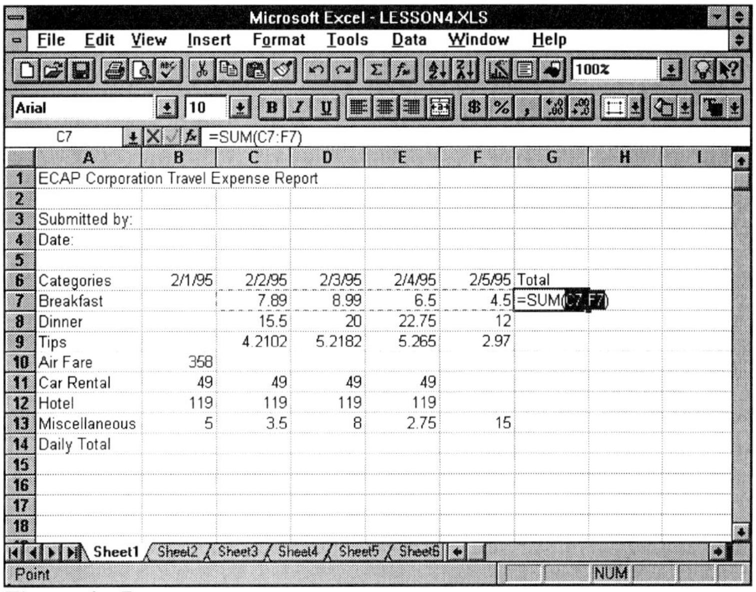

Figure 4 - 7

4. Select the correct range, **B7:F7.**

   ***B7:F7** replaces **C7:F7** in the function in cell **G7** and in the Formula Bar (Figure 4 - 8).*

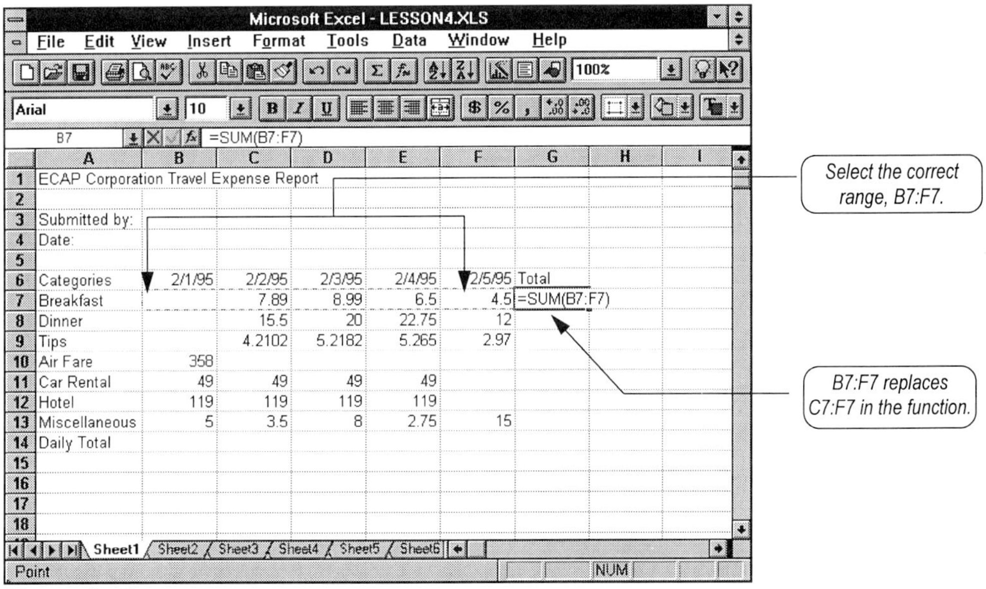

Figure 4 - 8

5. Click on the **AutoSum** button again or press **ENTER** or click on the **enter box** to enter the corrected function.
6. Use the **fill handle** to copy the function down column **G** through cell **G13**.

7. Use the **AutoSum** button to enter the sum of the daily expenses in cell **B14**. Be sure to adjust the range that *Excel* suggests for the function to **B7:B13** so that the formula will copy correctly.
8. Use the **fill handle** to copy the sum function across row **14** to column **G** (Figure 4 - 9).

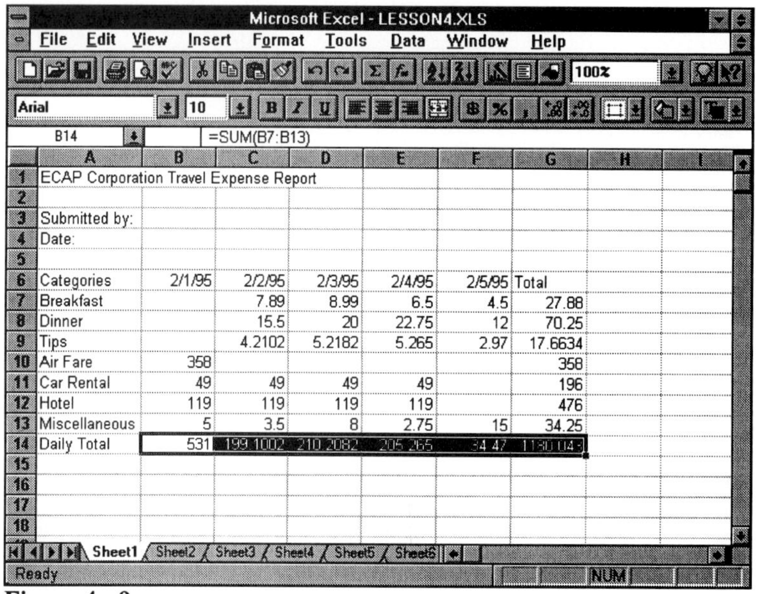

Figure 4 - 9

9. Use **FILE/Save As** to save the name using the filename: **travel**

CREATING MULTI-LINE LABELS IN ONE CELL

Next you are going to create a new section of the worksheet. The section will analyze the amount spent on meals. In previous projects when a column label was wider than the width you wanted the column to be, you typed each part of the label into different cells. The **Wrap Text** check box on the **Alignment** tab of the **Format Cells** dialog box lets you enter more than one line of text in a single cell.

To create a multi-line label in one cell:

- Enter the label into the cell.
- Choose **FORMAT/Format cells** or choose **Format Cells** from the Quick Menu.
- Choose the **Alignment** tab if it is not already selected.
- Check on the **Wrap Text** check box and click on **OK**.

Activity 4.5: Creating Multi-line Column Labels in One Cell

1. Select cell **A19. (HINT**: Press **CTRL+HOME** and then press **PAGE DOWN**. Move the cursor if necessary.)
2. In cells **A19, B19, C19**, and **D19**, enter the column labels for the section of the worksheet analyzing the food costs:

Cell	***Label***
A19	**Expense**
B19	**Minimum Spent**
C19	**Maximum Spent**
D19	**Average Spent**

The column labels overflow into the next cell (Figure 4 - 10) and are truncated if that cell is filled. You will fix that by using an alignment option that you have not yet used.

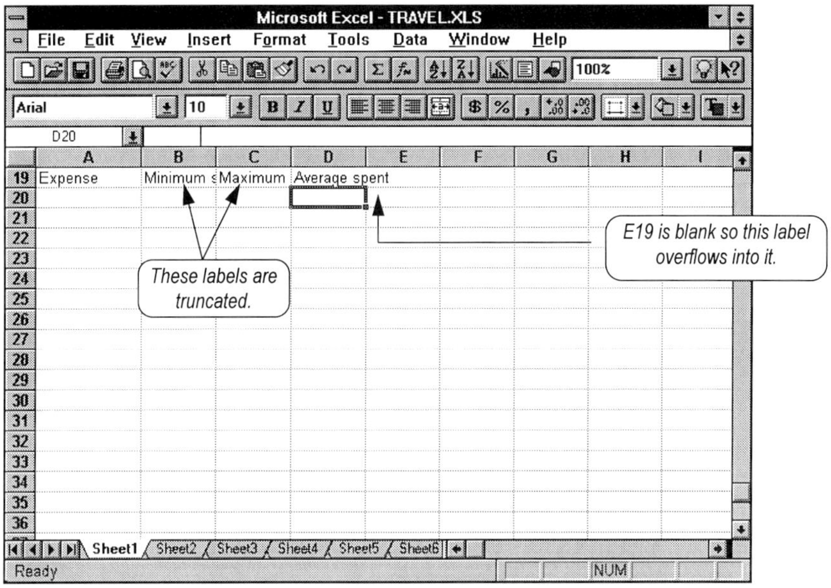

Figure 4 - 10

3. Select cells **B19:D19.**
4. While pointing somewhere in the range **B19:D19**, click the right mouse button.

   The shortcut menu for a range of cells appears (Figure 4 - 11).

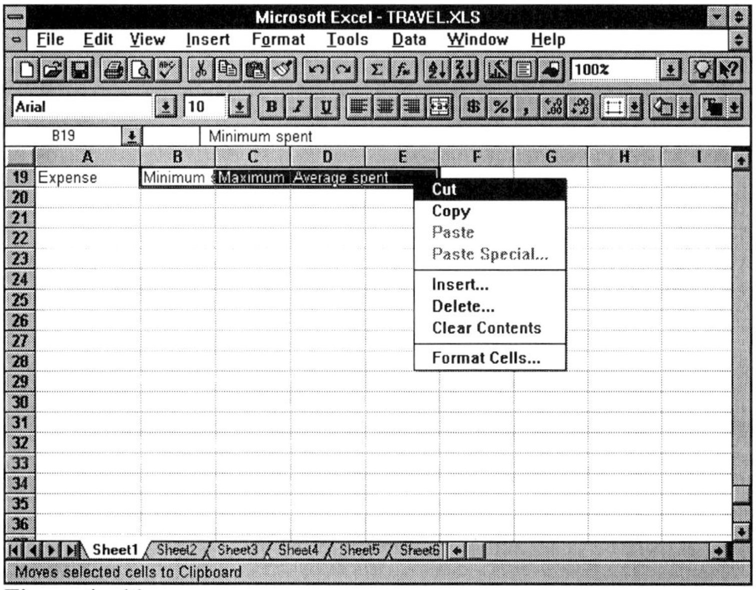

Figure 4 - 11

5. Choose **Format Cells**.
6. Click on the **Alignment** tab in the **Format Cells** dialog box.
7. Click on the **Wrap Text** check box to mark it (Figure 4 - 12).

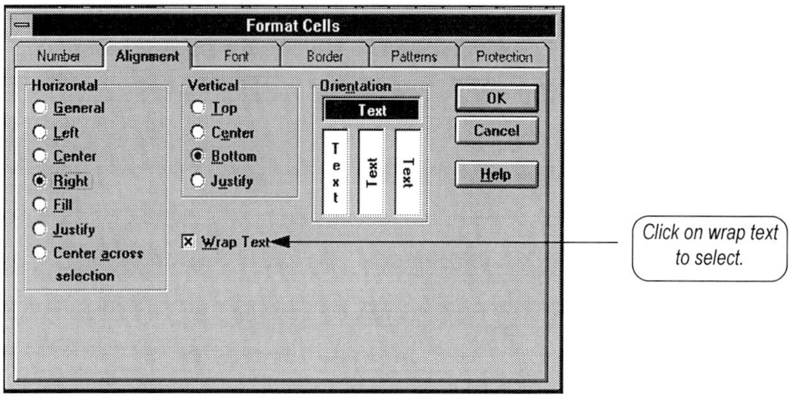

Figure 4 - 12

8. Click on **OK**.
9. Copy cells **A7:A8** to **A20:A21** (Figure 4 - 13).

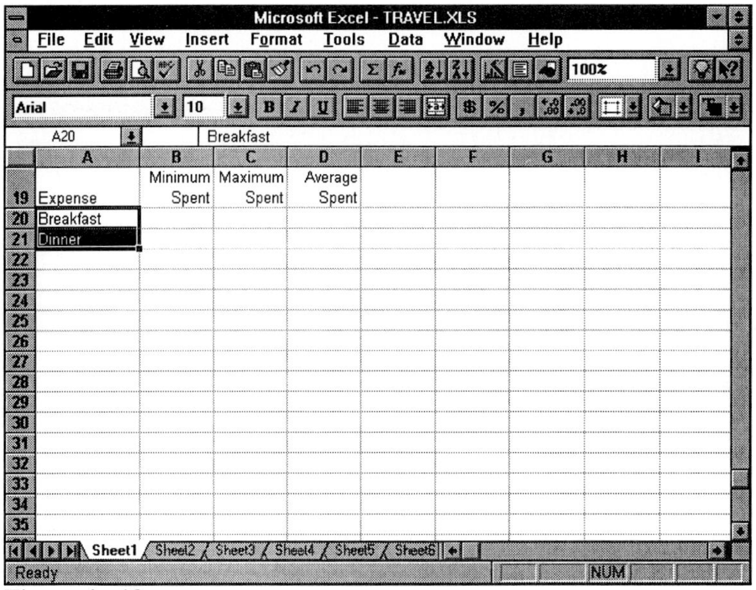

Figure 4 - 13

FUNCTIONS

Analyzing Data with the MIN, MAX, and AVERAGE Functions

You've finished your basic expense calculations. Now you are ready to do some analysis on your expense accounts. ECAP corporation sets a $20 limit on the amount spent daily for breakfast and dinner. (Lunch expenditures are not reimbursed since they are considered normal daily expenses.) In order to see how reasonable this limit is, you want to find the least, most, and average amount spent on meals each day.

Among the more than 400 functions included with *Excel* are statistical functions that let you find the minimum (=**MIN**), maximum (=**MAX**), or average (=**AVERAGE**) value of a range. All functions have the same format as the **SUM** function. They begin with an equal sign (=) followed by the function name. The function name is then followed by a set of parentheses that contains the values that the function will use in its predefined calculations. The values included within the parentheses are called the *arguments* of the function. The arguments of the **MIN, MAX,** and **AVERAGE** function, like that of the **SUM** function, are the range(s) of cells to be added or averaged or from which the minimum or maximum value is to be found.

To enter the MIN, MAX, or AVERAGE functions manually:

- Type an equal sign followed by the name of the function and a left parenthesis.
- Use pointing to select the range to be used in the function. (If more than one range is included, select the first range and keep the **CTRL** key depressed while pointing to the next range(s).)
- Type the closing right parenthesis and press **ENTER** or click on the **enter box**.

Activity 4.6: Using the MIN, MAX and AVERAGE Functions to Analyze Data

1. Select cell **B20**.
2. Type: =**min(**
3. Scroll the screen up until row 7 is visible. Select the range containing the daily breakfast costs, **C7:F7** (Figure 4 - 14).

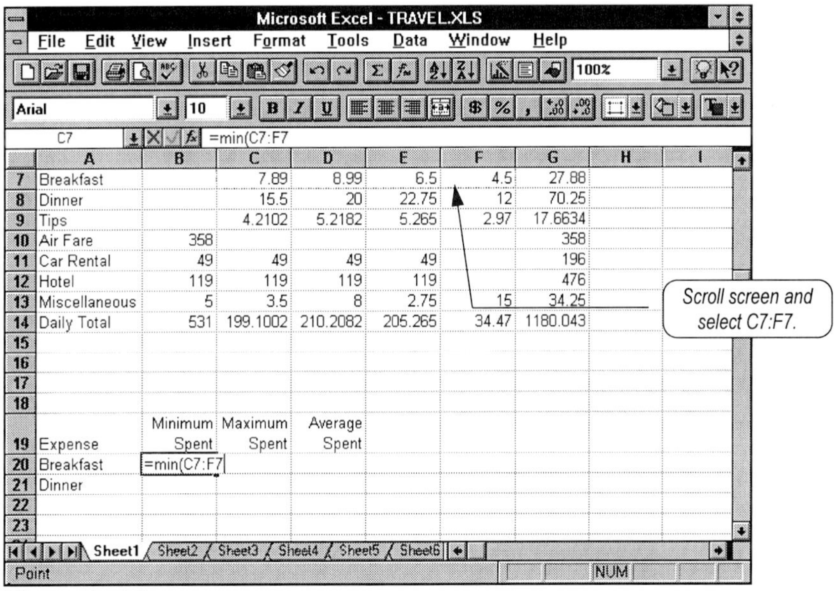

Figure 4 - 14

4. Type: **)** and click on the **enter box** or press **ENTER**.

   *The function =MIN(C7:F7) appears in the Formula Bar. The smallest value in the range C7:F7, **4.5**, appears in cell **B20**.*

5. Use the same procedure to enter the formula for the maximum spent for breakfast (**=max)** in cell **C20**.

*When **C20** is selected, **=MAX(C7:F7)** appears in the Formula Bar and the maximum amount in the range **(8.99)** appears in the cell.*

6. Enter the formula for the average spent for breakfast (**=average)** in **D20**.
7. Select the range containing the three functions, **B20:D20**.
8. Use the **fill handle** to copy the formulas down to cells **B21:D21** (Figure 4 - 15).

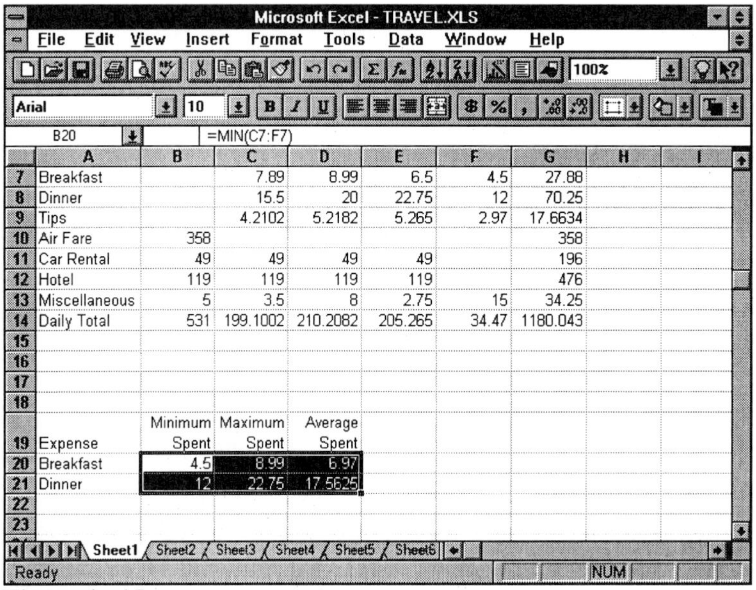

Figure 4 - 15

9. In **A22** enter the row label: **Total**
10. Use the **AutoSum** tool to calculate the sum of the minimum spent in cell **B22**.
11. Use the **fill handle** to copy the sum formula from **B22** to **C22** and **D22**.
12. **Save** the file again using the existing name.

Entering the System Date

Often you want to include the completion date on your worksheet. The **TODAY** function allows you to enter the *system date* on your worksheet. The system date is a pre-set date which is automatically updated, and which should be set to the current date. The date entered by the **TODAY** function is updated whenever you open the worksheet so that it will always display the current date.

Using the Function Wizard

You don't have to know the syntax of the **TODAY** function. *Excel* includes a number of aids, called *wizards*, which guide you through the basic steps required to complete a task. The **Function Wizard** button on the Standard Toolbar aids you in entering functions. It is useful for entering functions that you have never used before, or for entering functions with complicated syntax, or anytime you have forgotten the exact name or format of a function. Since the definition of the selected function is displayed in the **Function Wizard** dialog box, the **Function Wizard** can also be used to familiarize yourself with *Excel*'s many functions.

To use the Function Wizard to enter a function:

- Select the cell to contain the function.
- Click on the **Function Wizard** button  or select **INSERT/Function.**
- Click on the function category. If you are unsure of the category, select **All**. Select **Recent** if you have used the function recently.
- Click on the function name.
- Click the **Next** button.
- Enter values for each of the arguments. If the argument is a range of cells, you may type the range or highlight the range on the worksheet. When an argument box is active, a description of the argument is displayed. Press the **TAB** key or click in the next box to move from box to box.
- Click on the **Finish** button when you are done.

Activity 4.7: Using the Function Wizard to Enter the System Date

You want to include the System Date in cell **B4** so that the date the worksheet is printed appears on the worksheet.

1. Select **B4**.

2. Click on the **Function Wizard** button or select **INSERT/Function.**

   *The **Function Wizard - Step 1 of 2** dialog box will appear (Figure 4 - 16). The Most Recently Used category will probably be selected in the **Function Category** list box. **TODAY** may or may not appear in the **Function Name** box, depending on whether or not someone has recently used the **TODAY** function on your computer.*

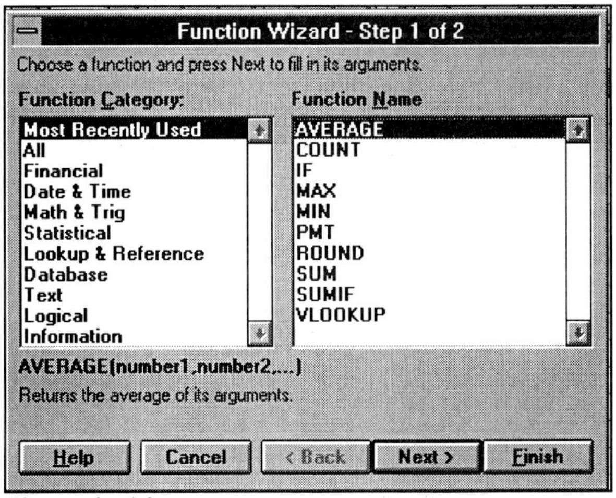

Figure 4 - 16

3. Click on **Date & Time** in the **Function Category** list box.

   *The date and time functions will be displayed in the **Function Name** list box (Figure 4 - 17).*

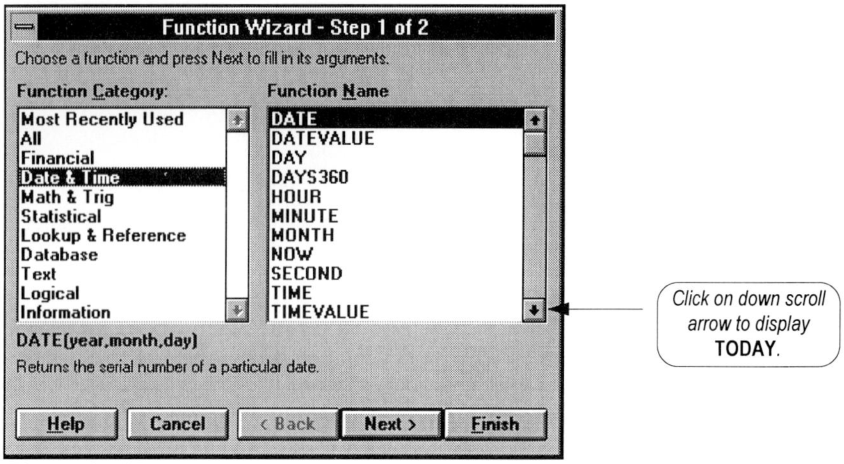

Figure 4 - 17

4. Click on the  on the vertical scrollbar of the **Function Name** list box until **TODAY** is visible. Click on **TODAY**.
5. Click on the **Next** button.

   *The **Function Wizard-Step 2 of 2** dialog box is displayed (Figure 4 - 18).*

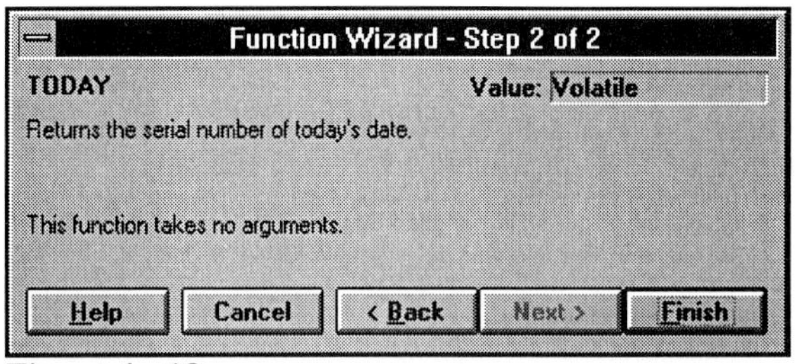

Figure 4 - 18

6. The **TODAY** function is very simple—it contains no arguments. You have finished entering the function, so click on **Finish**.

   *The function **=TODAY()** is entered in the Formula Bar. Notice that Excel has begun the function with an equal sign and that the function name is followed by a set of parentheses even though they are empty. The current date should appear in cell **B4**. If the date is not today's date, tell your lab instructor so that the system date on your computer can be changed.*

Activity 4.8: Formatting the Worksheet

In this activity you will format and print the worksheet.

1. Change the font size of the worksheet title, **ECAP Corporation Travel Expense Report** to **12** point. Make the title **Bold. Center** the title **across columns A:G**.
2. Make the column labels in row **6 bold. Right align** the column label **Total**.
3. Format **B7:G13** using the **Comma Style** with two decimal places.

4. Format **B14:G14** using the **Currency Style** with two decimal places.
5. Increase column widths if necessary.
6. Add a bottom border under rows **6** and **13** (Figure 4 - 19).

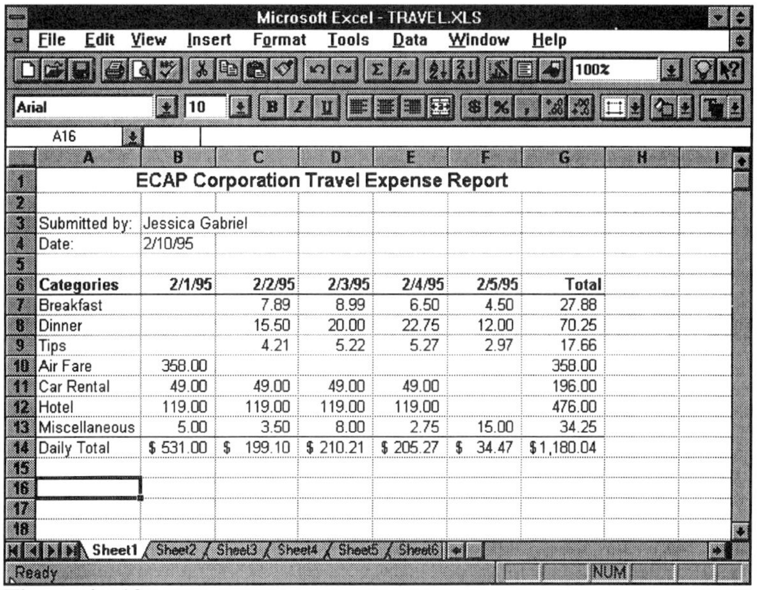

Microsoft Excel - TRAVEL.XLS

	A	B	C	D	E	F	G
1		ECAP Corporation Travel Expense Report					
2							
3	Submitted by:	Jessica Gabriel					
4	Date:	2/10/95					
5							
6	**Categories**	**2/1/95**	**2/2/95**	**2/3/95**	**2/4/95**	**2/5/95**	**Total**
7	Breakfast		7.89	8.99	6.50	4.50	27.88
8	Dinner		15.50	20.00	22.75	12.00	70.25
9	Tips		4.21	5.22	5.27	2.97	17.66
10	Air Fare	358.00					358.00
11	Car Rental	49.00	49.00	49.00	49.00		196.00
12	Hotel	119.00	119.00	119.00	119.00		476.00
13	Miscellaneous	5.00	3.50	8.00	2.75	15.00	34.25
14	Daily Total	$ 531.00	$ 199.10	$ 210.21	$ 205.27	$ 34.47	$1,180.04

Figure 4 - 19

7. Format the second section of the worksheet in cells **A19:A22** to match **A6:G14** as in Figure 4 - 20.

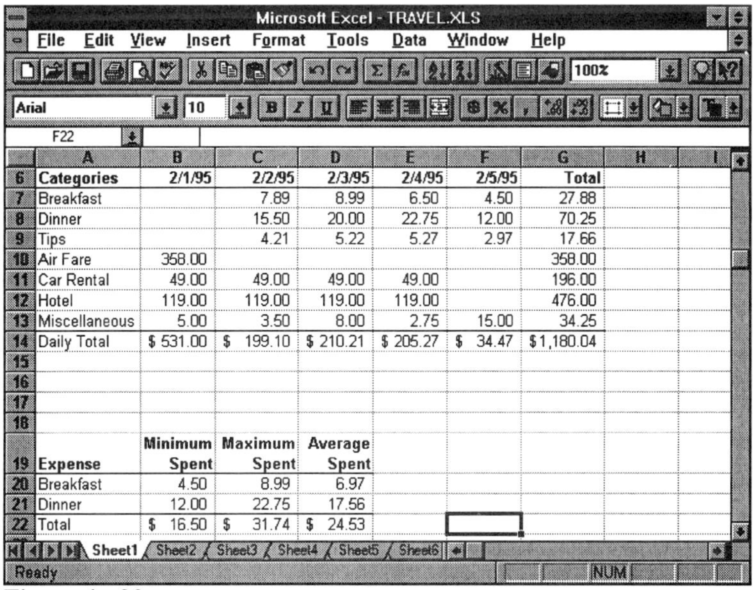

Microsoft Excel - TRAVEL.XLS

	A	B	C	D	E	F	G
6	**Categories**	**2/1/95**	**2/2/95**	**2/3/95**	**2/4/95**	**2/5/95**	**Total**
7	Breakfast		7.89	8.99	6.50	4.50	27.88
8	Dinner		15.50	20.00	22.75	12.00	70.25
9	Tips		4.21	5.22	5.27	2.97	17.66
10	Air Fare	358.00					358.00
11	Car Rental	49.00	49.00	49.00	49.00		196.00
12	Hotel	119.00	119.00	119.00	119.00		476.00
13	Miscellaneous	5.00	3.50	8.00	2.75	15.00	34.25
14	Daily Total	$ 531.00	$ 199.10	$ 210.21	$ 205.27	$ 34.47	$1,180.04
19	**Expense**	**Minimum Spent**	**Maximum Spent**	**Average Spent**			
20	Breakfast	4.50	8.99	6.97			
21	Dinner	12.00	22.75	17.56			
22	Total	$ 16.50	$ 31.74	$ 24.53			

Figure 4 - 20

8. **Save** the worksheet using the current name.

Activity 4.9: Printing the Worksheet

1. Use **FILE/Page Setup** to change the **Header** to **None**.
2. Print the worksheet.
3. Press **CTRL+`** to display formulas.
4. Print the worksheet again with formulas displayed.
5. Press **CTRL+`** again to redisplay values.
6. **Save** the worksheet again.

SUMMARY

In this lesson you learned how to use parentheses to change the order in which calculations are performed in a formula. You also learned how to use a few of *Excel's* more than 400 functions. Use the **Function Wizard** on your own to explore some of *Excel's* other functions.

KEY TERMS

Argument
AVERAGE
Function Wizard
MAX
MIN
Order of operations
Series
System Date
TODAY
Wizards
Wrap Text

INDEPENDENT PROJECTS

The independent projects will provide you with opportunities to review creating formulas and functions. In addition Project 4.1 shows you how to use a range including nonadjacent cells in a function. Project 4.2 uses the **FORMAT/Cells** command to format numbers.

Independent Project 4.1: Analyzing First Quarter Sales

Your company has branches in seven cities. You have been given a worksheet that contains the sales for the seven cities for the first quarter and have been asked to perform some analysis on the data. When you have completed the project your worksheet should resemble Figure 4 - 21.

FIRST QUARTER SALES

Branch	January	February	March
Boston, MA	$ 897,453	$ 723,432	$ 632,143
New York City, NY	567,345	765,435	764,621
Philadelphia, PA	154,325	123,234	175,276
Pittsburgh, PA	234,516	256,473	321,456
Richmond, VA	983,214	765,456	832,435
Washington, D.C.	345,123	476,587	432,435
White Plains, NY	164,361	324,156	123,456
Total Sales:	$ 3,346,337	$ 3,434,773	$ 3,281,822
Average Sales:	$ 478,048	$ 490,682	$ 468,832
Minimum Sales:	$ 154,325	$ 123,234	$ 123,456
Maximum Sales:	$ 983,214	$ 765,456	$ 832,435
Range of Sales:	$ 828,889	$ 642,222	$ 708,979
1st Quarter Total Sales:	$ 10,062,932		
1st Quarter PA Sales:	$ 1,265,280		
1st Quarter NY Sales:	$ 2,709,374		

Figure 4 - 21

Use Figure 4 - 21 and the instructions below to complete the project:

1. Open the file **indpr4_1.xls**.
2. In **B13** enter a function to total the **January** sales. Copy it across the row.
3. In **B14** enter a function to calculate the **Average January** sales. Copy it across the row.
4. In **B15** enter a function to calculate the **Minimum January** sales. Copy it across the row.
5. In **B16** enter a function to calculate the **Maximum January** sales. Copy it across the row.
6. In **B17** enter a formula to calculate the range of **January** sales (i.e. the difference between the highest and lowest sales). Copy it across the row.
7. In **B19** enter a function to calculate the total of the first quarter sales (January, February and March) for all of the cities.
8. In **B20** enter a function to calculate the total of the first quarter sales for both of the Pennsylvania cities. (What range will you use in the formula?)
9. In **B21** enter a function to calculate the total of the first quarter sales for both of the New York cities. **HINT:** This is harder than the previous step because the New York cities are not next to one another. Therefore, to select a range that has nonadjacent parts, you can highlight the first part and then depress the **CTRL** key while you highlight the second part of the range.
10. When you create a formula, the result of the formula usually is formatted to match the first cell in the formula range. Therefore, the total, average, minimum and maximum were all formatted for currency while the PA and NY totals used the comma style. Format the PA and NY values using **Currency Style**, 0 decimal places.
11. Save your worksheet using the name: **quarter1**
12. Print your worksheet without gridlines. Include your name and other identifying information in the header in place of **sheet 1**.
13. Print your worksheet again displaying formulas. Close and save the worksheet.

Independent Project 4.2: Analyzing Weather Information

You work for a home heating company. You are given a worksheet which contains the high and low temperatures and the amount of snowfall for the past week. You must enter formulas and functions to calculate the average temperature for each day in Fahrenheit and Centigrade. They also want you to calculate the degree days for each day. Degree days is a concept used by heating companies to see how far the average temperature was above or below 65 degree Fahrenheit. You have also been told to calculate the average of each of the measurements for the week and the total number of degree days and snowfall. When completed compare your worksheet to Figure 4 - 22.

Weather Information						
	Temperature (Fahrenheit)			Degree	Average	Snowfall
Day	Low	High	Average	Days	Centigrade	(inches)
5-Dec	15	35	25.0	40.0	-3.9	0.75
6-Dec	26	43	34.5	30.5	1.4	5.00
7-Dec	28	42	35.0	30.0	1.7	1.50
8-Dec	10	38	24.0	41.0	-4.4	0.00
9-Dec	-2	10	4.0	61.0	-15.6	0.25
10-Dec	-5	8	1.5	63.5	-16.9	0.00
11-Dec	10	25	17.5	47.5	-8.1	0.00
Average	11.7	28.7	20.2	44.8	-6.5	1.1
Low for Week	-5					
High for Week	43					
Total Degree Days	313.5					
Total Snowfall	7.50					

Figure 4 - 22

Use Figure 4 - 22 and the instructions below to complete the project:

1. Open the file **indpr4_2.xls**.
2. First, you will replace the days of the week by dates. Beginning in cell **A7** enter the series of dates beginning with: **12/5**

   The date will appear in the default date format for a date containing only a month and a day.
3. Left align all of the dates that you have just entered.
4. In **D7** enter a function to compute the average of the **Low** and **High** temperatures for the day.
5. In **E7** enter a formula to compute the **Degree Days**. The degree days is equal to the **65** minus the **Average** temperature of the day.
6. In **F7** enter a formula to convert the **Average Fahrenheit Temperature** to the **Average Centigrade** temperature. The average Centigrade temperature is equal to **5/9** of the difference between the **Average Fahrenheit** temperature and **32**.
7. Copy all of the functions and formulas to the appropriate cells.
8. You need to format the new numbers. Use **FORMAT/Cells,Number** instead of the **Comma Style** button. Make sure the **Number** tab of the **Format Cells** dialog box is active. Choose **Number** from the **Category** list box and **#,##0** from the **Format Code** list box. The code **#,##0** will insert commas to separate thousands. It also precedes negative numbers with a minus sign which is appropriate for temperatures. Click on **OK** after selecting the correct code.

   *Codes like #,##0_);(#,##0) and the format used by the **Comma Style** button indicate negative numbers enclosed in parentheses which is not appropriate for temperatures.*
9. Increase the decimal places to one.
10. In **B15** enter a function to calculate the average **Low** temperature. Copy the function across the row. Format the numbers as you did in step 8.
11. In **B16** enter a function to calculate the lowest Fahrenheit temperature of the week.
12. In **B17** enter a function to calculate the highest Fahrenheit temperature of the week.
13. In **B18** enter a function to calculate the total number of degree days for the week.
14. In **B19** enter a function to calculate the total snowfall for the week.
15. Save your worksheet using the name: **weather**
16. Print your worksheet without gridlines. Include your name and other identifying information in the header in place of **sheet 1**.
17. Print your worksheet again displaying formulas. Close and save the worksheet.

Independent Project 4.3: Analyzing Stock Sales

You have been asked to analyze the success of an investment portfolio. You have sold a number of stocks in 1994 and you want to analyze the profitability of the stocks that you sold. In completing this project you will create some complex formulas and explore date arithmetic. When complete your worksheet should resemble Figure 4 - 23 although spacing will be different.

1. Open **indpr4_3.xls**.
2. In **E5** enter a formula to compute the **Total Cost** of the stocks. The Total Cost is equal to the **Number of Shares** multiplied by the **Cost per Share**. Copy the formula down the column.

INVESTMENT PORTFOLIO
STOCKS SOLD IN 1994

Purchase Date	Number of Shares	NAME	Cost per Share	Total Cost	Date of Sale	Sales Price per Share	Proceeds	Gain (Loss)	Years Held	% Annual Return on Investment
10/12/92	100	*Jiffy Data Processing*	56.26	5,626	10/15/94	65.25	6,525	899	2.0	8%
9/30/85	100	*Books Galore*	109.12	10,912	11/12/94	62.50	6,250	(4,662)	9.1	-5%
12/15/88	500	*Dinosaurs, Inc.*	29.58	14,790	12/5/94	45.50	22,750	7,960	6.0	9%
10/2/92	200	*My Life Insurance*	22.12	4,424	4/2/94	75.87	15,174	10,750	1.5	162%
1/5/91	300	*Toys, Toys, Toys*	20.21	6,063	1/19/94	32.50	9,750	3,687	3.0	20%
9/4/88	500	*Best Travel Agency*	68.38	34,190	7/15/94	62.25	31,125	(3,065)	5.9	-2%
6/24/89	250	*Strawberry Fields*	10.28	2,570	8/27/94	21.50	5,375	2,805	5.2	21%
7/6/93	1,000	*Fly By Night Airlines*	19.45	19,450	11/7/94	12.50	12,500	(6,950)	1.3	-27%
5/5/94	600	*ECAP, Corp.*	9.74	5,844	7/23/94	17.75	10,650	4,806	0.2	380%
12/8/90	400	*Nationwide*	109.73	43,892	5/16/94	125.50	50,200	6,308	3.4	4%
10/4/84	800	*Best Buys*	54.87	43,896	12/17/94	62.50	50,000	6,104	10.2	1%
		Total Gain (Loss)	$ 28,642							
		Maximum Gain (Loss)	$ 10,750							
		Minimum Gain(Loss)	$ (6,950)							
		Average % Return on Investment	52%							
		Maximum % Return on Investment	380%							
		Minimum % Return on Investment	-27%							

Figure 4 - 23

3. In **H5** calculate the **Proceeds** which is equal to the **Number of Shares** multiplied by the **Sales Price per Share.**
4. In **I5** calculate the **Gain(Loss)** which is the difference between the **Proceeds** and the **Total Cost** and should be positive if the **Proceeds** are higher than the **Total Cost.**
5. In **J5** calculate the **Years Held**. In *Excel* every date you enter is associated with a number, so you can use dates in calculations. When you subtract dates the answer is the number of days between the two dates. Therefore, in order to find the **Years Held** you must divide the difference between the **Date of Sale** and **Purchase Date** by **365**.
6. In **K5** calculate the **% Annual Return on Investment** (without considering compounding)**.** The **% Annual Return on Investment** equals the **Gain(Loss)** divided by both the **Total Cost** and the **Years Held.**
7. Copy the formulas in **H5:K5** down the columns.
8. In cell **D17** use a function to calculate the total **Gain (Loss)**.
9. In cell **D18** use a function to calculate the maximum **Gain(Loss)**.
10. In cell **D19** use a function to calulate the minimum **Gain(Loss)**.
11. After completing the last three functions, you decide that calculating the average, minimum and maximum % annual return on investment might give you a different perspective on your data. In cell **C21** enter the label: **Average % of Return on Investment**. Change its alignment to **Wrap Text** so that it fits in the cell without widening the column. Add similar labels in **B22** and **B23** for maximum and minimum % return on investment.
12. Enter the appropriate functions in cells **D21:D23**.
13. Format the worksheet and increase column widths appropriately.
14. Save the worksheet using the name: **invest**
15. Print the worksheet without gridlines or the **Sheet 1** header and with a header or footer containing identifying information about you. The **Page Setup** was changed in **indpr4_3.xls** so that the worksheet will print in landscape orientation (sideways). This procedure will be explained in Lesson 5.
16. Based on the **Gain(Loss)** which stock made the largest gain? Based on the **% Annual Return on Investment** which stock made the largest gain?
17. Print the worksheet again with formulas displayed. Close and save the worksheet.

Independent Project 4.4: Analyzing Airline Flights

You work for Fly By Night Airlines. You have been asked to set up a worksheet analyzing flights which left White Plains Airport on December 15. The file **indpr4_4.xls** contains data on the Unrestricted (Full Price) fare for each flight and on the number of tickets sold at each of three rates. All flights use the same type of airplane. Maximum capacity is 150 passengers. You are to calculate:

- Number of tickets sold for each flight
- Percent of seats sold
- Revenue generated by each flight
- Average number of tickets sold in each category (Full Price, 20% Discount, and 50% Discount)
- Average number of tickets sold for each flight
- Average percent of seats sold
- Average revenue generated per flight
- Total revenue for all of the flights.

1. Your project should include:
   - A table specifying the calculations that you need to perform to obtain the results requested.
   - A paper and pencil design of the worksheet showing how you will organize the calculations that you need to include, and the column labels you will add.
   - A printout of the completed formatted worksheet. Remove gridlines and include information identifying you in the header or footer.
   - A printout of the worksheet displaying formulas.
2. Save the worksheet using the name: **flights**

Lesson 5 Absolute and Relative Cell References

Objectives

In this lesson you will learn how to:

- Enter numbers as text
- Determine when to use Absolute cell references
- Determine when to use Mixed cell references
- Create a formula containing Absolute cell references
- Copy Absolute cell references
- Use a function as part of a formula
- Print a worksheet that is larger than one piece of paper
- Freeze columns and rows
- Perform simple What-If Analysis
- Use **TOOLS/Goal Seek**

PROJECT DESCRIPTION

In this project you will complete the worksheet, **5YR.XLS,** which projects ECAP Manufacturing Corporation's sales, expenses and pretax income for the next five years. These projections are based on last year's actual sales, and a set of assumptions about the anticipated growth rate and expenses.

In the previous lessons worksheets were used to record and analyze existing data. In this lesson you will use the worksheet to make projections. This is one type of *What-If* analysis. Since formulas automatically recalculate whenever the values in the cells they reference are changed, you can systematically change a set of values and see how these changes affect the end result. *Excel* has many advanced tools which can help you manage complex what-if analyses. However, in this project you will use a very simple what-if analysis. A set of assumptions has already been entered into **5YR.XLS**. You will create formulas which project the sales, expenses and pretax income over the next five years. Then you will change the assumptions and let *Excel* recalculate the results!

In the process of completing the project you will also expand on previously developed skills. You will learn how to incorporate a function into a formula. Since the completed worksheet does not fit on one screen, you will also learn how to freeze part of the worksheet so that designated columns and/or rows remain on the screen as you scroll the worksheet. Finally, you will learn some techniques for printing worksheets that don't naturally fit on one page.

When this project is completed, the worksheet **5YR.XLS** will resemble Figure 5 - 1.

ECAP MANUFACTURING CORPORATION

FIVE YEAR PROJECTION

ASSUMPTIONS

Sales with Growth	104%	of previous year's sales
Returns & Allowances	2%	of sales
Materials	17%	of net sales
Labor	25%	of net sales
Overhead	150%	of labor
SGA	12%	of net sales

	CURRENT	PROJECTIONS					1995-1999
	1994	1995	1996	1997	1998	1999	Totals
Gross Sales	$1,345,560	$1,399,382	$1,455,358	$1,513,572	$1,574,115	$1,637,079	$7,579,506
R&A	26,911	27,988	29,107	30,271	31,482	32,742	151,590
Net Sales	1,318,649	1,371,395	1,426,251	1,483,301	1,542,633	1,604,338	7,427,916
Materials	224,170	233,137	242,463	252,161	262,248	272,737	1,262,746
Labor	329,662	342,849	356,563	370,825	385,658	401,084	1,856,979
Overhead	494,493	514,273	534,844	556,238	578,487	601,627	2,785,469
SGA	158,238	164,567	171,150	177,996	185,116	192,521	891,350
Income Before Taxes	$ 112,085	$ 116,569	$ 121,231	$ 126,081	$ 131,124	$ 136,369	$ 631,373

Figure 5 - 1

Activity 5.1: Getting Started

1. Start *Excel.*
2. **Open** the file **lesson5.xls**. Maximize *Excel* and **LESSON5.XLS** if necessary.

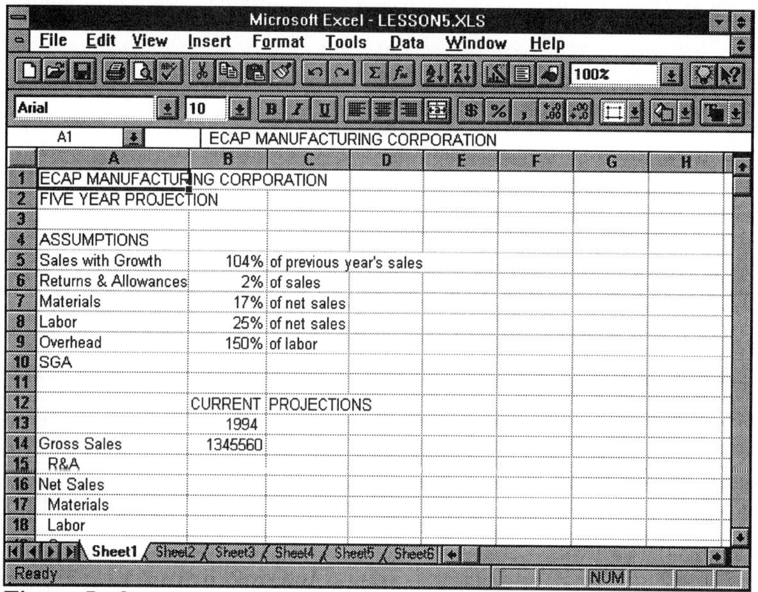

Figure 5 - 2

***LESSON5.XLS** contains assumptions about the projected sales, the expenses for returns as a percent of gross sales, materials, and labor as a percent of net sales, and the overhead rate as a percent of labor costs (Figure 5 - 2).*

3. The data on **SGA** (Sales, Growth and Administrative costs) has been omitted.

   a. In **B10** enter: **12%**

   b. In **C10** enter: **of net sales**

   *The percentage (**12%**) and the text associated with it (**of net sales**) must be entered in separate cells. If a cell contains text in addition to values, it cannot be used in calculations.*

ENTERING NUMBERS AS TEXT

The first step in completing the worksheet is to enter the five years for which you want to make projections. If you just type the year names (1995, 1996, etc.), *Excel* will treat them as values since they only contain numerals. However, if you precede the number with an apostrophe ('), *Excel* will treat the number as text.

To enter a number as text:

- Type an **apostrophe** (').
- Then type the number.

Activity 5.2: Entering Numbers as Text

In this activity you will enter the labels for columns **C:G**, which will contain your projections.

1. In cell **C13**, type: **'1995** and click on the **enter box** or press **ENTER**.

   *Since you preceded **1995** with an apostrophe, it is left justified in the cell.*

2. Select cell **C13**, if it is not already selected, and drag the **fill handle** to cell **G13**.

   *Excel still recognizes **1995** as a date and fills the remaining cells with the series, **1996, 1997...** (Figure 5 - 3).*

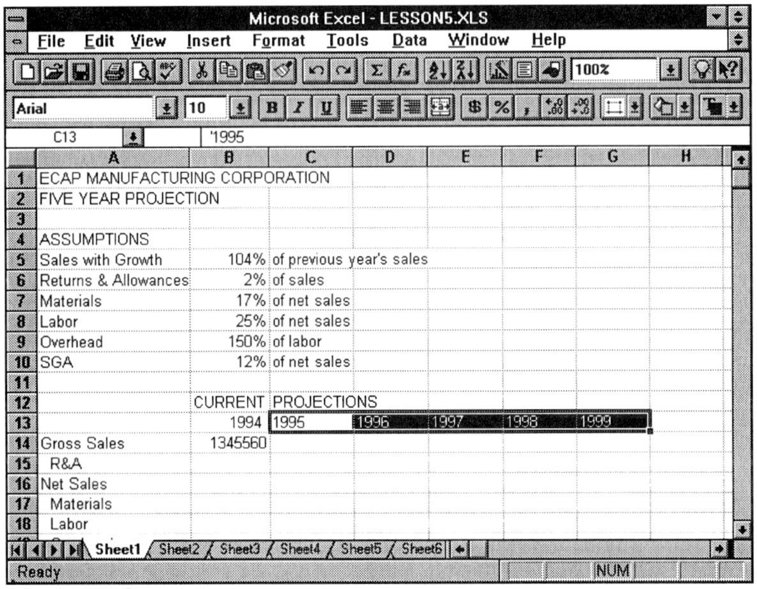

Figure 5 - 3

CELL REFERENCES

Your next step is to enter the formulas for the projected sales and expenses. However, you have a problem. In order to calculate the projected 1995 sales, you need to multiply last year's (1994) sales by the anticipated growth. For cell **C14** this formula would be **=B14*B5**. Then you want to copy the formula across row **14** to calculate the projected sales for 1996 to 1999.

As you saw in Lesson 3, when a formula is copied across a row, *Excel* automatically adjusts the cell references for each column. Therefore, the formula **B14*B5** would become **C14*C5**, **D14*D5**, etc. The first cell reference, **B14**, should adjust since it always refers to the previous year's sales and this changes (the previous year's sales for 1995 is in **B14** , but the previous year's sales for 1996 is in **C14**, etc.) However, the second cell reference, **B5**, refers to the projected sales and this value is always in **B5**.

Excel deals with this situation by letting you create formulas with different types of cell references. You can include *relative, absolute* or *mixed* cell references in formulas. In Lessons 3 and 4 you only used *relative* references. This is the most commonly used reference and is the default. In this lesson you will use *absolute* cell references. *Mixed* references are the most complicated to understand and the least frequently used; therefore, they will be described briefly, but not used in this book.

Relative Cell References

As we discussed in Lesson 3, if you just enter a cell reference into a formula, *Excel* automatically adjusts the column or row reference so that the same relationship is maintained between the cell containing the formula and the cells to which it refers. As indicated in Figure 5 - 4 if the formula in cell **C14** is copied one column to the right, each of the cell references adjusts so that the column reference is the letter after the one included in the original reference. Therefore, **B5** becomes **C5** and **B14** becomes **C14**.

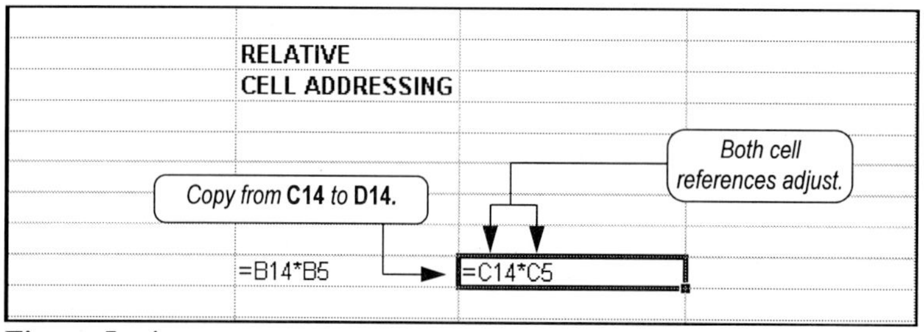

Figure 5 - 4

Absolute Cell References

To specify that a cell address should not change when it is copied, you must make the cell reference absolute when you enter it into the formula. *Absolute* cell references contain dollar signs before both the column and the row location (i.e. **$B$5**). Thus, as Figure 5 - 5 indicates, when **=B14*$B$5** is copied to **D14**, the reference to **$B$5** does not change. Since most formulas refer to more than one cell, some of the cell references in a formula may be absolute while references to other cells are relative.

While an absolute cell reference can be entered by typing a **$** before the column and row names, an easier way to make a cell reference absolute is to press the **F4** key as soon as you have pointed to the cell. **F4** is a toggle key. If it is pressed one time, dollar signs are inserted before the row and column designations (**$B$5**). If it is pressed a second time, the dollar sign is only inserted before the row number (**B$5**). A third press inserts the dollar sign only before the column name (**$B5**) and a fourth press removes all dollar signs (**B5**). Continued key presses repeat the cycle.

When the **$** precedes only part of the cell address, the reference is *mixed.* When mixed formulas are copied, the relative part adjusts while the absolute part remains the same.

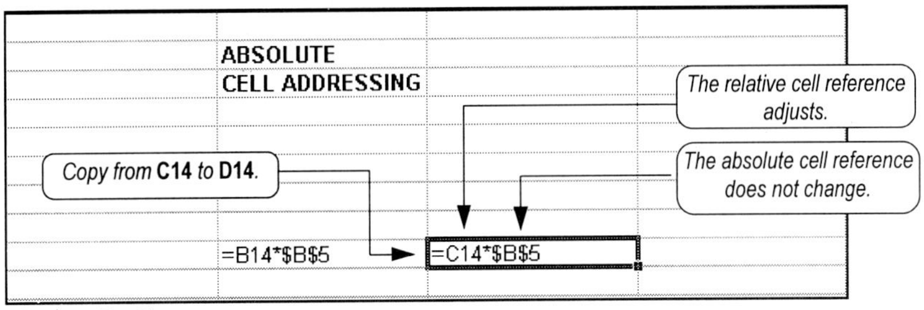

Figure 5 - 5

Mixed Cell References

Mixed cell references are references that are half relative and half absolute. If the column is relative and the row is absolute (**B$4**), then the column changes when the formula is copied but the row does not. If the column is absolute and the row is relative **($B4),** then the row changes when the formula is copied, but the column does not. Mixed references are often used when you need to copy a formula both across and down the worksheet. This typically happens when you are trying to see the effect of changing two variables on your data. Figure 5 - 6 and Figure 5 - 7 illustrate what happens to mixed references when they are copied.

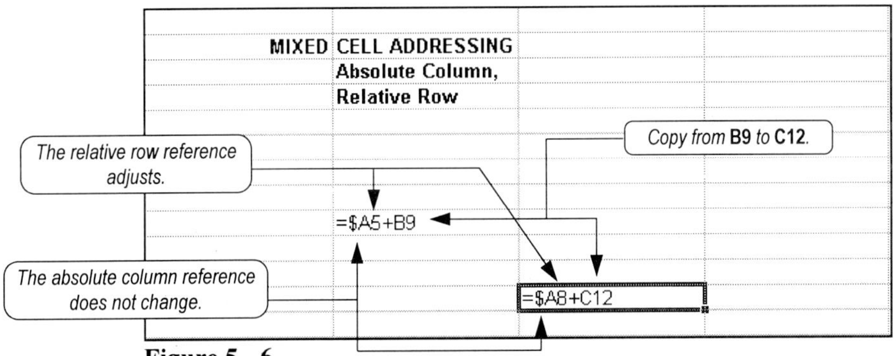

Figure 5 - 6

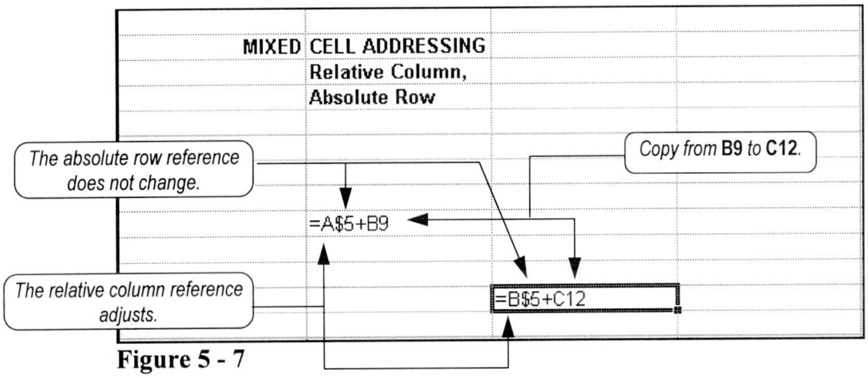

Figure 5 - 7

Creating Absolute References

To enter a formula using absolute cell references:

- Select the cell to contain the formula.
- Begin the formula by typing an equal (=) sign.
- Click on the first cell containing data that should be part of the formula. If this part of the formula should be absolute, press **F4** one time.

  Dollar signs will precede both the column and row names.
- Type a mathematical operator.
- Repeat the last two steps until the formula is complete. Only use **F4** with those cell references that should not change when the formula is copied.
- Click on the **enter box** or press **ENTER**.

Activity 5.3: Entering Formulas with Absolute Cell References

In this activity, you will create formulas for the 1995-1999 sales and the 1994-1999 expense categories. Since all of these formulas will depend on the assumptions at the top of the worksheet, they will involve absolute cell references. You will also enter a formula for the net sales; this formula will only use relative cell references.

1. To create a formula to multiply the previous year's sales by the expected growth:
   a. Select cell **C14**.
   b. Type: =
   c. Click on cell **B14**.
   d. Type the mathematical operator: *
   e. Point to cell **B5**.
   f. Press the **F4** key once.

   B5 *becomes the absolute cell reference,* ***$B$5*** *(Figure 5 - 8).*

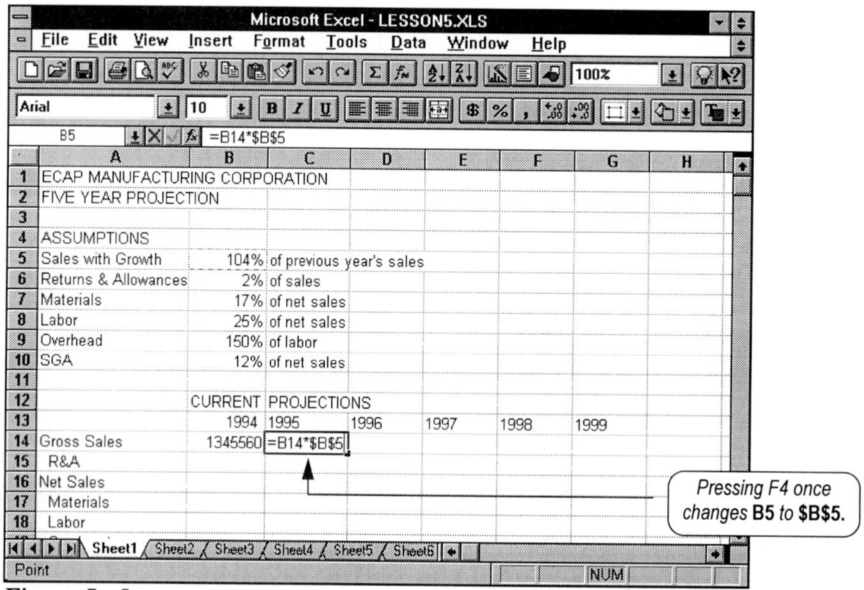

Figure 5 - 8

g. Click on the **enter box** or press **ENTER**.

*The value in cell **C14** should be **1399382.4**.*

h. Make sure **C14** is still highlighted and drag the **fill handle** across row **14** to copy the formula to cells **D14:G14**.

i. Click on **D14**.

*The relative part of the formula, **B14** has adjusted to **C14**, while the absolute part of the formula remains **$B$5** (Figure 5 - 9).*

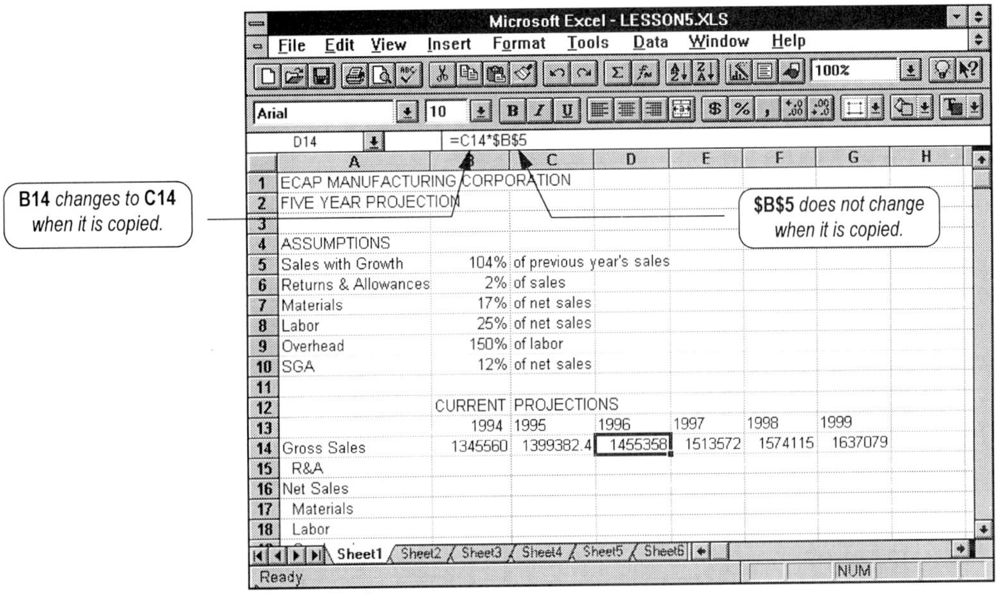

Figure 5 - 9

2. In cell **B15** use the steps above to create a formula to calculate the 1994 returns by multiplying the 1994 Gross Sales (**B14**) by the expected return rate (**B6**). Remember to make **B6** absolute so that it can be copied across the row.

   *When **B15** is highlighted the Formula Bar will display the formula **=B14*$B$6** while the cell displays the result of the formula (**26911.2**).*

3. Use the **fill handle** to copy the formula in **B15** across the row through **G15**.

4. In cell **B16** you want to create a formula to subtract the returns and allowances from the Gross Sales. Unlike the last formula, neither of these cell references should be absolute. Therefore, use pointing to enter the formula: **=B14-B15**

   *The value in cell **B16** should be **1318648.8**.*

5. Select **B16** if it is not already selected and use the **fill handle** to copy the formula across row **16**.

6. In **B17** create a formula to calculate the 1994 Materials Expense by multiplying the 1994 Net Sales (**B16**) by the Materials rate (**B7**). Make the reference to the Materials rate absolute.

   *The value in cell **B17** should be **224170.3** and the formula should be = **B16*$B$7**.*

7. In cell **B18** create a formula to calculate the 1994 Labor Expense by multiplying the 1994 Net Sales (**B16**) by the Labor rate (**B8**). Make the reference to the Labor rate absolute.

   *The value in cell **B18** should be **329662.2**.*

8. In cell **B19** create a formula to calculate the 1994 Overhead Expense by multiplying the 1994 Labor Expense **(B18)** by the Overhead rate ((**B9**). Make cell references absolute as necessary.

   *The value in cell **B19** should be **494493.3**.*

9. In cell **B20** create a formula to calculate the 1994 SGA expenses by multiplying the 1994 Net Sales (**B16**) by the SGA rate (**B10**). Make cell references absolute as necessary.

   *The value in cell **B20** should be **158237.86**.*

10. Highlight **B17:B20** and use the **fill handle** to copy the formulas across the rows through column **G**.

    Your worksheet should resemble Figure 5 - 10.

✓ ***PROBLEM SOLVER**:* If **#VALUE!** appears in any of the cells, delete the formula in the cell displaying **#VALUE!**, check your original formulas, make all of the references to the cells containing the assumptions absolute, and copy the formulas.

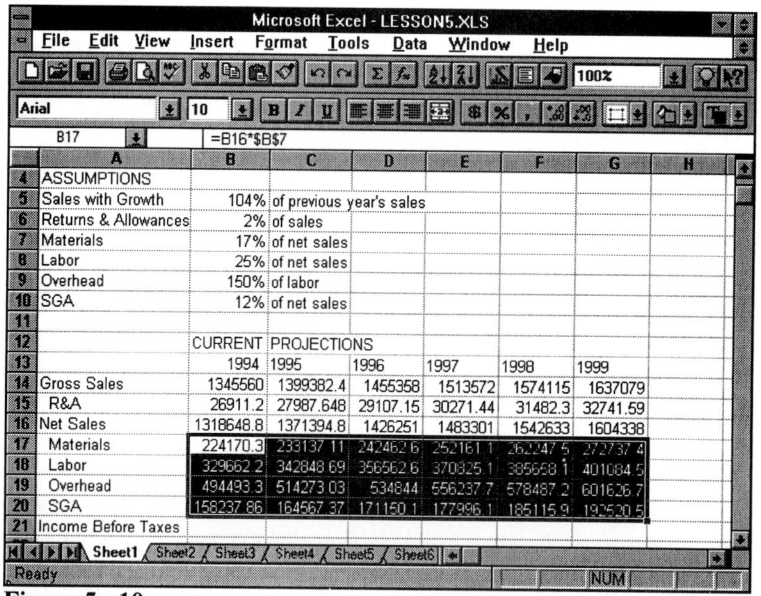

Figure 5 - 10

INCLUDING FUNCTIONS IN FORMULAS

Next, you need to calculate the pretax income. This is equal to the Net Sales minus the four expenses. You could calculate this by subtracting each of the expenses from the sales. This formula would be: Net Sales minus Materials minus Labor minus Overhead minus SGA or =**B16-B17-B18-B19-B20**. However, another, quicker way to calculate this is to subtract the sum of the expenses from the sales.

So far all of your formulas have included just cell references and operators (e.g. =**C3*C4**) or just a function (e.g. =**sum(B17:B20)**). However, it is possible for the same formula to include cell references, operators and functions. Therefore, the following formula can be used to calculate the pretax income: =**B16-sum(B17:B20)**.

Activity 5.4: Including a Function in a Formula

In this activity you will calculate the pretax income. Then you will calculate the predicted 1995-1999 totals for the sales, each of the expense categories and the pretax income.

1. Select cell **B21**.
2. Type: =
3. Point to the 1994 net sales, **B16**.
4. Subtract the sum of the expenses by typing: **-sum(** and then pointing to the range, **B17:B20** (Figure 5 - 11).

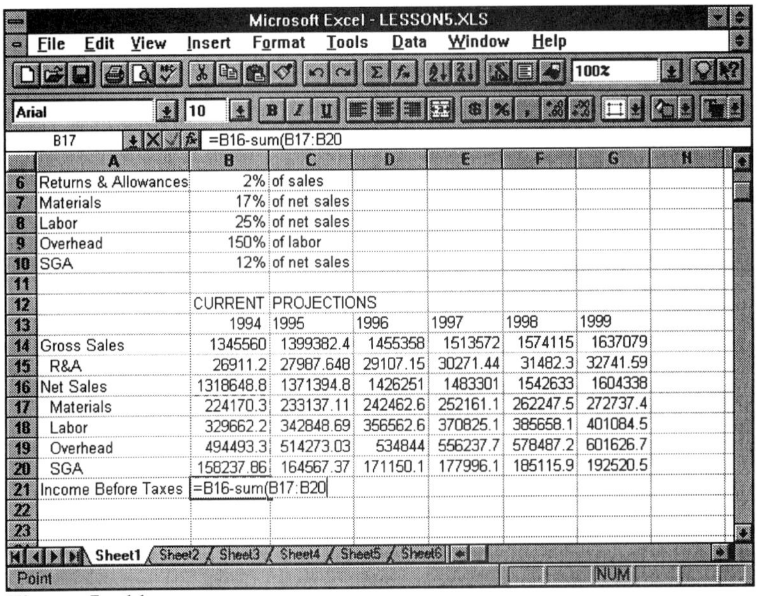

Figure 5 - 11

5. End the formula by typing:) and clicking on the **enter box** or pressing **ENTER**.

   The value of the formula, ***112085.15****, is entered in cell* ***B21****. When a function is not the only component of the formula, you must type the closing parenthesis before entering the function.*

6. Copy the formula across row **21** (Figure 5 - 12).

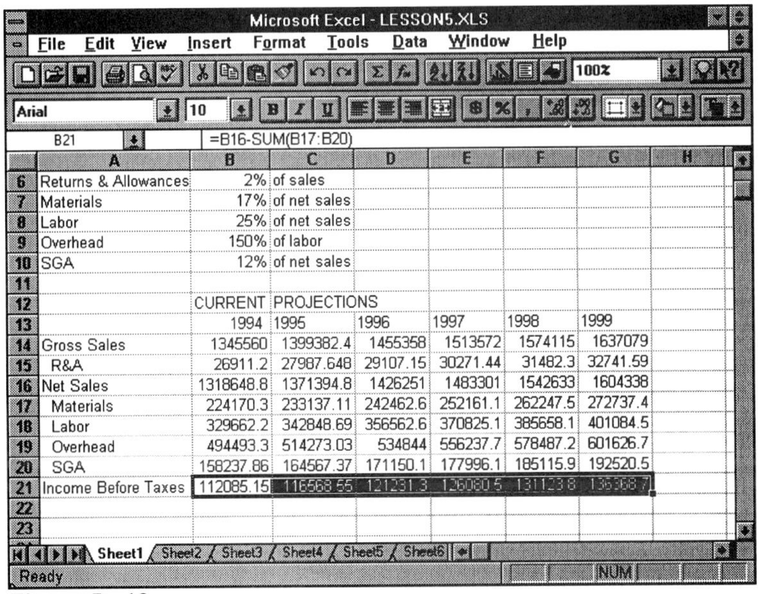

Figure 5 - 12

7. To identify the last column, enter **1995-1999** in **H12** and **Totals** in cell **H13.**

8. In **H14** enter a **sum** function to add the 1995-1999 predicted sales figures. You cannot use the range that the **AutoSum** function will enter because it will include the 1994 figure. Therefore, to create the sum for just 1995-1999:

   a. Select **H14.**

   b. Click on the **AutoSum** button.

   The range ***B14:G14*** *will be automatically entered into the function* ***(Figure 5 - 13).***

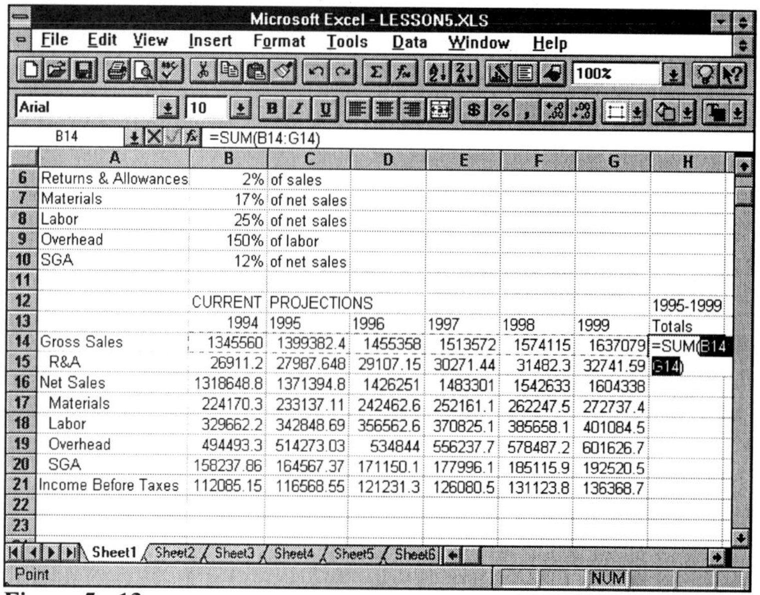

Figure 5 - 13

   c. Highlight the correct range, **C14:G14.**

   The range you selected will replace Excel's guessed range in the function.

   d. Enter the formula by clicking on the **enter box** or pressing **ENTER.**

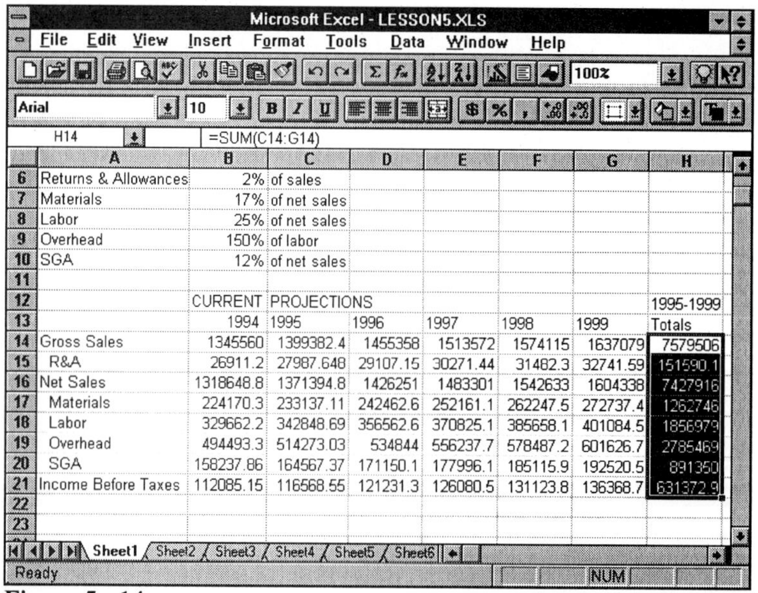

Figure 5 - 14

9. Copy the formula in cell **H14** down the column to cells **H15:H21** (Figure 5 - 14).
10. Use **FILE/Save As** to save the worksheet using the name **: 5yr**

Activity 5.5: Formatting the Worksheet

1. Center the heading **PROJECTIONS** over columns **C** through **G**.
2. Center align **CURRENT** in cell **B12**, **1995-1999** in cell **H12**, and **Totals** in **H13**. Center align each of the dates (**1994**, **1995**, etc.) in their cells.
3. Format the values in **B14:H14** and **B21:H21** using the Currency Style with no decimal places.
4. Select **B14:H21** and use **FORMAT/Column,Autofit** selection to display all values.

   If you are using Arial 10 point font, the worksheet may be too big to fit on the screen.
5. Format the values in **B15:H20** for Comma Style with no decimal places.

   PROBLEM SOLVER: *If you touch the sides of the window when using the mouse to define a range, the window may start to scroll very quickly. To avoid this, gently bump the side of the window and then move the mouse slightly in the other direction. Also remember that if you define a range which is smaller or larger than the desired range, use the* ***SHIFT+ARROW*** *keys to shrink or expand the range.*
6. Add bottom borders under cells **A13:H13** and **A20:H20**.

   *Figure 5 - 15 shows columns **A** through **G** of your worksheet.*

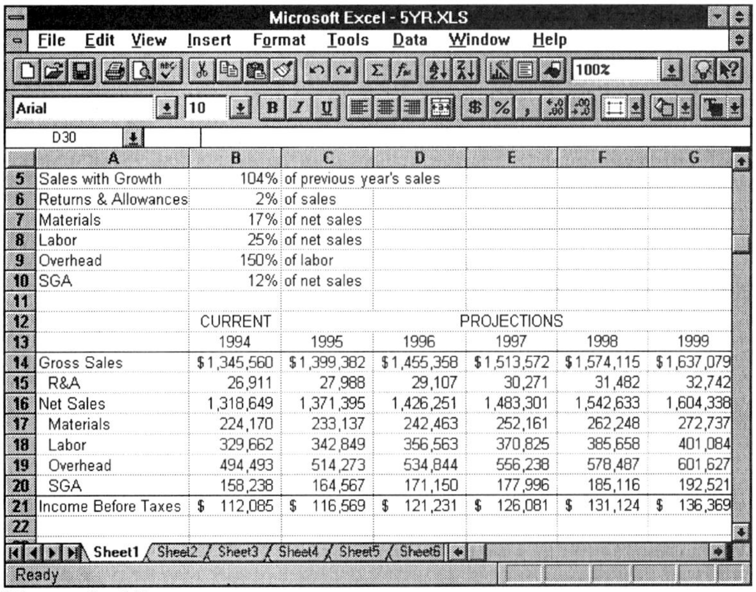

	A	B	C	D	E	F	G
5	Sales with Growth	104%	of previous year's sales				
6	Returns & Allowances	2%	of sales				
7	Materials	17%	of net sales				
8	Labor	25%	of net sales				
9	Overhead	150%	of labor				
10	SGA	12%	of net sales				
11							
12		CURRENT			PROJECTIONS		
13		1994	1995	1996	1997	1998	1999
14	Gross Sales	$1,345,560	$1,399,382	$1,455,358	$1,513,572	$1,574,115	$1,637,079
15	R&A	26,911	27,988	29,107	30,271	31,482	32,742
16	Net Sales	1,318,649	1,371,395	1,426,251	1,483,301	1,542,633	1,604,338
17	Materials	224,170	233,137	242,463	252,161	262,248	272,737
18	Labor	329,662	342,849	356,563	370,825	385,658	401,084
19	Overhead	494,493	514,273	534,844	556,238	578,487	601,627
20	SGA	158,238	164,567	171,150	177,996	185,116	192,521
21	Income Before Taxes	$ 112,085	$ 116,569	$ 121,231	$ 126,081	$ 131,124	$ 136,369
22							

Figure 5 - 15

7. **Save** the worksheet again using the same name.
8. Click on the **Print Preview** button or select **FILE/Print Preview**.

   Only part of the worksheet is displayed as it is too wide to fit on one piece of paper.
9. Click on the **Next** button to see the rest of the worksheet.
10. Click on the **Close** button to return to the worksheet.

PRINTING A LARGER WORKSHEET

Most worksheets which you create will be too big to fit on a single sheet of paper when you print. *Excel* will automatically divide the worksheet into pages. However, you often want to modify *Excel*'s decisions. Depending on the size of the worksheet and your needs, there are several ways to print worksheets which appear to be too large to fit on a page. Some of the changes that you can make using **PRINT/Page Setup** are:

- Change the orientation of the paper from portrait (the way the pages in this book are printed) to landscape (rotating the print so that the width of the page is 11 inches and the length is 8 1/2 inches).
- Decrease the margins.
- Tell *Excel* to **scale** the worksheet so that it fits on a specified number of pages (**Fit to** option on the **Page** tab of the **Page Setup** dialog box).
- Using **Print Titles** (on the **Sheet** tab of the **Page Setup** dialog box) to repeat one or more columns or rows on each page of the printout.

Since your worksheet will fit on a piece of paper if you turn it sideways, or in what is called *landscape orientation,* you will print it that way.

To print a worksheet in landscape orientation:

- Select **FILE/Page Setup**.
- Click on the **Page** tab if it is not already selected.
- Click on the **Landscape** option button.
- Make any other desired changes to the page setup, click on **OK** and print the document.

Activity 5.6: Printing in Landscape Orientation

1. Select **FILE/Page Setup**.
2. On the **Sheet** tab turn off **Gridlines**.
3. Click on the **Page** tab.
4. Click on the **Landscape** option button (Figure 5 - 16).

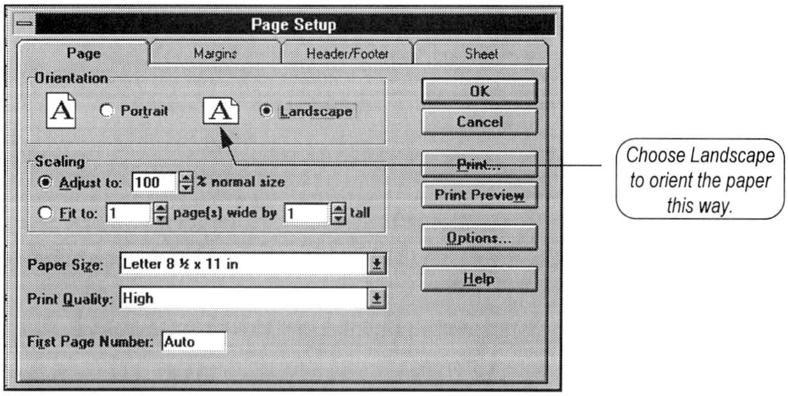

Figure 5 - 16

5. Click on the **Header/Footer** tab. Create a **Custom Header** which says: **Created by (your name)** in the left section. Delete **&[Tab]** from the center section.
6. Click on **OK**.
7. Print the document.
8. Press **CTRL+`** to display formulas.
9. Print the document.
10. Press **CTRL+`** to redisplay values.
11. **Save** the file again using the same name.

FREEZING COLUMNS AND ROWS ON THE SCREEN

If you have changed the column widths to fit the formatted values, you probably cannot see the whole worksheet Therefore, *Excel* lets you freeze one or more columns and/or rows on the screen so that they remain visible as you scroll the rest of the screen.

To freeze columns or rows:

- Click on the cell immediately to the right of any columns that you want to remain visible and immediately below any rows that should remain visible.
- Choose **WINDOW/Freeze Panes**.

To reset the screen so that all columns/rows scroll:

- Choose **WINDOW/Unfreeze Panes**.

CHANGING ASSUMPTIONS

We now want to see how your projections change if you change assumptions. What effect will the changed projections have on your projected 1995-1999 totals? When your worksheet was created, assumptions were placed on the worksheet. You could have instead created a formula for the next year's sales by multiplying the previous year's sales by 104%. However, that would not be good worksheet design. The assumptions were included on the worksheet so that it would be easy for anyone looking at the worksheet to see what the assumptions were, and so that if you change the assumptions, all of the formulas that depend on them will automatically change. This lets us use the worksheet for simple **What-If** analysis.

Activity 5.7: Viewing the Effects of Changed Assumptions

After the 5-Year Projection worksheet was created, it was shared with company officials. Some of them suggested that the assumptions weren't accurate. What would be the effect on the five year totals if the projected sales including growth was 106% instead of 104%? What if material costs could be held to 15% of net sales instead of 17%? In this activity you will see what the effects of these changes would be.

1. Scroll the screen so that row **4** is the top row on the screen.
2. To keep the assumptions, the row labels in column **A**, and the column labels in rows **12** and **13** on the screen at all times, click in cell **B14**.

3. Choose **WINDOW/Freeze Panes** (Figure 5-17).

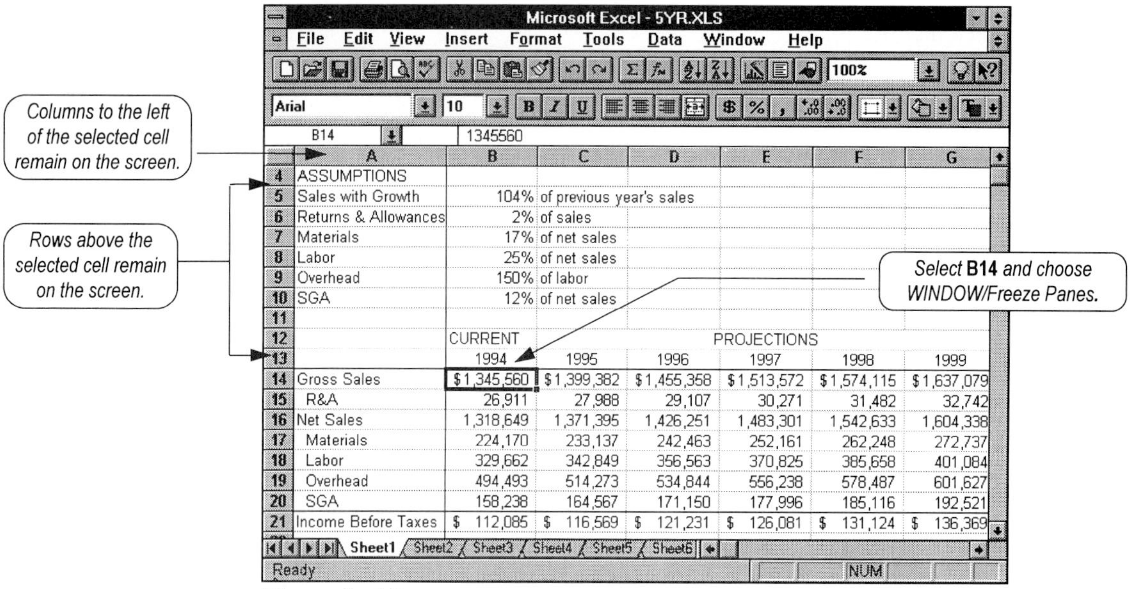

Figure 5 - 17

4. In cell **B5** enter: **106%**.
5. Compare your worksheet with your printout of the original worksheet. How many cells change? Scroll the screen so that you can see the values in all of the columns.
6. Change the materials percent in **B7** to **15%**.
7. Scroll the screen to see which values changed.
8. Choose **WINDOW/Unfreeze Panes** to remove the panes.
9. Use **FILE/Save As** to save the worksheet using the name: **new5yr**
10. Print the worksheet. Close the file.

SUMMARY

In the lesson you increased your ability to create useful formulas by learning to control if a formula adjusts when it is copied. You also learned new skills for viewing and printing larger worksheets. The problem you solved in this lesson involved using worksheets to make projections rather than analyze existing data. Independent Project 4.4 introduces another technique used in making projections.

KEY TERMS

Absolute cell reference
F4
Freezing panes
Landscape orientation
Mixed cell reference
Portrait orientation

INDEPENDENT PROJECTS

The four independent projects in Lesson 5 provide practice entering complex formulas that use relative and absolute cell referencing. Some projects also give you practice using and printing larger worksheets. In addition Independent Project 5.1 expands on your ability to create series and Independent Project 5.4 introduces Goal Seeking in What-If analyses.

Independent Project 5.1: Completing a Sales Worksheet

You work for a company which sells T-shirts. You are told to create a worksheet which compares the sales of each of three salespersons in the month of March. You are given a worksheet which contains all of the raw data. You need to compute the percent of sales for each salesperson for each week of the month; and each salesperson's total sales and total commission.

When you finish this project, your worksheet should resemble Figure 5 - 18.

T-Shirt Sales March						
Week of:	Blasek	% of Sales	Pierce	% of Sales	Selwyn	% of Sales
3/6/95	$ 300	23%	$ 645	34%	$ 724	43%
3/13/95	435	33%	267	14%	341	20%
3/20/95	234	18%	546	29%	234	14%
3/27/95	346	26%	432	23%	402	24%
Total	$ 1,315		$ 1,890		$ 1,701	
Comm%	25%		27%		29%	
Comm$	$ 328.75		$ 510.30		$ 493.29	

Figure 5 - 18

Use Figure 5 - 18 and the following instructions to help you complete the project:

1. Open **indpr5_1.xls**.
2. In **A6** enter: **Week of:**
3. In **A7** enter: **3/6/95**
4. You want to create a series, but instead of including every day you only want to include every seventh day (the beginning of each week). Therefore, when you point to the **fill handle**, press the **right** mouse button as you drag down to **A10**.
5. A shortcut menu will appear. Choose **Series**. The **Series** dialog box, which contains many options for creating series, appears. The pointer is in the **Step Value** text box. Type: **7** and then click on **OK**. A series of dates, 7 days apart will be entered.
6. **Left align** the dates that you just entered and format **Week of:** to match the other column labels.
7. In cell **B11** calculate the total sales for Blasek.
8. Copy the function to cells **D11** and **F11**. Remember, if you use **EDIT/Copy** and **EDIT/Paste** you can copy to more than one cell. To copy to the last cell either press **ENTER** instead of using **EDIT/Paste** or press the **ESC** key after pasting to the last cell, so that the copy command is ended and the moving border is removed from the cell(s) that were copied.
9. Enter the formula for the amount of commission for Blasek in cell **B16**. The commission is equal to the total sales multiplied by the commission percentage.
10. Copy the formula to cells **D16** and **F16**.
11. Format all three cells for Currency Style with 2 decimal places.
12. In cell **C7** calculate the percent of the month's sales that Blasek made in the first week of the month. The percent is equal to the Blasek's first week's sales divided by Blasek's total sales for the month. Make cells absolute as necessary so that the formula will adjust correctly when copied to the other weeks in the month.

13. Copy the formula to cells **C8:C10**.
14. Format the column using Percent style with no decimal places.
15. Create similar formulas for the other two salespersons. Format the results to match those in column **C.**
16. Since the **EDIT/Copy** and **EDIT/Fill** commands (or dragging the **fill handle**) copy cell formats as well as contents, part of the bottom border in row **10** is missing. Replace the bottom border under row **10**.
17. Save your worksheet using the name: **tshirt**
18. Print the worksheet with appropriate changes to the page setup.
19. Print the worksheet again displaying formulas.
20. Close and save the worksheet.

Independent Project 5.2: Completing a Sales Worksheet

Nationwide Sporting goods wants to project 1995 sales based on 1994 sales. The calculated projections will be based on an assumed growth rate and an assumed inflation rate, both of which have been entered into your worksheet. You will use the cells containing these assumptions in your formulas so that you can easily recalculate sales projections if the assumptions change. In order to complete the worksheet you will create some complex formulas using absolute cell addressing.

When you finish **projectn.xls**, your worksheet should resemble Figure 5 - 19.

Nationwide Sporting Goods			
Projected 1995 National Sales			
ASSUMPTIONS			
Growth Rate =	8.0%		
% Inflation =	3.6%		
	DOLLAR VOLUME SOLD		
		1995	1995
PRODUCT	1994	(in 1995 $)	(in 1994 $)
Baseball Bats	$ 16,928	$ 18,282	$ 17,647
Olympic Frisbees	21,064	22,749	21,959
Golf Club Sets	29,374	31,724	30,622
Athletic Wear	23,618	25,507	24,621
Kayaks	13,833	14,940	14,421
Tennis Raquets	19,818	21,403	20,660
Camping Equipment	23,332	25,199	24,323
Football Pads	30,251	32,671	31,536
Boxing Gloves	9,370	10,120	9,768
Totals	$ 187,588	$ 202,595	$ 195,555

Figure 5 - 19

Use Figure 5 - 19 and the following instructions to help you complete the project:

1. Open the file **indpr5_2.xls**. Cell **B6** contains the assumed growth rate and cell **B7** contains the assumed inflation rate. Sales data for 1994 has been included.
2. In cell **C12** enter a formula for the projected 1995 baseball sales in 1995 dollars. The projected sales are equal to the 1994 sales multiplied by the sum of 1 plus the projected growth rate. Remember to use absolute cell references for any cells which should not change

when the formula is copied down the column. Use parentheses when necessary for correct calculation.

3. Copy the formula from **C12** to the other cells in column **C**.
4. In **D12** enter a formula to calculate projected 1995 baseball sales in 1994 dollars, which is equal to the 1995 projected baseball sales divided by the sum of 1 plus the assumed inflation rate.
5. Copy the formula in **D12** down the column through **D20**.
6. Format **C13:D20** for Comma Style with no decimal places. Replace the bottom border under the cells in row **20**. Format **C12:D12** for Currency Style with no decimal places.
7. In **B21** enter a function to sum the 1994 product sales.
8. Copy the function from **B21** to **C21:D21** and format for Currency Style with no decimals.
9. Save the worksheet using the name: **projectn**
10. Change the page setup to remove gridlines and insert appropriate headers and footers. Print the worksheet.
11. Print the worksheet again displaying formulas.
12. Change the assumed **Growth Rate** to **6.5%** and the assumed **% Inflation** to **4.5%**.
13. Print the changed worksheet.
14. Save the worksheet as: **project2** and close.

Independent Project 5.3: Completing a Grading Worksheet

You are a teacher. **Indpr5_3.xls** contains the raw data on your students' test and project scores. You need to calculate a grade for each test and the average of the projects. The final grade is a weighted combination of the test average, final and average project scores. The data for each test is the number wrong. You need to calculate the score for each test, the average score for the midterm tests, the weighted scores for the three grade components and the final grade. The total number of points possible on each test and the weights for each of the three grade components are shown at the top of the worksheet.

When you finish this project, the first 29 rows of your worksheet should resemble Figure 5 - 20 although the formatting may be different.

CS202 Fall Semester Grades

Total points	
Test 1	44
Test 2	40
Final	36
Grade weights	
Tests	30%
Final	35%
Projects	35%

	Test 1		Test 2		Test Average		Final			Projects		
Student Initials	Points Missed	Grade	Points Missed	Grade	Average Grade	Weighted Grade	Points Missed	Grade	Weighted Grade	Average Grade	Weighted Grade	Final Grade
ab	2.50	94	2.00	95	95	28	6.25	83	29	9.40	33	90
cc	10.00	77	16.50	59	68	20	18.00	50	18	8.38	29	67
bg	16.30	63	14.25	64	64	19	15.00	58	20	7.40	26	65
sg	2.00	95	1.00	98	96	29	5.00	86	30	10.00	35	94
mh	1.25	97	1.00	98	97	29	4.00	89	31	9.20	32	93
mj	6.75	85	5.00	88	86	26	2.25	94	33	8.50	30	88
gj	2.50	94	2.00	95	95	28	7.75	78	27	9.50	33	89
rj	21.00	52	11.50	71	62	19	13.75	62	22	8.95	31	71
kl	4.00	91	1.50	96	94	28	3.00	92	32	9.70	34	94
cm	1.00	98	2.50	94	96	29	2.00	94	33	9.60	34	95
um	4.25	90	4.50	89	90	27	14.25	60	21	9.00	32	80
fm	3.00	93	1.00	98	95	29	2.75	92	32	8.30	29	90
wp	4.50	90	3.00	93	91	27	2.00	94	33	10.00	35	95
ap	3.50	92	2.00	95	94	28	5.50	85	30	9.80	34	92
br	7.50	83	2.00	95	89	27	5.75	84	29	9.80	34	90
jr	1.00	98	-	100	99	30	-	100	35	9.70	34	99

Figure 5 - 20

Use Figure 5 - 20 and the following instructions to help you complete the project:

1. Open the file **indpr5_3.xls**. Cells **B4:B6** contain the total possible points for each test. Cells **B8:B10** contain the weights that you give each of the three components of the final grade.
2. Scroll to the right so that you can see all of the columns in the worksheet.
3. Make **A1** the active cell again.
4. Since the worksheet is so wide, the first thing that you should do is freeze panes so that you can see the student initials, the total points per test and the grade weights at all times. Scroll the screen so that row **3** is the first row visible. Click on **C14** and **freeze panes**.
5. The formula for the Test 1 Grade (**C14**) should divide the difference between the total points possible (**B4**) and the points missed (**B14**) by the total points possible (**B4**) and then multiply by **100**. Remember to make any cell references that should NOT change when the formula is copied, absolute. Also use parentheses where necessary. You may want to write down the formula before you create it.
6. Copy the formula down column **C**. Use Figure 5 - 20 to check results.
7. Create a formula for Test 2 in cell **E14** similar to the formula for Test 1 and copy it down the column.
8. In **F14** create a formula for the average test grade. Since the two test grades are not next to each other, it is probably easier to enter a formula which adds the two test grades and then divides the sum by 2, than it is to use the average function. Copy the formula down the column.
9. In **G14** enter a formula which calculates the weighted test grade. The weighted test grade is equal to the average test grade multiplied by the weight for test grades (cell **B8**). Copy the formula down the columns.
10. In **I14** create a formula for the final grade. This should be similar to the formulas for the grades on tests 1 and 2. Copy this formula down the column.
11. In **J14** calculate the weighted final grade and copy it down the column.
12. In **L14** create a formula for the weighted project grade. Since the projects were graded on a scale from 1 to 10 instead of 1 to 100, the weighted project grade equals the average project grade multiplied by the weight multiplied by 10. Copy the formula down the column.
13. In **M14** create a formula for the final grade. The final grade is equal to the total of the weighted test average grade, the weighted final grade and the weighted projects grade. Copy the formula down the column.
14. Unfreeze panes.
15. Format all of the grades and weighted grades that you calculated using Comma Style with no decimal places.
16. Format the three columns that are labeled **Points Missed** and the **Average Grade** for **Projects** for Comma Style with 2 decimal places.
17. Save the worksheet as: **grades**
18. Print the worksheet with appropriate headers and footers. Use Landscape orientation.
19. Print the worksheet again displaying formulas. Make sure the header or footer contains a page number.
20. Close and save the worksheet.

Independent Project 5.4: Completing a Common Size Income Statement

You are an employee of ECAP Corporation. You have been asked to create a "Common Size Income Statement" for 1993 and 1994. Common Size Income Statements show the costs and expenses for a period in relation to the sales for that period. The purpose of common size statements is to emphasize relationships rather than numbers. These statements are important when performing financial statement analysis. **Indpr5_4.xls** contains the data that you need for your analysis. You need to add the formulas and format the results of the formulas.

1. When finished, your worksheet should contain:
   - The following formulas:

Result	Calculation
Gross Profit for 1993 and for 1994	Net Sales minus Cost of Goods Sold
Operating Income for 1993 and for 1994	Gross profit for the year minus General & Administration and Selling Expenses
Income before Taxes for 1993 and for 1994	Operating Income for the year minus Interest Expense
%1993 and %1994	For each item, its percent of the Net Sales

Table 6 - 1

   - In all cases, create formulas that use appropriate cell referencing so that they can be copied down columns or across rows.
   - Appropriate formatting.

2. Save the file as: **income**
3. Print the worksheet using appropriate page setup and identifying headers or footers.
4. Print the worksheet showing formulas.
5. Use your worksheet to answer the following question: Was before tax income in 1994 lower than in 1993 simply because sales were lower, or were there other reasons?
6. In the chapter you performed what-if analysis by changing assumptions. There are no explicitly stated assumptions in this worksheet, but you can still perform what-if analysis. Change the value for Cost of Goods Sold in 1994 until it is the same percent of Net Sales as it was in 1993. **HINT**: You can arrive at the appropriate value for Cost of Goods Sold by trying various numbers until the percent is the same as it was for 1993, or you can use the **TOOLS/Goal Seek** command to let *Excel* calculate the value for you. Use **Help** in the **Goal Seek** dialog box to help you fill in the dialog box (you want to set the cell containing the %1994 Cost of Goods Sold to 60% by changing the 1994 Cost of Goods Sold).
7. After you make that change, what is the income before taxes? Is it a higher or lower percent of net sales than the 1993 income before taxes?
8. Save your worksheet as **income2.xls**. Print the worksheet. Use a header or footer which indicates that the value of the cost of goods sold is a goal and not the actual figure.

Lesson 6

Charts

Objectives

In this lesson you will learn how to:

- Differentiate between the types of charts
- Define the parts of a chart
- Use the ChartWizard to create charts
- Embed a chart in the worksheet
- Format the text in a chart
- Create a three-dimensional chart
- Create a chart on its own sheet
- Change the type and AutoFormat of the chart
- Format Y-axis values
- Edit data used in a chart
- Print charts
- Switch between sheets in a workbook
- Rename sheets in a workbook
- Print multiple sheets in a workbook

CHARTING

Often the best way to get an understanding of the patterns in worksheet data is by creating a picture — or chart of the data. *Excel* makes this task easy by providing the ChartWizard to help you create the chart. Once the chart is created, you can easily enhance or edit it. More importantly, since the chart is linked to the worksheet, changes made to the worksheet are instantly reflected in the chart.

Excel has 14 different types of charts: area, bar, column, line, pie, doughnut, radar, XY scatter, 3-D area, 3-D bar, 3-D column, 3-D line, 3-D pie, and surface. Each type has at least one *subtype* or variation that can also be created. In addition, combination charts mixing column and line charts or column and area charts can be created. The most common types of charts are described in Table 6 - 1.

PROJECT 1 DESCRIPTION

In this lesson you will add charts to the worksheets created in Lessons 1 and 3. In the project in Lesson 1 you created a worksheet that calculated the hours worked by three consultants as well as their salaries, billing amount, and profit generated. Now you are going to enhance that worksheet by adding a chart. You have been told to create a chart that shows the proportion, or percent, of the profit contributed by each employee. The most common chart used to illustrate how a total is divided into parts is a *pie* chart. You will *embed*, or place, the pie chart immediately below the worksheet data on the same sheet as the data. When finished your worksheet will resemble Figure 6 - 1.

Type of Chart	Example	Use
Pie, 3-D Pie	Figure 6 - 1	Compares the percent of the total contributed by each part; can only be used to compare one series of data.
Column, 3-D Column	Figure 6 - 22	Compares noncontinuous items; the value of each item is displayed as a vertical column.
Bar, 3-D Bar	Figure 6 - 32	The same as a column chart except that each item is displayed horizontally.
Line, 3-D Line	Figure 6 - 33	Compares items, usually over time; used to show trends in data.
Area, 3-D Area	Figure 6 - 34	Shows the continuous change in volume of multiple data series; usually shows changes over time.
Stacked Column	Figure 6 - 36	A subtype of the column chart, the columns are stacked for all series being compared on top of each other so that the totals can also be compared.
100% Column	Figure 6 - 35 Nos. 5, 10	A subtype of the column chart, 100% columns compare each data series as a percent of the whole.
Combination	Figure 6 - 42	Uses two different formats, usually bar and line or bar and area, to compare data of different types or to make one series of data stand out from the rest.

Table 6 - 1: Types of Charts

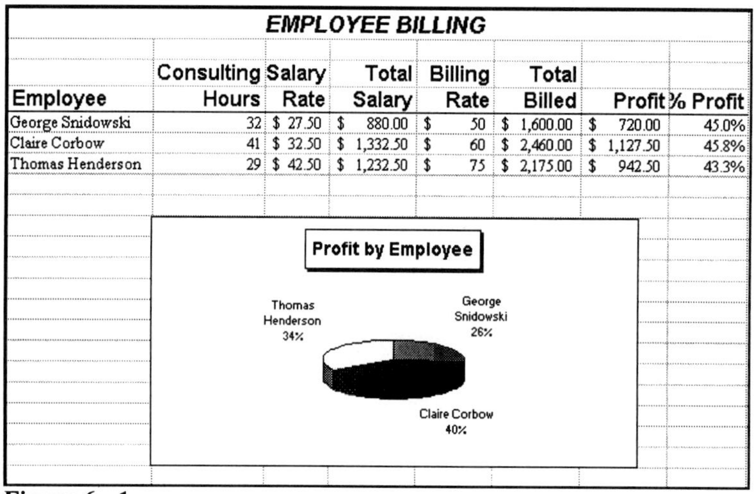

Figure 6 - 1

A PIE CHART

Pie charts are often the easiest to understand. Pie charts contain only one *data series*. A *data series* is a series of related data such as the hours worked by the employees or the profit generated by each employee. In *Excel* the data for each series is from a single worksheet row or column. Each value (or cell) in the series is called a *data point*. In our pie chart the data series is the profit resulting from the three employees' consulting. It is located in cells **G5:G7** . The profit generated by each employee is a data point and will be represented by a wedge of the pie. A pie chart must include information that identifies each wedge or slice of the pie.

In your pie chart the employee names are the identifying information. In a pie chart this information can be included right next to each wedge or in a *legend* that lists each employee name and the color or pattern used in the wedge for that person. *Excel* also allows you to add a title for the chart while you are creating it.

USING THE CHARTWIZARD

The ChartWizard works just like the FunctionWizard. Just as the FunctionWizard provides a series of steps that help you enter a function, the ChartWizard guides you through the creation of a chart.

To use the ChartWizard to create a new chart embedded on the worksheet:

- Select a worksheet range. The range should include the data series to be charted. It often also includes the information for the legend and for some of the titles used on the chart.
- Click on the **ChartWizard** button or select **INSERT/Chart,On This Sheet.**

  The mouse pointer will change to a
- To let the **ChartWizard** size the chart for you, position the mouse pointer where you want the upper left corner of the chart to be and click the mouse button. To position the chart yourself, place the mouse pointer at the point where you want the upper left corner of the chart to be. Click and drag until the rectangle formed is the size and shape that you want the chart to be. Release the mouse button.
- In the **ChartWizard - Step 1 of 5** dialog box, confirm that the correct range has been entered and click on the **Next** button.
- In the **ChartWizard - Step 2 of 5** dialog box, click on the chart type of your choice and click on the **Next** button.
- The **ChartWizard - Step 3 of 5** dialog box displays the *AutoFormats* (predefined formats) available for the chart type you selected. Click on your preferred format for the chart and click on the **Next** button.
- The **ChartWizard - Step 4 of 5** dialog box displays a sample chart of your data using the chart type and format you have selected. *Excel* has guessed that each data series is in either a row or a column. If this guess is incorrect, click on the other option. If you have included any text that can be used for labels on the chart, tell *Excel* how many rows and/or columns are to be used for each kind of label. When the Sample Chart is correct, click on the **Next** button.
- The **ChartWizard - Step 5 of 5** dialog box also includes a Sample Chart. Indicate whether or not you want a legend. Type a **Chart Title**, if desired. If you are creating a chart that has X and Y axes (we will discuss these later), type titles for these axes. Click on **Finish**.

If you notice a mistake in your chart when you are in any of the **ChartWizard** dialog boxes, use the **Back** button to return to previous dialog boxes.

Activity 6.1: Creating a Pie Chart

In this activity you will create a pie chart that shows the percent of the total profit contributed by each employee.

1. Start *Excel* and open **consult2.xls**. (If you have not completed Lesson 2, you can use **consult.xls**.)
2. The data for the chart is the nonadjacent range **A5:A7** and **G5:G7.** Select the range **A5:A7**. Press the **CTRL** key and, while keeping it depressed, select the range **G5:G7** (Figure 6 - 2).

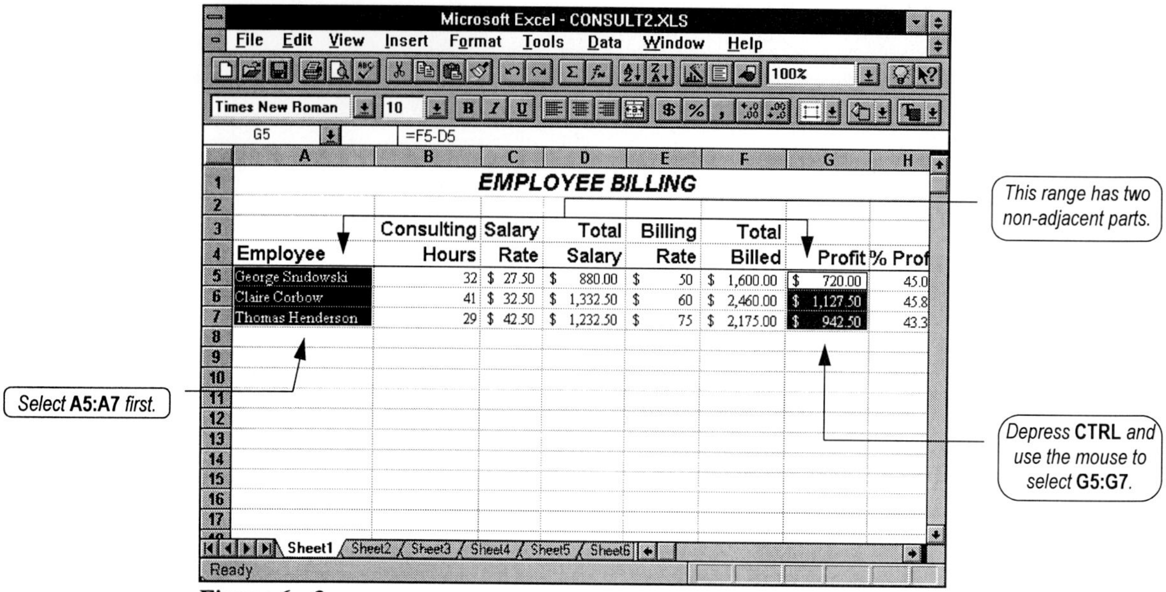

Figure 6 - 2

3. Choose **INSERT/Chart,On This Sheet** or click on the **ChartWizard** button.

   The mouse pointer changes to a + *when you move the pointer onto the worksheet grid.*

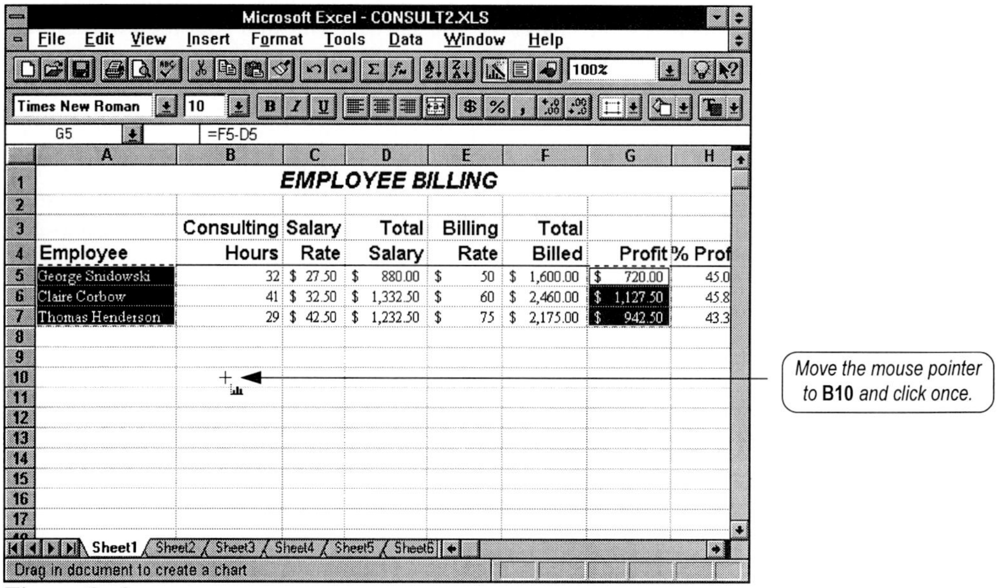

Figure 6 - 3

4. Point anywhere in cell **B10** (Figure 6 - 3) and click the left mouse button once to let *Excel* automatically place the chart.

   The first ***ChartWizard*** *dialog box (Figure 6 - 4) appears. The range you selected is entered in the* ***Range*** *text box.*

5. In the **ChartWizard - Step 1 of 5** dialog box, click on **Next**.

Figure 6 - 4

6. In the **ChartWizard - Step 2 of 5** dialog box, click on the **Pie** (Figure 6 - 5) and then click on **Next**.

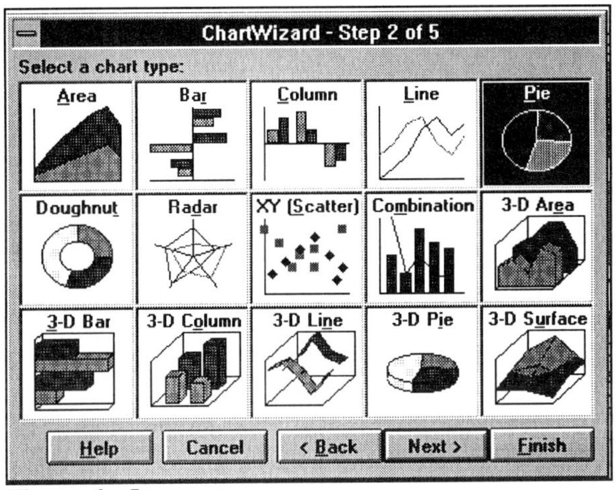

Figure 6 - 5

7. In the **ChartWizard - Step 3 of 5** dialog box, click on the format number **6** (Figure 6 - 6) to display the percent represented by each employee's part of the profit. Click on **Next**.

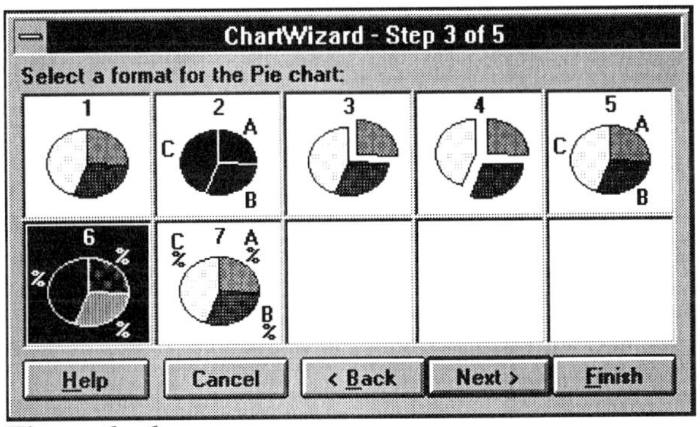

Figure 6 - 6

8. To make **ChartWizard - Step 4 of 5** dialog box resemble Figure 6 - 7:
   a. The data series is in a **Column** (**G**—the profits generated by each employee), not a row. If the Rows option button is selected, click on **Columns.**

b. The **First 1 Column** (**A**—the names of the employees) will be used as the pie slice labels and the **First 0 Rows** are used for the chart title. If you need to change either of these numbers, click on the ▲ to increase the number in the spin box or the ▼ to decrease the number.

c. When your dialog box matches Figure 6 - 7 click on **Next**.

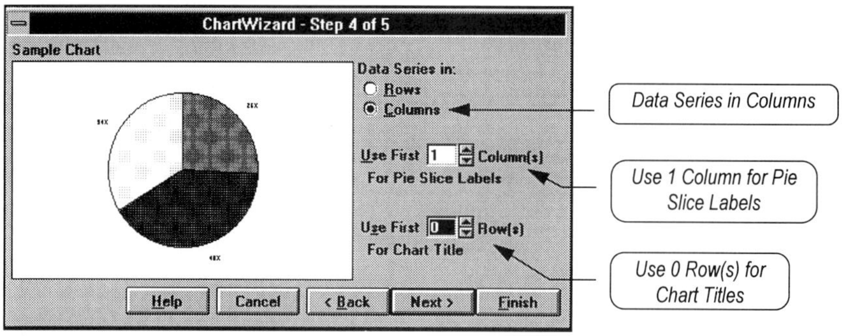

Figure 6 - 7

9. In the **ChartWizard - Step 5 of 5** dialog box, click on the **Yes** option button to add a legend.

   A legend identifying each wedge of the pie is added to the Sample Chart (Figure 6 - 8).

10. Click in the **Chart Title** text box and type: **Profit by Employee**

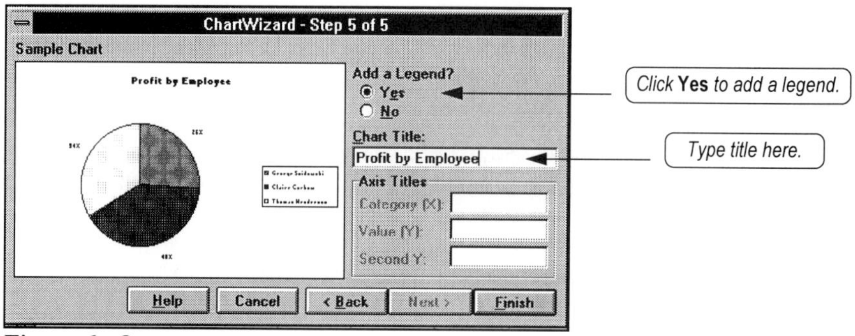

Figure 6 - 8

*The Axis Titles are all in light print, and therefore unusable, because **Pie** charts do not have X and Y axes.*

11. The dialog box should resemble Figure 6 - 8. Click on **Finish**.

    *Excel centers the chart under the data on the worksheet beginning in the cell you clicked in. The **Chart** tool bar is also displayed. It may be displayed as a rectangle on the screen as in Figure 6 - 9 or it may be along one of the borders of the worksheet. The chart is selected (as indicated by the selection squares on the corners and sides of the chart).*

12. Point to each of the buttons on the Chart toolbar. Look at the name of the button and read the description of the button that appears on the Status Bar.

13. Click anywhere on the worksheet outside of the chart.

The worksheet is no longer selected. The selection squares and the Chart toolbar no longer appear on the screen.

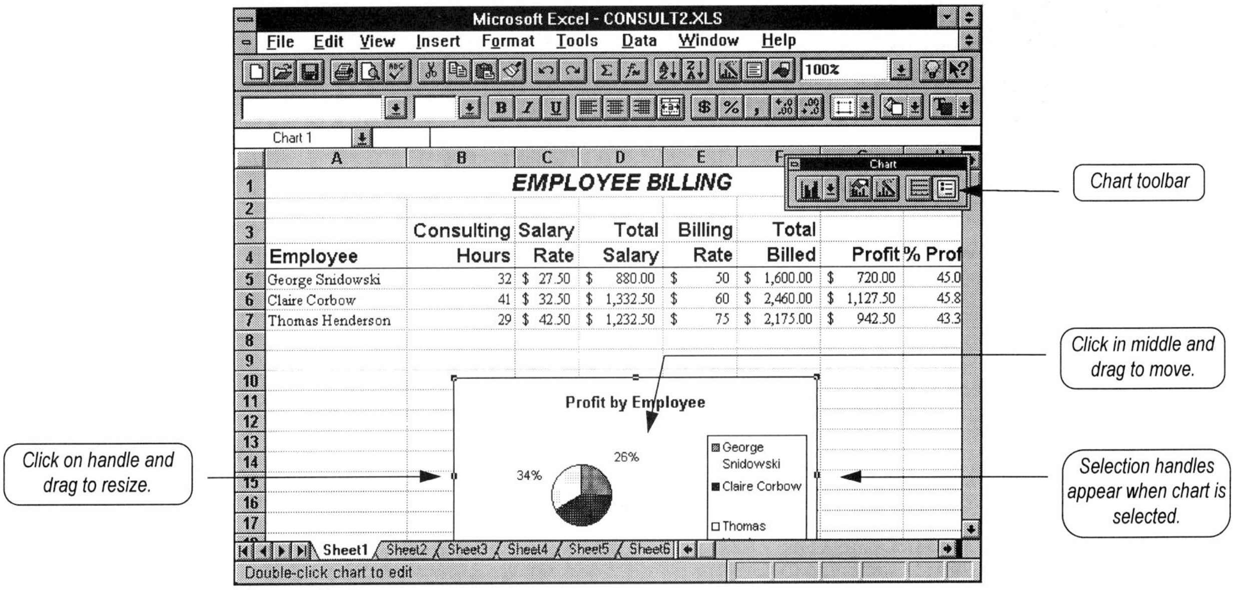

Figure 6 - 9

14. Use **FILE/Save As** to save the worksheet with the file name: **consultp.xls**

MOVING AND SIZING EMBEDDED CHARTS

Embedded charts can be moved and sized on the worksheet.

To move an embedded chart:

- Click on the chart once to select it, if it is not already selected.
- Point with the mouse anywhere in the chart. Click and drag the chart to the new location.

To resize an embedded chart:

- Click on the chart once to select it, if it is not already selected.
- Point with the mouse to any of the selection squares on the chart borders.
- When the mouse pointer changes to a ↔, drag until the chart is the size and shape you want.

Activity 6.2: Moving and Resizing an Embedded Chart

1. Click anywhere on the chart to select it.
2. Point to the middle of the chart and drag it so that its left border is touching the left border of the worksheet and the top border is along the gridline between rows **9** and **10** (Figure 6 - 10).

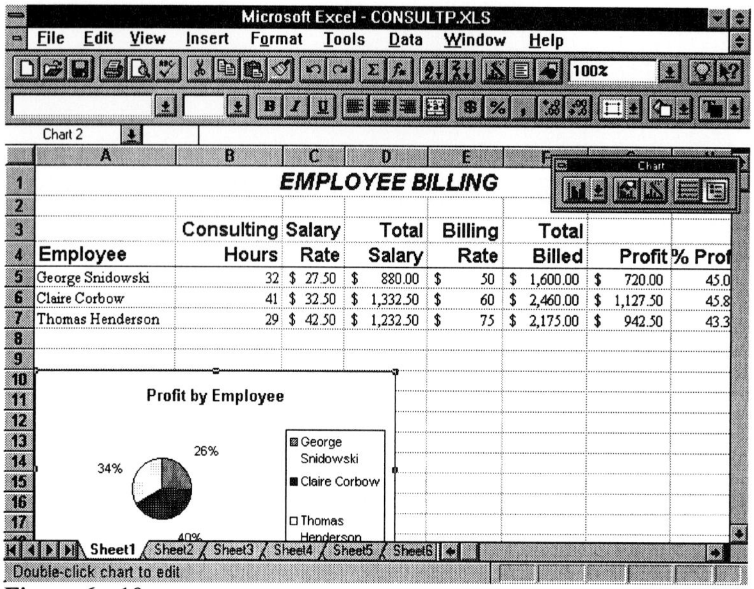

Figure 6 - 10

3. Click the on the vertical scroll bar to scroll the worksheet until row **21** is visible.
4. Point to the selection square in the bottom right corner of the chart frame. When the mouse pointer changes to a ↔, click and drag until the right border is approximately on the line between column **E** and **F** and the bottom border is on the gridline between row **21** and **22.** Release the mouse button.
5. Point to the middle of the chart, make sure the pointer is a and drag it again so that the left frame border is on the gridline between columns **A** and **B** (or wherever the chart is approximately horizontally centered on your worksheet) as in Figure 6 - 11.

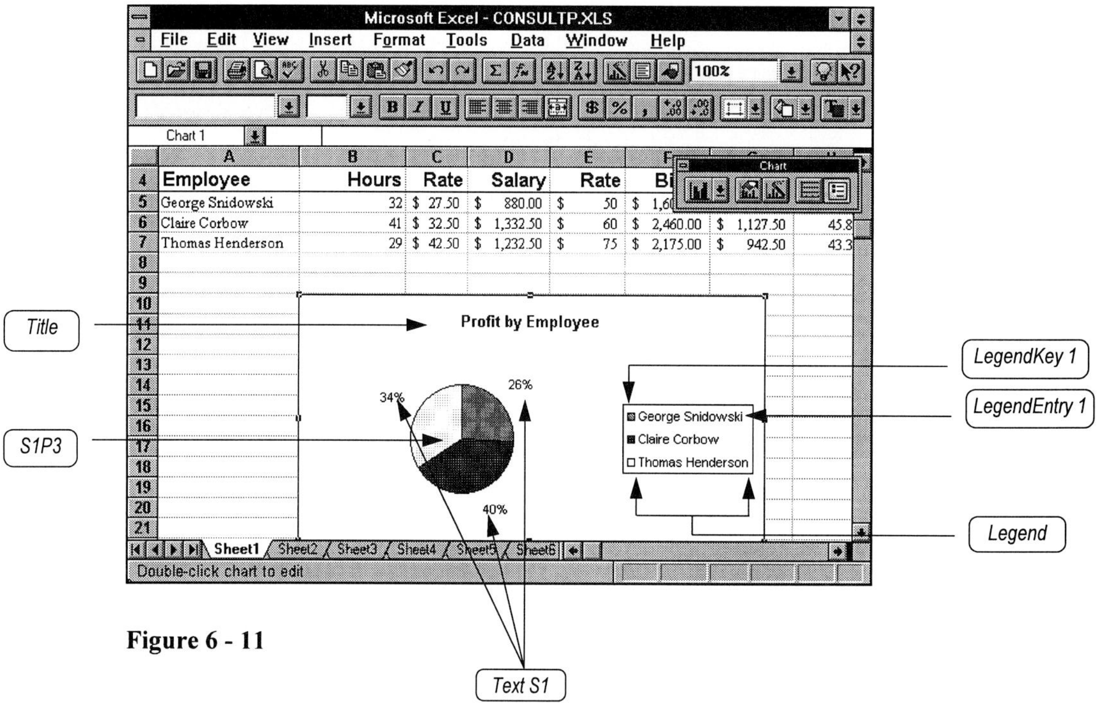

Figure 6 - 11

6. Click outside of the chart to deselect it.

MODIFYING AN EMBEDDED CHART

Once created an *Excel* chart can be modified in many ways. The chart type can be changed. You can insert, delete, or change titles, legends, data points, and gridlines. Fonts and colors can be changed, and borders, arrows, and other graphic objects can be added. You will have an opportunity to use a few of these options in this project and the next one. Once you learn the procedures, however, you can experiment with other changes using **Help** when you run into problems. Figure 6 - 11 indicates *Excel's* names for the different parts of the chart that can be modified. *Excel* calls each of these parts of the chart *items*.

To select an embedded chart so that it can be modified:

- Double-click on the chart.

  The chart is surrounded by a different frame and the names and contents of the menus change to the chart menus.

To select a new AutoFormat for the chart:

- Choose **FORMAT/AutoFormat**.
- Choose a new chart type from the **Galleries** list box if desired.
- Choose the **AutoFormat** of your choice and click on **OK.**

To format a part of the chart:

- Click on the part of the chart that you want to format. *Excel* indicates the selected part by surrounding it with small squares and displaying its name in the **name box** (left end) of the Formula Bar. To select one entry in a legend, data series, etc., click once to select the entire group and then click a second time on the specific item that you want to select.
- Click on the selected item with the **right** mouse button to display a shortcut menu. (You may click on the object with the **right** mouse button without first clicking with the **left** mouse button. However, when you are first using charts it is easier to first select the part of the chart with the left mouse button, make sure you have made the correct selection, and then click on that same selection with the right mouse button.)
- Choose the formatting command from the shortcut menu and make the desired changes to the dialog box.

CAUTION: *If you click outside of the chart frame during editing, the chart will no longer be selected. Double click on the chart again to select it.*

ALTERNATE METHODS: *You can also change the format of a chart item by a) double-clicking on the item and then making changes to the dialog box that appears; or b) clicking on the item and then using the Formatting Toolbar to make the changes; or c) clicking on the item and then using the **FORMAT** menu commands.*

Activity 6.3: Changing the Format of Parts of the Chart

After looking at the chart you decide that you would rather have a three dimensional pie instead of the current two-dimensional pie. Also, you would prefer the pie section labels to appear next to the wedges instead of in a separate legend. You also decide to format the title of the chart so that it stands out more.

1. Double-click anywhere in the chart.

   The frame of the chart should change. The Chart toolbar is displayed somewhere on the screen and the menu changes to those commands used with charts.

2. Press the **RIGHT ARROW** key on the keyboard once. One part of the chart will be selected (Figure 6 - 12). Look at the name of the selected item in the **name box** of the Formula Bar. Keep pressing the **RIGHT ARROW** key until **chart** appears in the **name box** again.

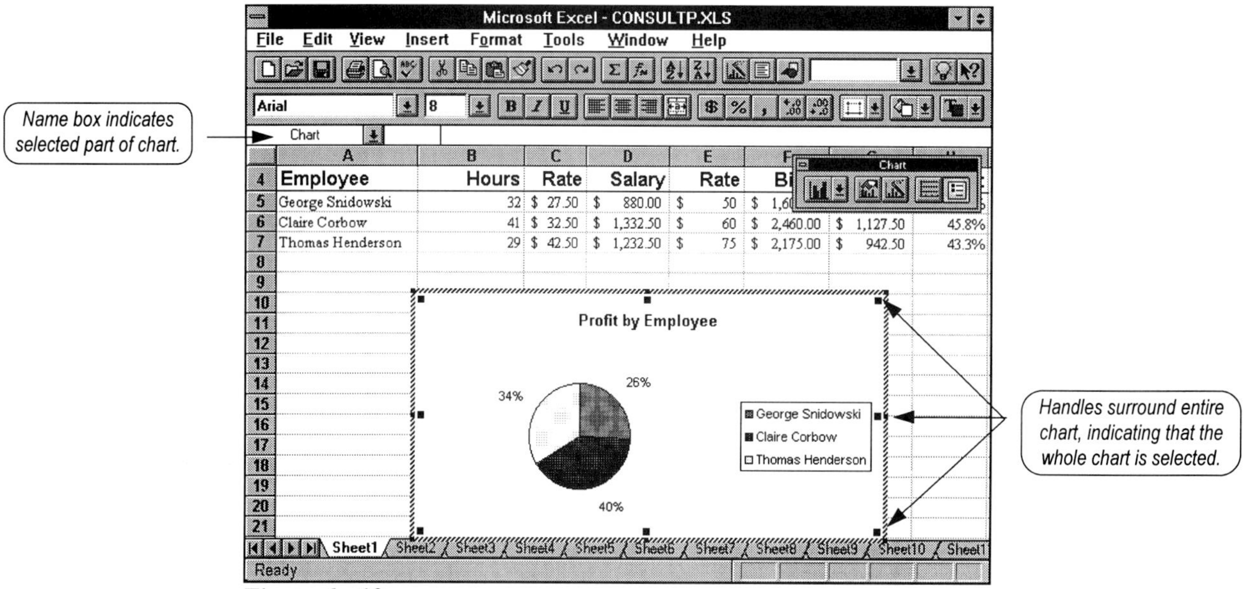

Figure 6 - 12

3. Choose **FORMAT/AutoFormat**.
4. In the **AutoFormat** dialog box scroll the **Galleries** list to display **3-D Pie**. Click on **3-D Pie**.
5. Choose format number 7 (Figure 6 - 13) to display labels and percents next to each pie slice. Click on **OK**.

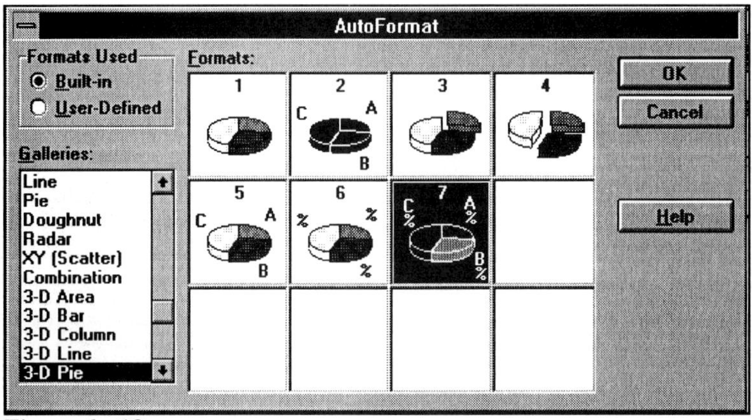

Figure 6 - 13

6. The legend is no longer necessary, so it should be deleted. Point anywhere in the legend and click once.

Small squares appear at the corners and sides of the legend and the item name, ***Legend,*** *appears in the* ***name box*** *(Figure 6 - 14).*

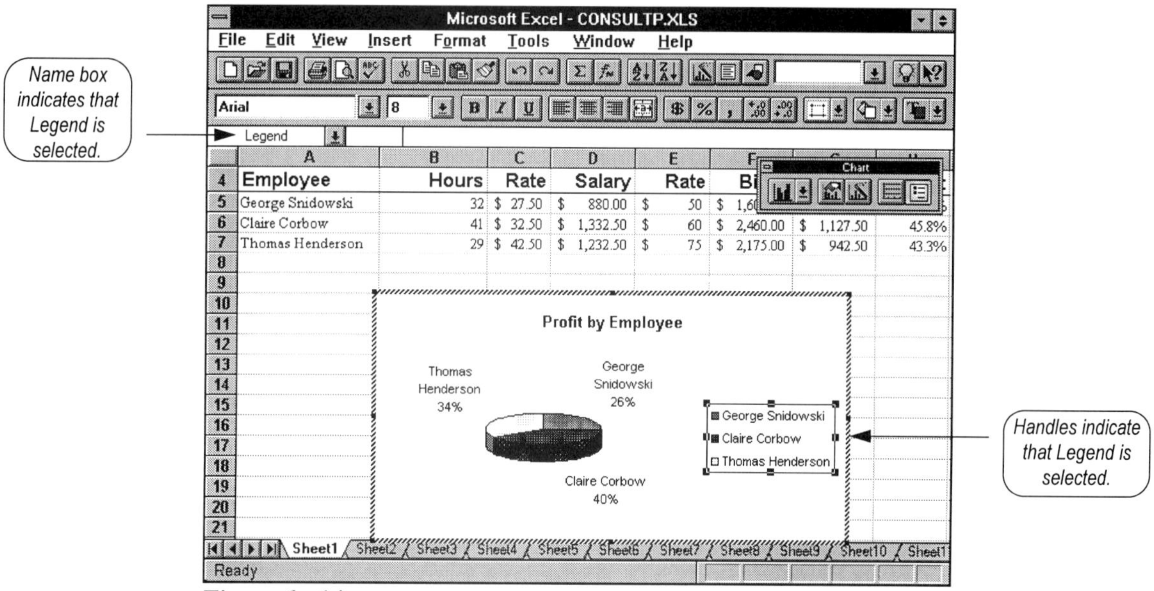

Figure 6 - 14

7. With the mouse pointer still pointing anywhere in the legend, click the **right** mouse button once to display the shortcut menu (Figure 6 - 15).

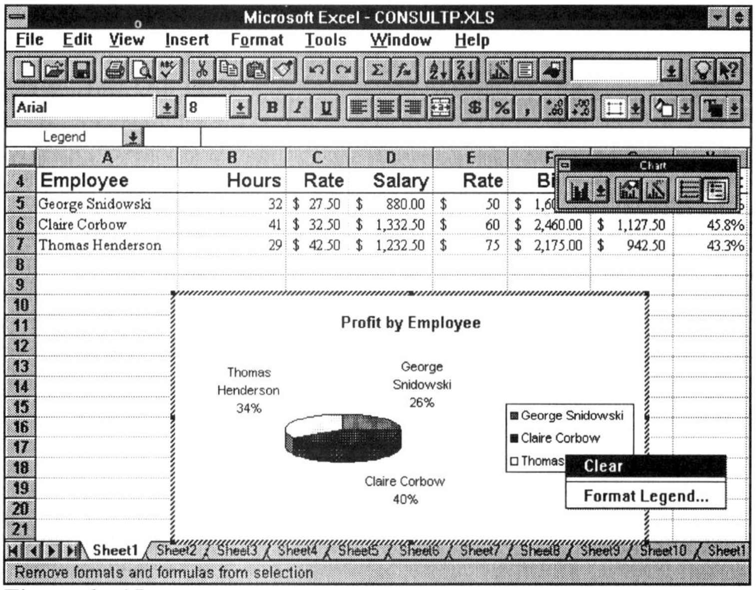

Figure 6 - 15

8. Click on **Clear** to remove the legend.
9. To center the pie chart in the frame, choose **FORMAT/AutoFormat**. Format **7** should still be chosen. Click on **OK**. (Figure 6 - 16 shows the pie chart without the rest of the screen.)

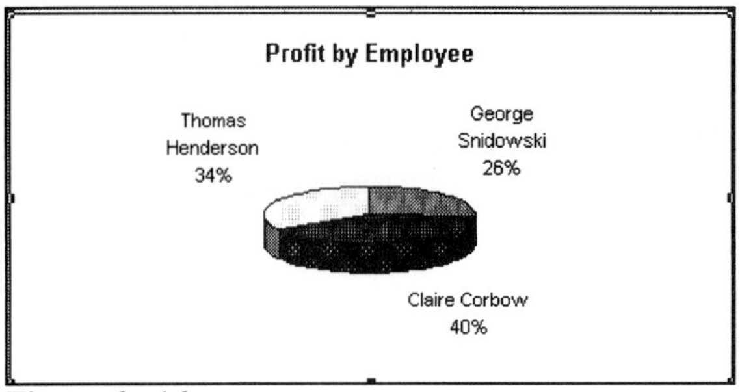

Figure 6 - 16

To enhance the chart title:

10. Click anywhere on the chart title.
11. While still pointing to the chart title, click the **right** mouse button (Figure 6 - 17).

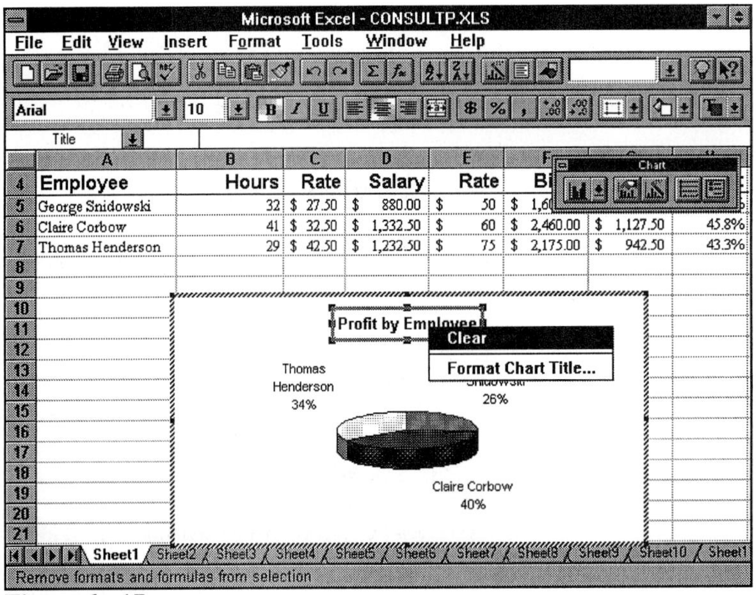

Figure 6 - 17

12. Select **Format Chart Title** from the shortcut menu.

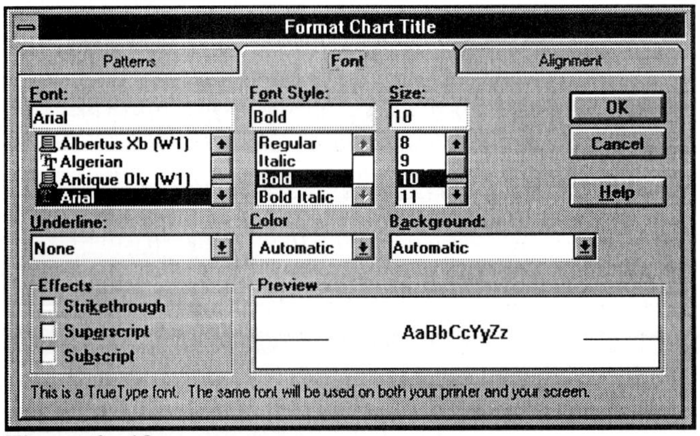

Figure 6 - 18

13. Click on the **Font** tab if it is not already selected.

    *The **Font** tab displays the same choices as you used in the worksheet when formatting cells (Figure 6 - 18).*

14. Choose a **Size** of **11**.
15. Click on the **Patterns** tab.
16. Click on the **Shadow** check box to mark the box.

    *As soon as you mark **Shadow**, the **Border** changes from **None** to **Automatic**, because a border must be inserted before it can have a shadow (Figure 6 - 19).*

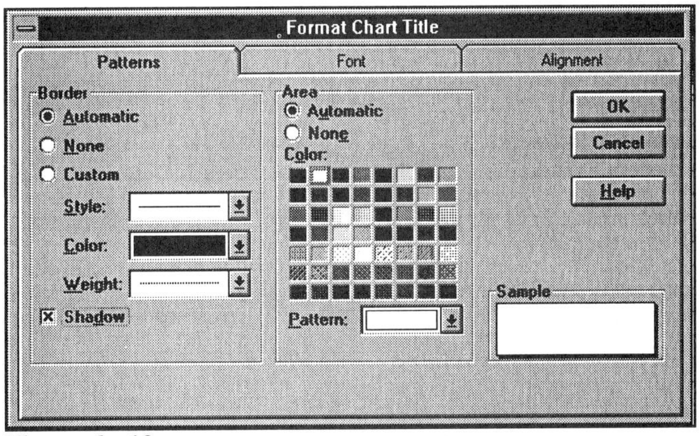

Figure 6 - 19

17. Click on **OK**.

    The title, Profit by Employee, is larger and is enclosed in a border with a shadow (Figure 6 - 20).

18. With the left mouse button, click on **George Snidowski** or any of the other labels.

    ***Text S1** (for Text, Series 1) appears in the **name box** on the Formula Bar. All three of the wedge labels should be selected (Figure 6 - 20) If only **George Snidowski** is selected, click on a blank part of the chart and then click back on George's name.*

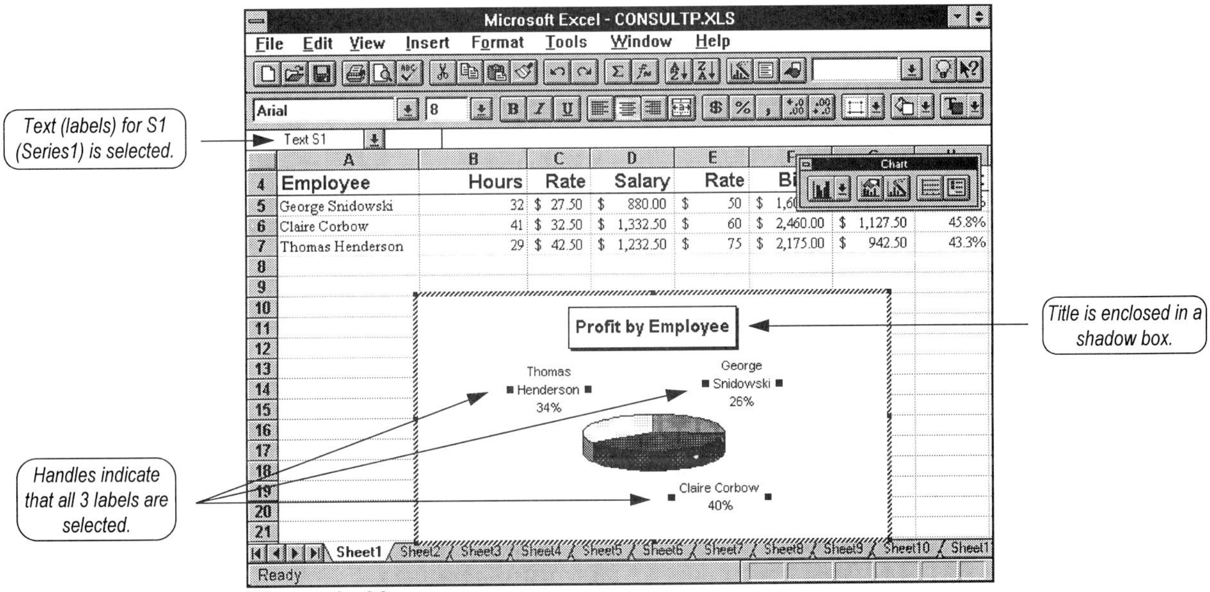

Figure 6 - 20

19. Click on the **Bold** button on the formatting toolbar.

    The wedge labels are in bold.

    PROBLEM SOLVER: If the titles become too wide to fit on one line, point to the selection square in the middle of the chart frame. When the mouse pointer changes to a ↔, click and drag until the chart is wide enough.

20. Click twice on the worksheet outside of the chart frame to exit from editing the chart (Figure 6 - 21).

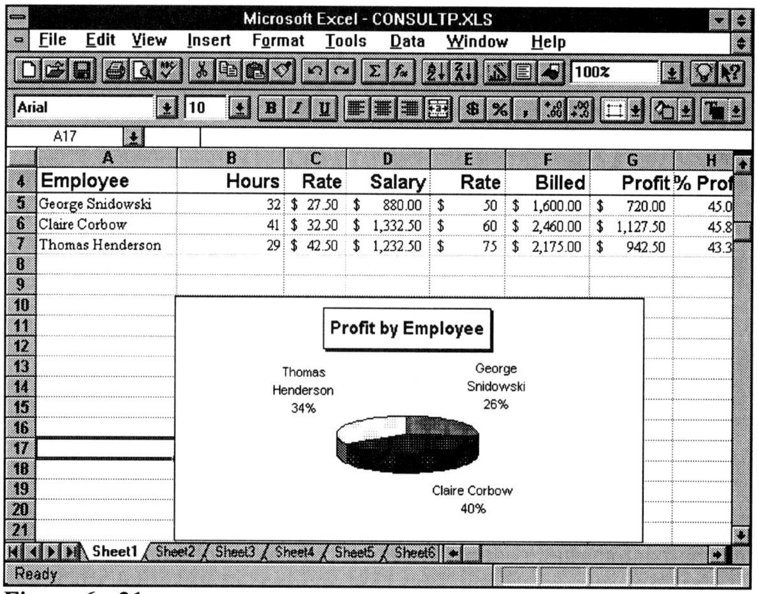

Figure 6 - 21

21. **Save** the worksheet again.

PRINTING AN EMBEDDED WORKSHEET

Now you're ready to print the worksheet and the chart. Printing a worksheet with an embedded chart is exactly the same as printing a worksheet that doesn't contain a chart.

Activity 6.4: Printing a Worksheet with a Chart

1. Click on the **Print Preview** button to see what your worksheet and chart will look like when printed.
2. **Print** the worksheet.
3. **Close** the file. **Exit** from *Excel* or continue with the next project.

PROJECT 2 DESCRIPTION

In the second project in this lesson, you will add a chart to the **NATN2.XLS** worksheet that you created in Lesson 3. The **NATN2.XLS** worksheet summarizes the 1994 sales by product and region. Column, bar, or line charts are usually used to show trends or compare data. You will create a column chart (Figure 6-22) to visually compare the sales of the products in the different regions. Unlike pie charts, column charts can contain data from more than one series and data is plotted on a grid with two axes, therefore you will learn some additional terms before creating the chart.

Since the **NATN2.XLS** worksheet has more than one section, it would be easier to create the chart on a separate sheet in the workbook. In the Introduction you learned that a workbook can contain more than one sheet. However, up to now you have used only one sheet in each of your projects. Therefore, while working on this project, you will learn how to move between different sheets and how to rename the sheets so that you can identify the content of each easily.

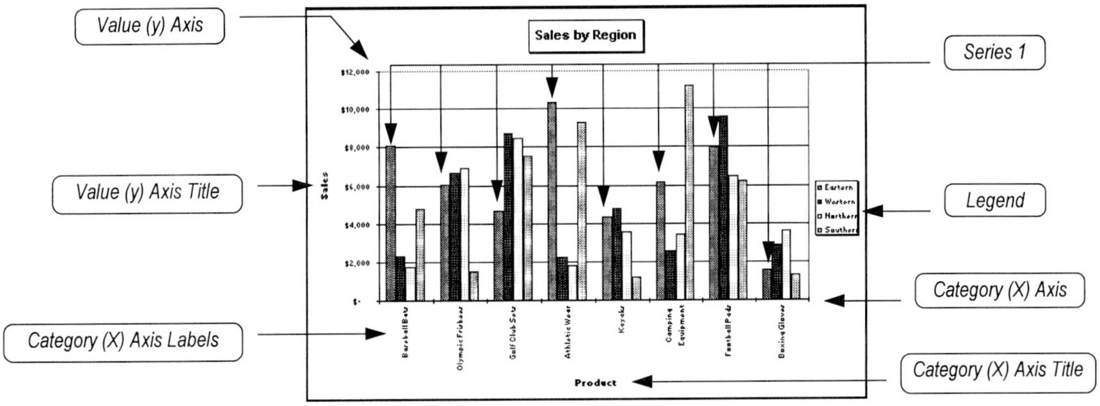

Figure 6 - 22

CREATING A COLUMN CHART

Excel refers to charts containing vertical bars as *column charts* and charts containing horizontal bars as *bar charts.* Some other programs refer to both types as bar charts. As Figure 6 - 22 indicates your column chart will contain four data series (one for each region of the country). Each data series has a value or bar for each of the products being compared. You will need to understand the following terms to understand the options in the **ChartWizard** dialog boxes.

- **X-axis** — Usually the horizontal axis, this is also called the *category* axis because it indicates the way in which you have classified the data being charted. Frequently the categories on the X-axis represent periods of time (days, months, quarters, etc.) because column, bar, and line charts are often used to see how data change over time. In your chart the categories on the x-axis are the different products. *Excel* refers to the category names as the *Category (X) Axis Labels.* In the chart you will create, the product categories are in column **A** of the worksheet.
- **Y-axis** — Usually the vertical axis, this is also called the *value* axis because it is used to measure each of the items being charted. When you create a chart, *Excel* automatically enters a scale of numbers along the Y-axis.
- **Data series** — A series of related data points contained in a single row or column. The pie chart that you created in Project 1 contained one data series. The column chart you will create in this project contains four data series — one for each region of the country. They are contained in columns **B, C, D,** and **E** of the worksheet. Each of the products represented on the X-axis will have one bar for each data series. Each data series is represented in a different color or pattern.
- **Legend** — As we saw in Project 1, the legend is a box containing the names of each data series (which *Excel* calls the *legend text*) and the pattern or color by which they are represented.
- **Titles** — The chart and the X- and Y-axes may have labels, or *titles* that help the viewer understand what the chart is illustrating.

Activity 6.5: Creating a Column Chart

1. Start *Excel* if necessary and open the file **natn2.xls**.
2. Select the cells representing the column labels for the four regions, the product names, and all of the associated values. If you completed Lesson 3, this range will be **A6:E14**.
3. Choose **INSERT/Chart,As New Sheet.**

   *You cannot use the **ChartWizard** button to create a chart as a new sheet.*
4. The **ChartWizard - Step 1 of 5** dialog box should indicate the range **=$A$6:$E$14**. Click on **Next** to accept this range.
5. In the **ChartWizard - Step 2 or 5** dialog box, click on the **Column** chart if it is not already selected. Click on **Next**.
6. In the **ChartWizard - Step 3 of 5** dialog box, click on column chart number **1**. Click on **Next**.
7. The **ChartWizard - Step 4 of 5** dialog box displays a sample chart (Figure 6 - 23). Only half of the X-axis category labels are displayed because they are too long to fit on the axis. That's okay, you'll fix that later. All of the default settings should be correct. Each of your data series is a **column**. The **First 1 Column** in the range **(A)** contains the **Category (X) Axis Labels** (the names of the products) and the **First 1 Row** contains the **Legend Text** (the names of the four regions). Click on **Next**.

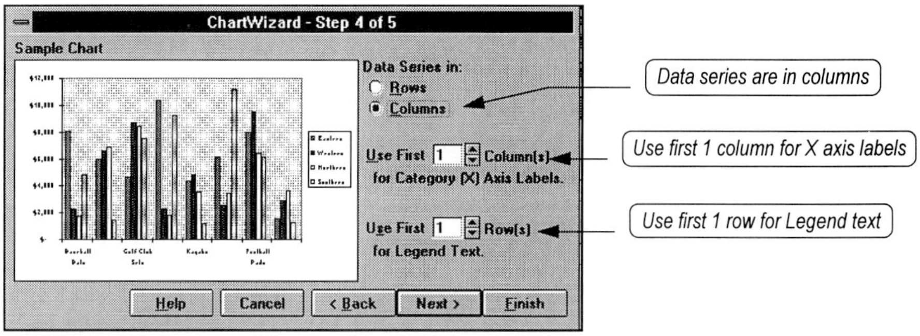

Figure 6 - 23

8. In the **ChartWizard - Step 5 of 5** dialog box, press the **TAB** key or click in the **Chart Title** box. Type: **Sales by Region**
9. Select the **Category (X)** text box and type: **Product**
10. Select the **Value (Y)** box, type: **Sales** (Figure 6 - 24*)*, and then click on **Finish**.

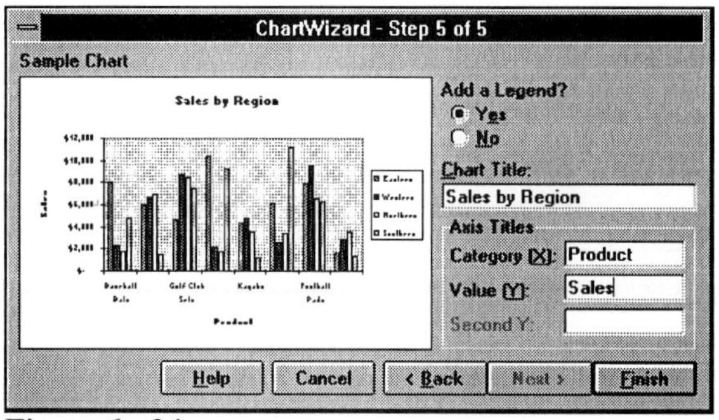

Figure 6 - 24

Your chart is displayed on its own Chart sheet (Figure 6 - 25). Notice that Excel has added a Chart tab to the tabs at the bottom of the workbook. You will learn how to go back to the worksheet after we have worked with the chart.

11. **Save** the file **As: natnchrt**

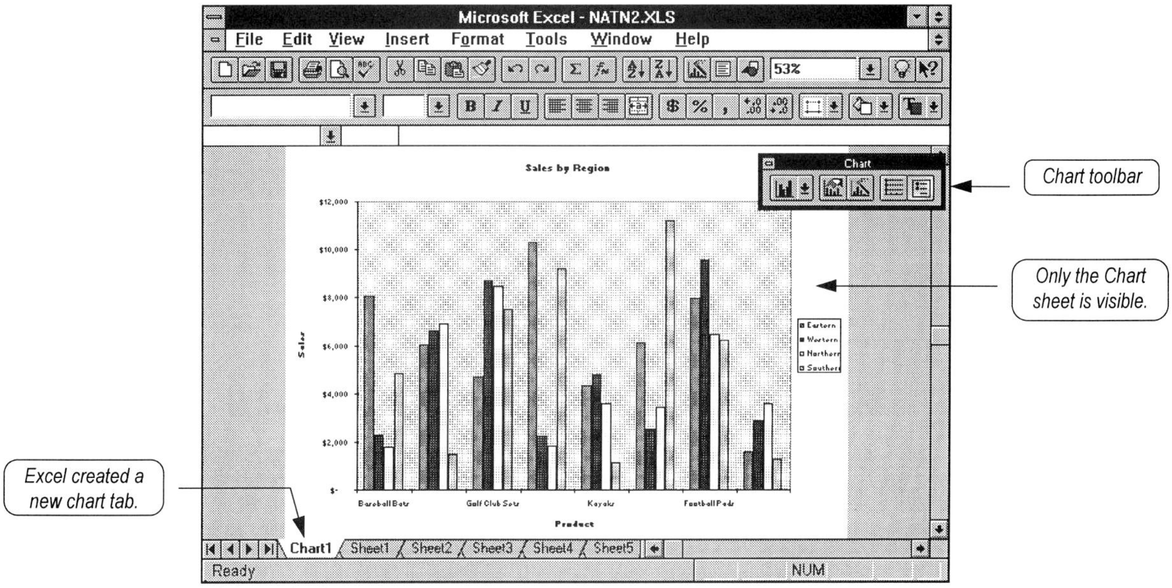

Figure 6 - 25

Activity 6.6: Formatting the Chart

In this activity you will change the alignment of the X-axis labels so that all of the Category (X) axis labels are displayed. You will also format the title, legend, and Value (Y) axis text. In the process you will use some of the alternate methods listed in the first project in this lesson for formatting parts of the chart.

1. Point to a part of the X-axis that is in between bars (Figure 6 - 26) and click the mouse button.

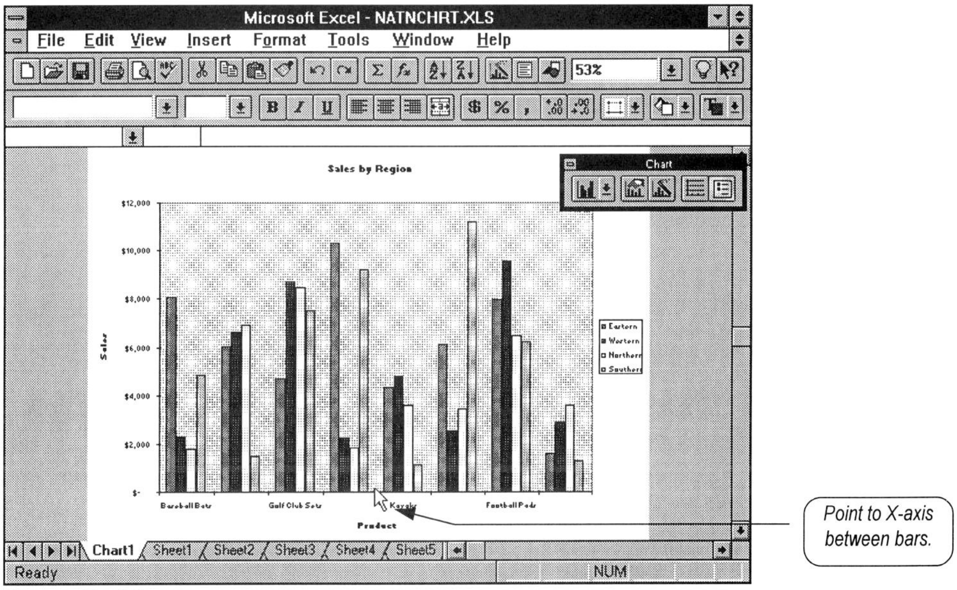

Figure 6 - 26

! ***Problem Solver:*** *Small squares should appear only at the two ends of the X-axis, and the* ***name box*** *of the Formula Bar should say* ***Axis 2****. If a different part of the chart is indicated in the* ***name box****, you have clicked in the wrong place. Repeat step 1.*

2. Still pointing to the same part of the X-axis, click the **right** mouse button. Choose **Format Axis** from the shortcut menu.
3. Click on the **Alignment** tab of the **Format Axis** dialog box (Figure 6 - 27).
4. Click on the middle vertical alignment (Figure 6 - 27). Click on **OK**.

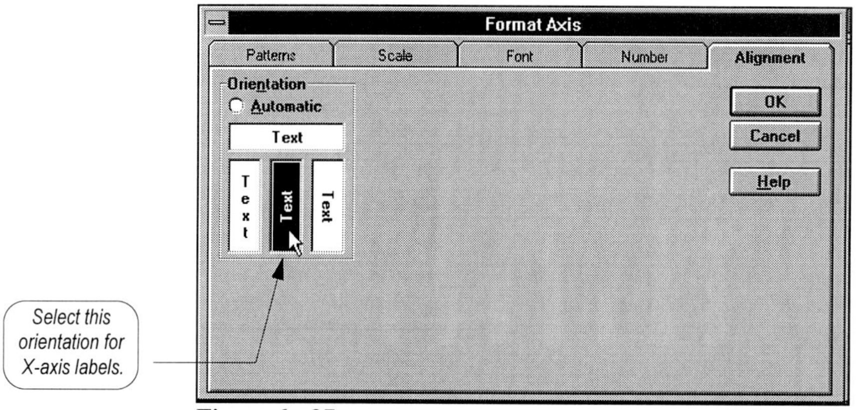

Figure 6 - 27

5. Point to part of the chart area that does not contain bars and click with the **left** mouse button. If the **name box** says **Plot** (Figure 6 - 28), you have selected the correct area. Click in the same place with the **right** mouse button.

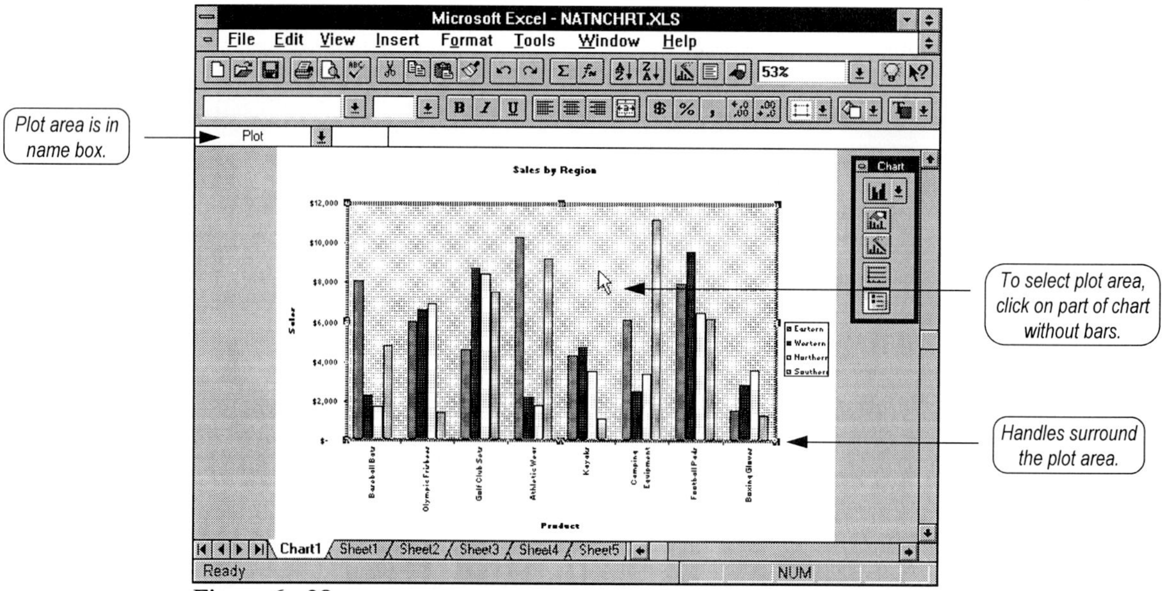

Figure 6 - 28

6. Choose **Format Plot Area** from the shortcut menu.
7. Click on the solid white box in the **Color** part of the **Area** section (Figure 6 - 29). Click on **OK**.

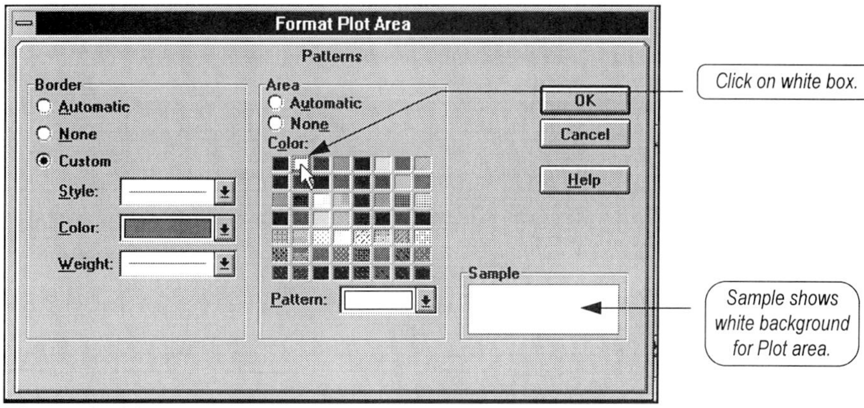

Figure 6 - 29

8. Click anywhere in the **Legend** with the **right** mouse button. Choose **Format Legend** from the shortcut menu. Choose the **Patterns** tab, mark **Shadow**, and click on **OK**.
9. Point slightly below the worksheet title, **Sales by Region** and double-click.

   *The **Format Chart Title** dialog box is displayed.*
10. Use the **Font** tab to change the Font size to **16.** Use the **Patterns** tab to add a **Shadow**. Click on **OK**.
11. Click once on the **Y-axis** title, **Sales**. Use the **Font Size** drop down box on the Formatting toolbar (Figure 6 - 30) to change the size to **12.**

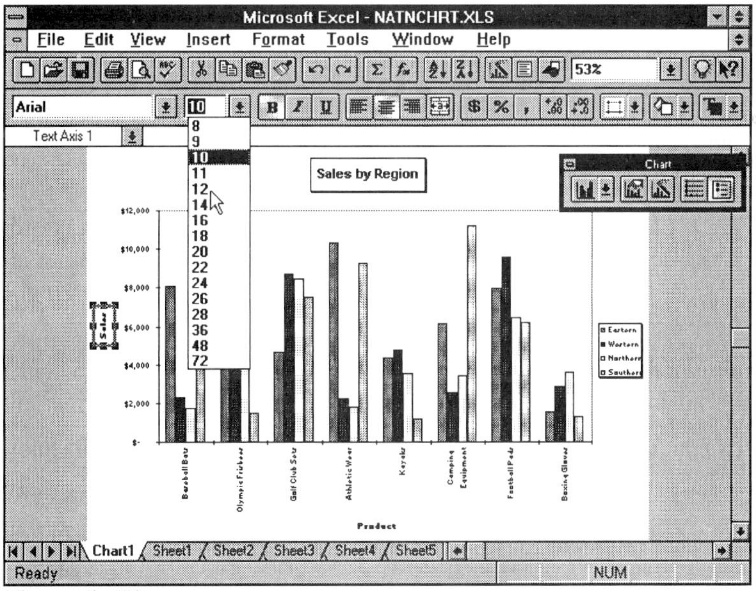

Figure 6 - 30

12. If you cannot see the X-axis label (**Products**), click on the ↓ on the vertical scroll bar until it is displayed. Click once on the X-axis label.
13. Use the **Font Size** button to change the font size of the X-axis title, **Product**, to **12** points.
14. Click on the Y-axis with the **right** mouse button.

   *The name box should say **AXIS 1**. If not, try selecting the Y-axis again.*

15. Choose **Insert Gridlines** from the shortcut menu.

    Gridlines are lines that go across the width or height of the chart. Major Y-axis gridlines go across the chart at the point of each value marked on the Y-axis. They help you read the value of the bars on the chart.

16. Choose **Major Gridlines** on the **Value (Y) Axis** (Figure 6 - 31) and click on **OK**.

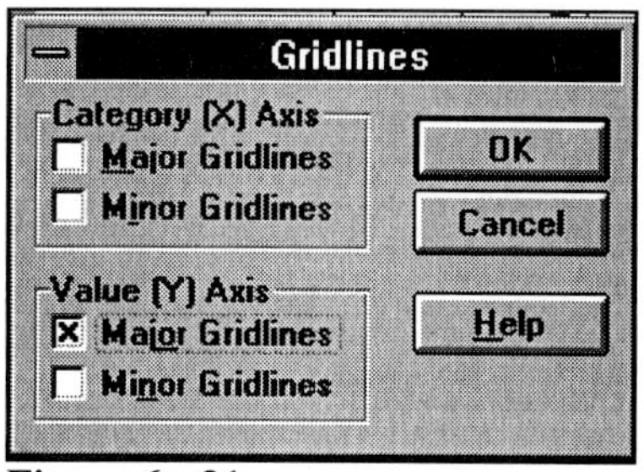

Figure 6 - 31

17. Save the workbook again using the current name.

PRINTING A CHART FROM A SEPARATE SHEET

Printing a chart from a chart sheet is performed in the same way as printing a worksheet or printing a chart that is embedded on a worksheet. The difference is that the default paper orientation is landscape.

Activity 6.7: Printing the Column Chart

1. Choose **PRINT/Preview** or click on the **Print Preview** toolbar button.

   The chart is displayed in landscape orientation (the page is wider than it is long). If you do not have a color printer, the colors in the bars and the legend are automatically changed to patterns.

2. Click on the **Print** button.
3. **Selected Sheets** should be marked in the **Print What** section of the **Print** dialog box. If it isn't, choose it. Click on **OK**.

CHANGING THE TYPE OF CHART

Different types of charts are better for different data. To help you understand the differences between charts, you will display the **natnchrt** data using different chart types and subtypes.

To change the chart type, use one of these three methods:

- Click on the drop-down arrow to the right of the **Chart Type** tool  on the Chart toolbar and then click on the chart type of your choice; *or*
- Choose **FORMAT/Chart Type**. The **Chart Type** dialog box lets you select a **2-D** or **3-D** chart and then select from the available chart types. The **Options** button in the dialog box also lets you select **Subtypes** of the chart and change other display options; *or*

- Choose **FORMAT/AutoFormat** and select a different chart type from the **Galleries** list box. This method also lets you select one of the AutoFormats for the chart type that you choose. The AutoFormats include all of the subtypes included in the Chart Type options, plus several formatting options such as the inclusion of gridlines.

Activity 6.8: Changing the Chart Type and Subtype

In this activity you will have the opportunity to see how changing the chart type affects your chart.

1. Choose **FORMAT/Chart Type**. Choose **Bar** and click on **OK**.

   *Your chart is rotated so that the columns are now horizontal bars. The **Category (X) Axis** is now the vertical axis and the **Value (Y) Axis** is now the horizontal axis (Figure 6 - 32).*

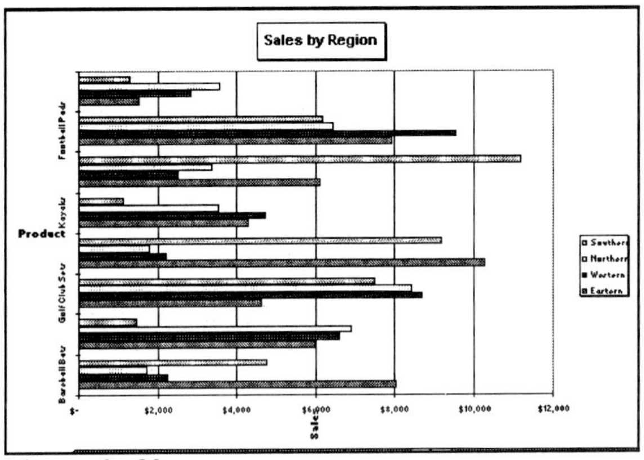

Figure 6 - 32

2. Click on the drop down arrow to the right of the **Chart Type** tool on the Chart toolbar. Click on the picture of a line chart.

   The line chart (Figure 6 - 33) can be used to compare the sales for the products in the different regions. However, line charts are more appropriate for showing trends over time, than for comparing unrelated items such as baseball bats and golf clubs.

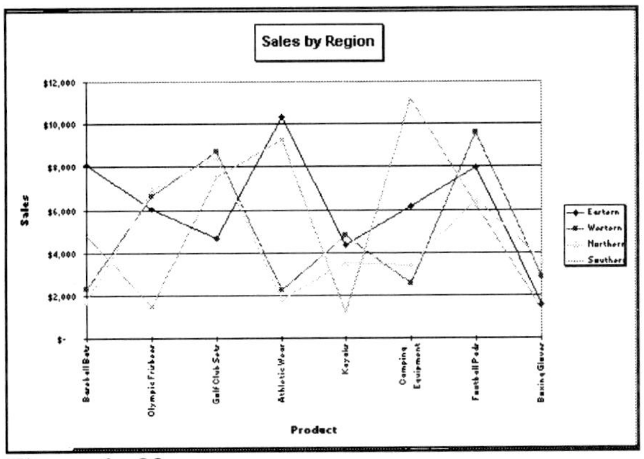

Figure 6 - 33

3. Use **FORMAT/Chart Type** or the **Chart Type** tool to change the chart type to an area chart.

   In an area chart (Figure 6 - 34) the areas for each of the data series at a given point are charted on top of each other. Thus each section of your area chart shows the volume of sales for one region and the top line of your area chart indicates the total sales for the all four regions. Like line charts, area charts are usually used to show changes over time rather than to compare different items.

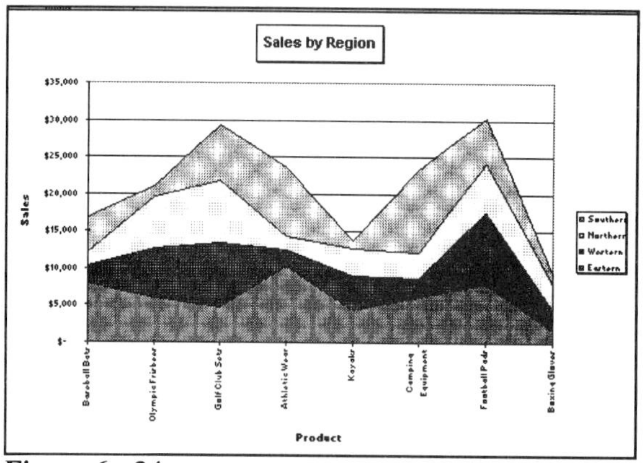

Figure 6 - 34

4. Choose **FORMAT/AutoFormat.** Choose **Column** from the **Galleries** list box (Figure 6 - 35).

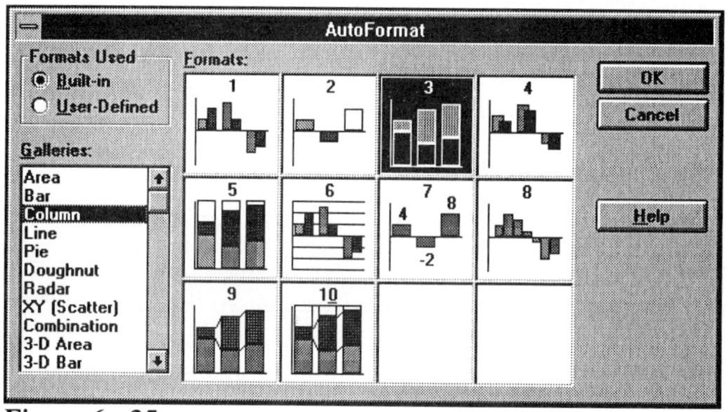

Figure 6 - 35

*Formats **3, 5, 9,** and **10** are different from the others in that the columns are stacked on top of each other rather than next to each other. Formats **3** and **9** represent **stacked column** charts. The column for each series in each category is stacked to create one column. This allows you to compare the totals more easily than a regular column chart does.*

*Formats **5** and **10** represent **100% column** charts. A **100% column** chart is a cross between a bar and a pie chart. It is made up of stacked columns as in the stacked column chart. However, each column is the same height. Each segment shows the percentage to the whole contributed by that segment, just as each wedge in the pie chart represents the percentage of the whole contributed by that segment.*

5. Choose format number **3**, a stacked column chart, and click on **OK**.

6. Click on the **Horizontal Gridlines** button on the Chart toolbar.

   In the stacked column chart it now becomes clear that the total sales for football pads was the highest, with golf club sales running a close second (Figure 6 - 36).

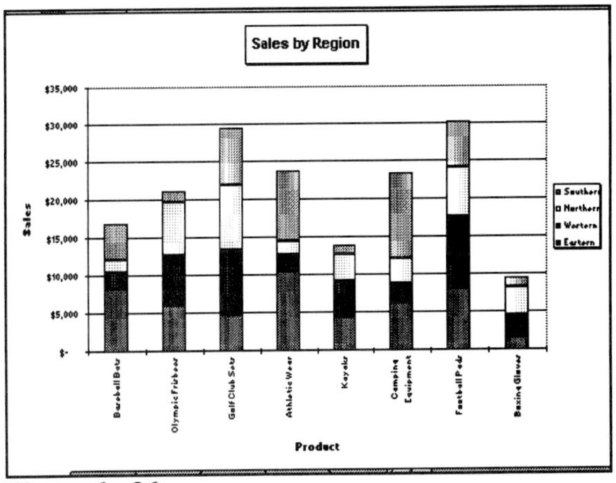

Figure 6 - 36

7. **Save** the file again using the existing name.

   Your saved file will contain the stacked column chart rather than the column chart that was saved the last time you saved the file.

WORKBOOK SHEETS

Next you will change some data in the worksheet and see how it affects the chart. Before you can do that, you need to know how to move around a workbook with more than one sheet.

A workbook can contain one sheet or as many as 255 sheets. In this workbook you have used two types of sheets — a worksheet and a chart sheet. Some workbooks have multiple worksheets. Multiple worksheets are used to keep related data together in one file. For example, in **natn2.xls** instead of placing the Projected vs. Actual part of the worksheet on the bottom of the first sheet, you could have placed it on a sheet of its own. In the future you might want to add another sheet containing sales data for 1995.

Similarly, it is often easier to manage your data if a chart is placed on a chart sheet within the workbook rather than embedded on the worksheet.

The sheets in a workbook are listed on tabs at the bottom of the workbook. The active sheet is always displayed on top, and the associated tab looks different from the other tabs. Sometimes, you may want to select more than one tab at a time so that multiple sheets can be printed or edited as a group. When you create a new workbook, a group of tabs is present even if the sheets they are associated with are empty. Therefore, it is a good idea to name the sheets that you are using.

To move between sheets:

- Click on the tab of the sheet that you want to select; *or*
- Press **CTRL+PAGE UP** to move to the previous tab and **CTRL+PAGE DOWN** to move to the next tab.

To rename a sheet:

- Point to the sheet tab and click the **right** mouse button to display the shortcut menu.
- Choose **Rename** from the shortcut menu.
- Type the new name in the **Rename Sheet** dialog box and click on **OK**. The name can have up to 31 characters. It can contain letters, numbers, and spaces but cannot be enclosed in square brackets or contain the following characters: : / \ * ?. It is preferable to keep the names short because long names cause the size of the tab to increase.

Activity 6.9: Using Multiple Sheets in a Workbook

1. Point to the **Chart 1** tab and click the **right** mouse button (Figure 6 - 37).

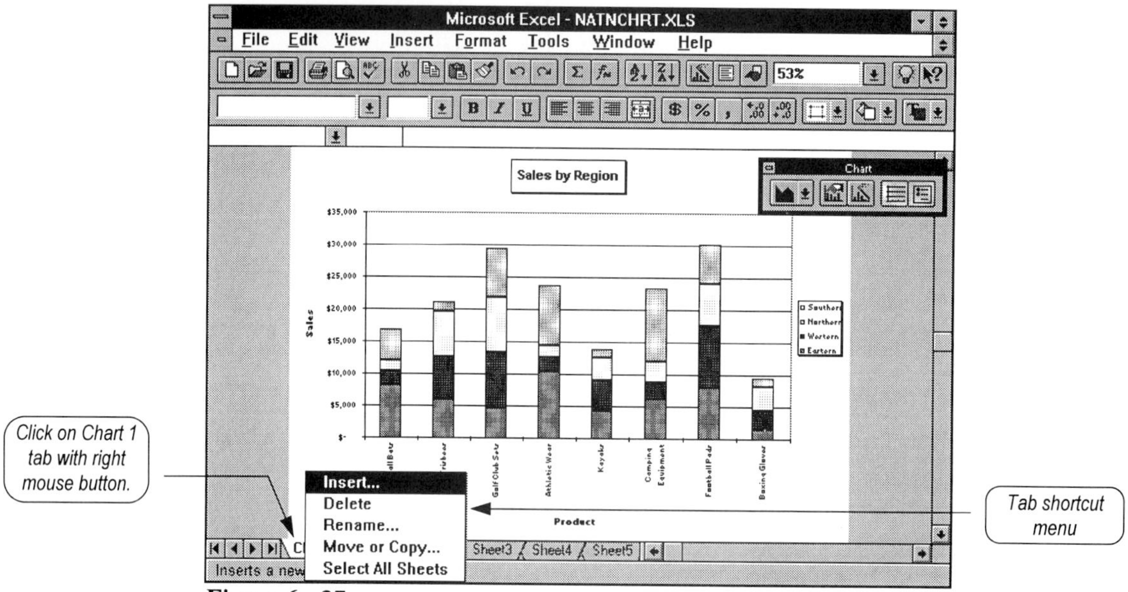

Figure 6 - 37

2. Choose **Rename** from the shortcut menu.
3. In the **Name** text box in the **Rename Sheet** dialog box, type: **Sales Chart** and click on **OK**.
4. Point to the **Sheet 1** tab and click with the **left** mouse button.

   The worksheet should be displayed.
5. Click on **Sheet 1** with the **right** mouse button.
6. Choose **Rename** from the shortcut menu and name the sheet: **1994 Sales** (Figure 6 - 38).

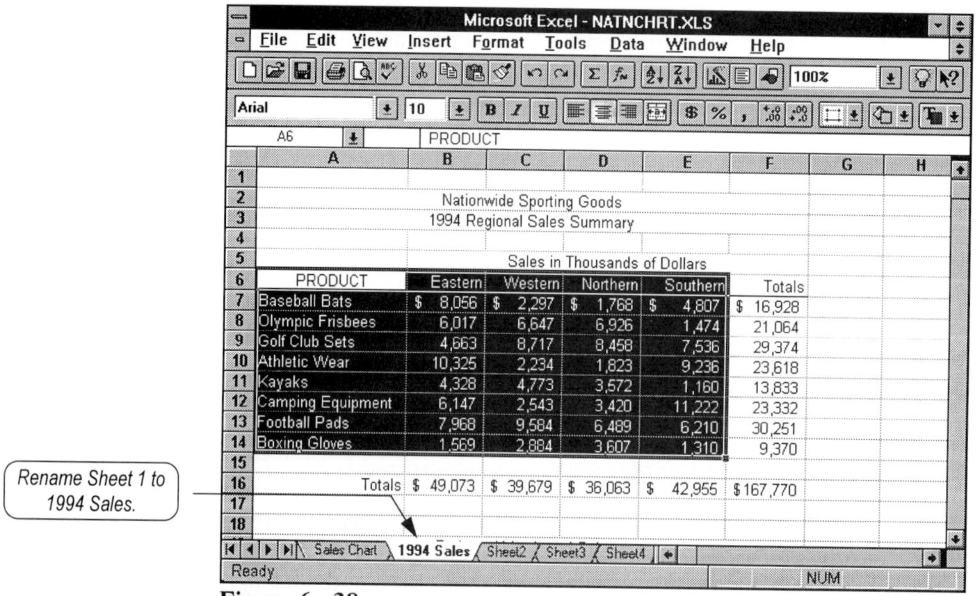

PRODUCT	Eastern	Western	Northern	Southern	Totals
Baseball Bats	$ 8,056	$ 2,297	$ 1,768	$ 4,807	$ 16,928
Olympic Frisbees	6,017	6,647	6,926	1,474	21,064
Golf Club Sets	4,663	8,717	8,458	7,536	29,374
Athletic Wear	10,325	2,234	1,823	9,236	23,618
Kayaks	4,328	4,773	3,572	1,160	13,833
Camping Equipment	6,147	2,543	3,420	11,222	23,332
Football Pads	7,968	9,584	6,489	6,210	30,251
Boxing Gloves	1,569	2,884	3,607	1,310	9,370
Totals	$ 49,073	$ 39,679	$ 36,063	$ 42,955	$ 167,770

Figure 6 - 38

7. **Save** the workbook again using the existing name.

PRINTING MULTIPLE SHEETS IN A WORKBOOK

Now you're ready to print your new chart, only this time you want to print the related worksheet data as well. Since the chart and the worksheet that you want to print are the only sheets in the workbook, you can either tell *Excel* to print the entire workbook or you can select the sheets that you want to print.

To print selected sheets in a workbook:

- Select the first sheet by clicking on it.
- Select additional nonadjacent sheets by pressing and holding down the **CTRL** key while you click on additional tabs.
- Select a range of sheets by selecting the first sheet and then holding down the **SHIFT** key before clicking on the last sheet tab.
- Choose **FILE/Print**. Make sure that the **Selected Sheet(s)** option in the **Print What** option box is selected. Make any desired changes to **Page Setup** and print the worksheets.

To print all sheets in a workbook:

- Choose **FILE/Print**.
- Choose the **Entire Workbook** option in the **Print What** option box. Make any desired changes to **Page Setup** and print the workbook.

Activity 6.10: Printing All of the Sheets in the Workbook

1. Choose **FILE/Print.**
2. Choose the **Entire Workbook** option in the **Print What** option box.
3. Click on the **Print Preview** button.

   The chart will be displayed since it is the first tab. It will be displayed in landscape orientation.
4. Click on the **Next** button.

   The worksheet will be displayed. It is in portrait orientation.
5. Click on the **Print** button to print both sheets of the workbook.

EFFECTS OF CHANGING DATA ON RELATED CHARTS

One of the advantages of creating a chart in *Excel* is that the charts are updated automatically when the data are changed.

Activity 6.11: Effects of Changing Data on the Related Chart

You receive the following revised sales data: sales of golf club sets in the northern region was really **8,958** and sales of football pads in the southern region was really **5,000**.

1. Change the value of the sales for golf club sets in the northern region (cell **D9**) to **8958** and the value for football pads in the southern region (cell **E13**) to **5000.**

   Compare your screen with the printout that you just made to see which valuess changed.

2. Click on the **Sales Chart** tab to display the revised chart. Compare your screen with the printout that you just made of the sales chart. Notice that the total sales represented by the golf club sales is now larger that that represented by the football pads (Figure 6 - 39).

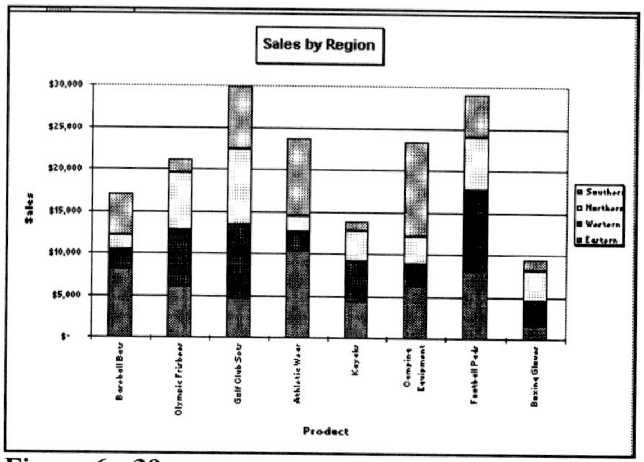

Figure 6 - 39

3. **Save** your file as: **ntncht2**
4. Print the revised worksheet and chart.
5. Close and save the worksheet.

SUMMARY

In this lesson you learned to create charts on the worksheet and on separate sheets. You also saw how easy it is to modify and format charts. More importantly you saw some of the different kinds of charts *Excel* can create and how they aid in data analysis. In the Independent Projects you will get more practice in seeing the different purposes of different charts and in using multiple sheets in a workbook.

KEY TERMS

100% column chart
Area chart
Autoformat
Bar chart
Category (x) axis labels
Chart galleries
ChartWizard
Column chart
Combination chart
Data point
Data series
Embed
Gridlines
Legend
Legend text
Line chart
Pie chart
Stacked column chart
Titles
Value (y) axis labels
Workbook sheets
X-axis
Y-axis

INDEPENDENT PROJECTS

The four independent projects in Lesson 6 will give you practice creating and formatting pie, column, line and mixed charts. You will also use workbooks which contain multiple worksheets or multiple chart sheets.

Independent Project 6.1: Charting a Sales Worksheet

You work for a clothing store. You are given a worksheet which shows the first quarter sales divided by department (men's. women's and children's). You have been asked to create a chart to compare total first quarter sales for the three departments. You decide that a pie chart will show the percent of sales accounted for by each department best.

When you finish the first chart, your worksheet should resemble Figure 6 - 40.

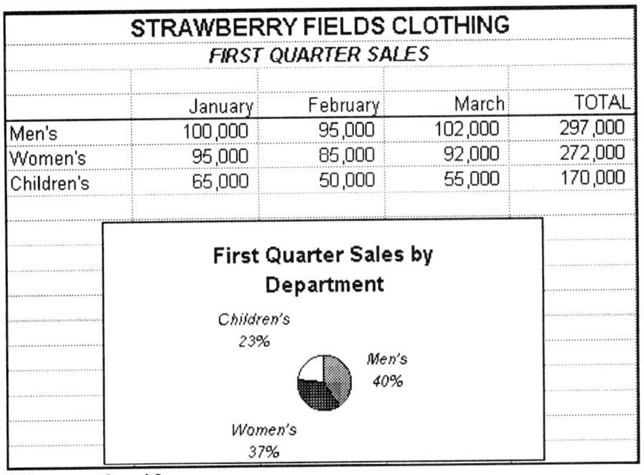

STRAWBERRY FIELDS CLOTHING				
FIRST QUARTER SALES				
	January	February	March	TOTAL
Men's	100,000	95,000	102,000	297,000
Women's	95,000	85,000	92,000	272,000
Children's	65,000	50,000	55,000	170,000

Figure 6 - 40

Use Figure 6 - 40 and the following instructions to help you complete the project:

1. Open **indpr6_1.xls**.
2. Use the **ChartWizard** to create a **pie** chart on the worksheet. Your range should include the labels in **A5:A7** and the totals in **E5:E7**.
3. Click in **B9** to let *Excel* automatically place your chart, beginning at that point.
4. Use **Format** 7 for the pie chart.
5. The **ChartWizard - Step 4 of 5** dialog box should indicate that the data series are in columns, the first **1** column is used as slice labels and the first **0** rows are used as the chart title.
6. Do not add a legend. Give the chart the title: **First Quarter Sales by Department**
7. Move the chart so that it is visible on the screen and approximately centered under the worksheet.
8. Double-click on the chart to edit it.
9. Make the slice labels (**Text S1**) **italic.**
10. Change the font size of the title to **11** point.
11. Save the file as: **Deptpie**
12. Print the worksheet (including the chart) without gridlines; use appropriate headers and footers.
13. The worksheet is reviewed and it is discovered that part of the women's department sales is missing. Change **February Women's** sales to **95,000** and **March Women's** sales to **104,000.**
14. Select the data labels (**Text S1**) and use the **Increase Decimal** button to add one decimal place to the percentages.
15. Save the worksheet as: **deptpie2**
16. Print the worksheet with the new data, totals, and chart. Close the file.

Independent Project 6.2: Charting a Sales Worksheet

In Independent Project 5.1 you added formulas to a worksheet to help analyze March sales' patterns for T-shirt company salespersons. In this project you will chart each of the three salesperson's sales to see if there are any trends indicating that some weeks have stronger sales than others. You will create your chart on a separate sheet.

Figure 6 - 41 shows the first chart that you will create. (If you use **indpr5_1.xls** instead of **tshirt.xls**, the **X-axis** labels and some of the formatting of the labels will be different.)

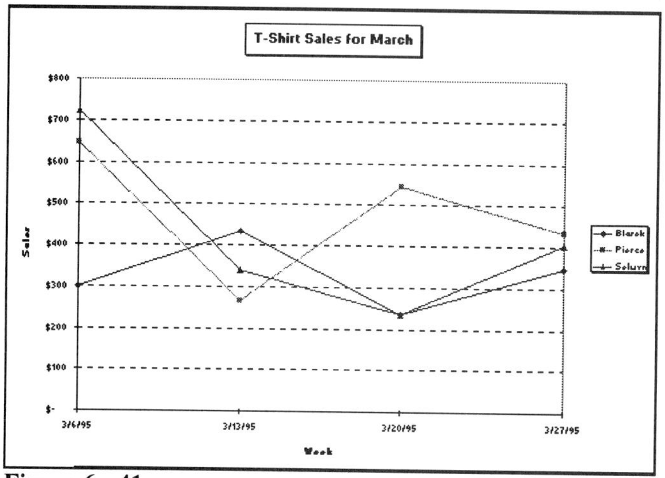

Figure 6 - 41

Use Figure 6 - 41 and the following instructions to help you complete the project:

1. If you completed Independent Project 5.1, open **tshirt.xls**. If you did not complete Independent Project 5.1, open **indpr5_1.xls**. The data that we are going to chart is on the original worksheet.
2. Select the range **A6:B10**. While it is still selected, add the ranges **D6:D10** and **F6:F10**.
3. Insert a chart as a new sheet.
4. Make your chart a line chart. Use the format that includes lines, markers, and horizontal gridlines.
5. Data series are in columns, the first 1 column is used for X Axis labels and the first 1 row is used for legend text.
6. Use the following titles:

   Chart Title: **T-Shirt Sales for March**
   Category (X): **Week**
   Value (Y): **Sales**

7. Format the plot area so that the Area color is white.
8. Format the chart title so that its font size is 14, and it has a border with a shadow.
9. Format the legend so that it has a border with a shadow.
10. Save the file as: **tchart**
11. Make **Sheet1** the active sheet. Change its name to **March Sales**.
12. Save the worksheet again using the current name.
13. Print the worksheet and the chart.

14. Do all of salespersons show the same pattern (i.e. are the same weeks best for each)?
15. Change the chart type to a **column** chart.
16. Print just the chart.
17. Change the chart to a **stacked column** chart.
18. Print just the chart.
19. Which of the three charts shows the total sales per week best? Which shows the trends for each salesperson best?
20. Close and save the worksheet.

Independent Project 6.3: Creating a Mixed Chart

In this project you will create a chart to compare automobile sales for each of three different manufacturers in nine states. In order to make it easier for the person viewing the chart to compare sales of individual manufacturers within and across states and to compare total sales for individual cars, you will create a mixed chart. The sales of each of the three automobile makers, Ford, GM and Chrysler, will be represented by bars, and the total sales will be shown as a line. The worksheet that you will chart is similar to the first part of the worksheet that you rearranged in Independent Project 3.2. In Independent Project 3.2 you re-arranged the worksheet so that sales of cars from each country were shown on a different part of the worksheet. In **indpr6_3.xls** each country's cars are located on a different sheet of the workbook. Therefore, you will also practice selecting and printing different sheets in the workbook.

When finished your chart should resemble Figure 6 - 42 although the formatting may be different.

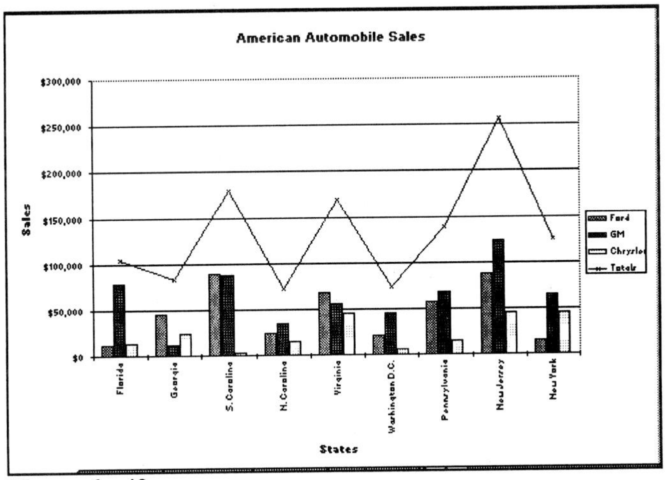

Figure 6 - 42

Use Figure 6 - 42 and the following instructions to help you complete the project:

1. Open **indpr6_3.xls**. Notice that the tabs at the bottom of the worksheet are labeled with the names of different countries.
2. Create a column chart of all of the data on American car sales on a new sheet. The range should include the names of the states, the names of the automobile manufacturers, and for each state, the sales for each manufacturer and the total sales for the state. Do NOT include the total sales for each manufacturer (row **14**).

3. In the **ChartWizard** dialog boxes choose a column style that includes horizontal gridlines, but does NOT stack the columns on top of each other. On the **ChartWizard - Step 4 of 5** box make sure that the selections are correct to produce the chart shown in Figure 6 - 42 except that the Totals will be represented as a tall bar, not a line. Some of the X-axis labels will not be displayed. Don't worry, you'll fix that later. Use the following labels:

   Chart Title: **American Automobile Sales**
   Category (X) Axis Title: **States**
   Category (Y) Axis Title: **Sales**

4. Select the X-axis (Axis 2), choose **Format axis** and change the alignment of the X-axis labels to one of the vertical alignments which will display all of the states.
5. Select the Plot area, and format it so that the Area color is white.
6. Select one of the bars in the Totals series (**S4**). Display the shortcut menu and change the **Chart Type** of just the **Selected Series** to **Line**.
7. If the line color is light, select the line, choose **Format Data Series** from the shortcut menu and use the **Patterns** tab to choose darker line and marker colors.
8. Increase the sizes of the Chart title, and X- and Y-Axis labels.
9. Save the file as: **autochrt**
10. Rename the **Chart1** tab to **American chart**.
11. Select the **American chart** and **American** tabs.
12. Choose **FILE/Print**. Make sure the **Selected Sheets** option is selected.
13. Choose the **Print Preview** button from the **Print** dialog box. On the Print Preview screen, use the **Next** or **Previous** button to preview both the chart and the related worksheet. Use the **Page Setup** button to remove **gridlines** from the worksheet and make any desired changes to the headers and footers. Print the chart and worksheet.
14. Save the file again using the existing name.
15. Switch to the sheet that shows **UK** sales.
16. Print just that worksheet.
17. Create a chart of **UK** car sales that matches the one that you created for American automobile sales. Format it similarly, change the name of its sheet tab and print the chart.
18. Save the file again using the current name and close the file.

Independent Project 6.4: Creating Two Charts

You are in charge of analyzing complaints received by the nine divisions of your company during the first quarter. In order to do this, you are going to create two charts, one to compare the total complaints received each month, and a second to compare the complaints per division per month. The data are in the file **indpr6_4.xls**.

When completed your project should include two charts:

A pie chart comparing the percent of the total 1st Quarter complaints occurring in each month.

1. Create the chart on a separate sheet.
2. Use the months as part of the wedge labels or in the legend. Create a title for the chart.
3. Format the chart as you wish.
4. Give the chart tab an appropriate name.

5. Print the complete worksheet and the chart.

A column chart comparing the complaints for each of the divisions in each month.

1. Create the chart on a separate sheet.
2. Choose any type of column chart that you want except for 100% column.
3. Provide appropriate titles and labels for the chart.
4. Format the chart as you wish.
5. Give the chart tab an appropriate name.
6. Print the chart.
7. Save the worksheet as: **compchrt**

Appendix: Featured Reference

The following table contains a summary of the main features presented in the lesson. As you know, most features in Excel can be performed in a variety of ways. Many of the menu bar commands can also be selected from The Quick Menus. Listed mouse shortcuts involve the use of the buttons on the Standard and Formatting Toolbars and other mouse techniques. Shortcut keys are keystrokes of function keys. Many features require that the text be selected prior to executing the command. If you need more detail on using these features, the table contains a reference to the lesson describing its use.

Table 6 - 1

Features	Menu Bar Commands	Mouse Shortcut	Shortcut Keys	
Alignment	FORMAT/Cells, Alignment	Align Center button Align Left button Align Right button Center Across Columns button	CTRL + 1 (Format Cells dialog box)	2
Bold	FORMAT/Cells, Font	Bold button	CTRL + B	2
Borders, add, change or remove	FORMAT/Cells, Borders	Border button	CTRL + 1 CTRL + SHIFT + _ (removes borders)	2
Center across Columns	FORMAT/Cells, Alignment	Center Across Columns button	CTRL + 1	2
Charts, changing type	FORMAT/Chart Type (or AutoFormat)	Chart Type button		6
Charts, creating	INSERT/Chart	ChartWizard button (on same sheet)	F11 (default type on new sheet)	6
Clear cell contents	EDIT/Clear, Contents	Drag fill handle up until selection is gray	DELETE	1
Clear contents and format	EDIT/Clear,All			
Column Width	FORMAT/Column	Drag right column header border (or double click border to AutoFit)		1
Column, Select		Click on column header	CTRL+SPACEBAR	1
Comma Format	FORMAT/Cells, Number	Comma Style button	CTRL + SHIFT + !	2
Copy cell contents to adjacent cells	EDIT/Fill	Drag fill handle	CTRL + R (fill right) CTRL + D (down)	3
Copy cell contents to nonadjacent cells	EDIT/Copy EDIT/Paste	Copy button Paste button; or Point to selection, press **CTRL** and drag to new location	CTRL + C CTRL + V	3
Currency Format	FORMAT/Cells, Number (Currency formats put $ next to number; Accounting formats place $ on left side of cell)	Currency Style button ($ is on left side of cell)	CTRL + SHIFT + $ ($ is next to number)	2

Features	Menu Bar Commands	Mouse Shortcut	Shortcut Keys	
Delete Rows/Columns	EDIT/Delete			3
Edit cell contents		Double-click on cell	F2	1
Exit Excel	FILE/Exit		ALT + F4	1
Font	FORMAT/Cells, Font	Font button	CTRL + 1	2
Font Size	FORMAT/Cells, Font	Font Size button	CTRL + 1	2
Footers	FILE/Page Setup, Header/Footer			
Formulas, displaying on worksheet	TOOLS/Options, View		CTRL +	1
Font Style	FORMAT/Cells,Font	Bold, Italic, Underline buttons	CTRL + B CTRL + I CTRL + U	2
Freeze (row/columns)	WINDOW/Freeze panes			5
Functions, Insert	INSERT/Function	Function Wizard button	SHIFT + F3	4
Gridlines, remove from printout	FILE/Page Setup, Sheet			2
Headers	FILE/Page Setup, Headers/Footers			2
Help on a specific topic	HELP/Search for Help on			1
Help, contents	HELP/Contents		F1	1
Help, context sensitive		Help button	SHIFT + F1	1
Insert Rows (Columns)	INSERT/Rows (Columns)			3
Italics	FORMAT/Cells, Font	Italic button	CTRL + I	2
Move cell contents	EDIT/Cut EDIT/Paste	Cut button Paste button; or Point to selection and drag	CTRL + X CTRL + V	3
New File, create	FILE/New	New Workbook button	CTRL + N	1
Open a file	FILE/Open	Open button	CTRL + O	1
Page Setup for printout	FILE/Page Setup			2
Percent Format	FORMAT/Cells, Number	Percent Style button	CTRL + SHIFT + %	2
Preview printout	FILE/Print Preview	Print Preview button		2
Print	FILE/Print	Print button	CTRL + P	1,2, 5
Row, Select		Click on row header	SHIFT+SPACEBAR	3
Save a file, using a different name	FILE/Save As		F12	2
Save a file, using same name	FILE/Save	Save button	CTRL + S	1
Series, create	EDIT/Fill, Series	Drag fill handle		5
Sort data	DATA/Sort	Sort Ascending/ Descending buttons		3
Spelling, Check	TOOLS/Spelling	Spelling button	F7	2
SUM function	INSERT/Function	AutoSum button	ALT + =	3
Underline	FORMAT/Cells, Font	Underline button	CTRL + U	2
Undo	EDIT/Undo	Undo button	CTRL + Z	1
Workbook, change tab		Click on new tab	CTRL + PAGE DOWN (UP)	6
Workbook, rename sheets	FORMAT/Sheet, Rename	Double-click sheet tab		6

Index

NOTES

NOTES

NOTES

NOTES

NOTES